76/-n

Yale Studies in English
Volume 166

SHAKESPEARE'S
METRICS

Dorothy L. Sipe

Yale University Press   New Haven and London   1968

Dedicated to the memory of

Professor Helge Kökeritz

and to my parents

PREFACE

Many Shakespeare scholars have added to their critical commentary
detailed but impressionistic analyses of the poet's versification. The
later plays, in particular, have been scrutinized (often in a modernized
text) and found to be laden with trisyllabic substitutions and other
rhythmic irregularities. These alleged deviations from an iambic pattern
have then been interpreted as signs of Shakespeare's growing impatience
with constraint and artifice. Sometimes they have even been used as evidence that he was progressively shifting toward purely accentual verse,
verse in which the lines have a fixed number of stressed syllables but a
widely varying number of unstressed syllables.

The present study is an attempt to restore a balance by demonstrat-
ing that, whatever the corrupting influence of Renaissance orthography
and modern editing, Shakespeare wrote carefully constructed _iambic_ verse
into which he introduced only those few minor variations considered permissible in his time. This means that his normative line consists of a
succession of iambic feet, each containing two, and only two, syllables:
the first unstressed, the second stressed. Thus, though occasional lines
include "licenses" (such as initial truncation and feminine endings)
which were acceptable to his contemporaries, Shakespearean blank verse
is overwhelmingly decasyllabic. Trimeter, tetrameter, and hexameter lines
sometimes occur as similarly "allowable" variations on the usual pentameter, and they too consist almost exclusively of disyllabic iambs. Only

vii

very rarely--and only under certain conditions specified by Renaissance
theorists--do we find the trisyllabic and monosyllabic feet so characteristic of purely accentual verse with its highly variable number of
unstressed syllables.

My evidence supporting these statements was gathered by investigation of Shakespeare's word choice: specifically, his choice between or
among etymologically related words differing from one another in number
of syllables but not in meaning (e.g. abide and bide). I adopted a
statistical method in the belief that it is impossible to make sound
critical and philological judgments about an author's metrical practice
until the observable facts have been collected and analyzed. Except for
variants involving accidence or compounding, all statistically significant words of the abide-bide type were included--a total of more than
1,500 words occurring in approximately 13,000 lines, or more than
one-sixth of the total number of verse lines in the plays.

Only 63 lines show use of a variant that creates a trisyllabic or
monosyllabic foot which could have been avoided had a synonym been
chosen. And even these few irregularities hold only if spelling is
taken as a rigid guide to the meter, with no allowance being made for
corruptions and obscurities inherent in the orthography of the time.
Thus, evidence is now available to demonstrate that in at least 99.5
per cent of the lines investigated, and presumably in a like percentage
of the rest of the dramatic verse, Shakespeare was carefully adhering
to an iambic prosody.

Even if this had been the only substantial result of my study, I
feel that it would justify the effort that was needed to carry out such
a systematic analysis. As it happened, however, exploration of Renaissance metrical theory revealed much external evidence pointing to the

same conclusion but never, to my knowledge, assembled before; it has been
summarized in two introductory chapters. And the massive collection of
synonymous variants illuminates the fascinating, ingenious ways in which
a great poet seeks out or creates desired word-forms. But most important
of all, my findings about Shakespearean versification lead to stylistic,
phonological, and lexical corollaries (presented in the final chapter)
which will, I hope, be provocative as well as persuasive.

I owe a special debt to Professor E. Talbot Donaldson of Columbia
University for his good-humored encouragement in many dark hours. And I
am grateful, too, to Professors Marie Borroff and William K. Wimsatt, Jr.,
of Yale University and Miss Patricia Craddock of Goucher College, all of
whom read the manuscript in unfinished form and suggested various improve-
ments. Finally, my sincere thanks go to Dr. Francis J. McCauley and the
late Dr. Hobart McV. Agnew, who helped me to envision the project and see
it through to completion.

D. L. S.

The University of Wisconsin

September 1967

CONTENTS

ABBREVIATIONS

Titles of Plays and Poems

AC	Antony and Cleopatra (1606)
AW	All's Well That Ends Well (1601)
AYLI	As You Like It (1600)
C	Coriolanus (1607)
CE	The Comedy of Errors (1590)
Cy	Cymbeline (1611)
H	Hamlet (1602)
1H4	Henry IV, Part 1 (1596)
2H4	Henry IV, Part 2 (1597)
H5	Henry V (1599)
1H6	Henry VI, Part 1 (1591)
2H6	Henry VI, Part 2 (1593)
3H6	Henry VI, Part 3 (1593)
H8	Henry VIII (1613)
J	King John (1595)
JC	Julius Caesar (1601)
L	King Lear (1605)
LC	A Lover's Complaint (1597)
LLL	Love's Labour's Lost (1588)
M	Macbeth (1605)

MA	Much Ado About Nothing (1599)
MM	Measure for Measure (1603)
MND	A Midsummer Night's Dream (1590)
MV	The Merchant of Venice (1596)
MW	The Merry Wives of Windsor (1598)
O	Othello (1604)
P	Pericles (1608)
PP	The Passionate Pilgrim (1599)
R2	Richard II (1593)
R3	Richard III (1594)
RJ	Romeo and Juliet (1592)
RL	The Rape of Lucrece (1593)
S	Sonnets (1600)
T	The Tempest (1610)
TA	Titus Andronicus (1588)
TC	Troilus and Cressida (1606)
TG	The Two Gentlemen of Verona (1591)
TmA	Timon of Athens (1607)
TN	Twelfth Night (1601)
TS	The Taming of the Shrew (1596)
VA	Venus and Adonis (1592)
WT	The Winter's Tale (1611)

Dates are those assigned by The Oxford English Dictionary, which were tentatively accepted when the words included in this study were classified as "neologisms" or "non-neologisms" in Shakespearean usage.

Other Abbreviations

a.	adoption of	OED	The Oxford English Dictionary
ad.	adaptation of	OF	Old French
adj.	adjective	om.	omit(s), omitted
adv.	adverb	OSp	Old Spanish
AF	Anglo-French	OTeut	Original Teutonic
conj.	conjunction	pl.	plural
Epil.	Epilogue	p.p.	past participle
f.	formed on	ppl.	participial
F	First Folio	prep.	preposition
F2-4	Second-Fourth Folios	Prol.	Prologue
Ff	Folios	pr.p.	present participle
fig.	figurative(ly)	pr.t.	present tense
Fr	French	p.t.	past tense
Ind.	Induction	Q	(First) Quarto
intr.	intransitive	Q2-3	Second and Third Quartos
It	Italian	Qq	Quartos
L	Latin	sg.	singular
lit.	literal(ly)	sp.	spell(s), spelled
ME	Middle English	Sp	Spanish
ModE	Modern English	trans.	transitive
OE	Old English	vbl.sb.	verbal substantive

Symbols

:-   is used, as in OED, to mean 'extant representative or regular phonetic descendant of.'

*   a) preceding words found in Shakespeare, identifies

words not cited by OED in quotations antedating

the Shakespearean use.

b) in etymologies, designates a hypothetical form.

//   marks the point at which a line of verse is broken

between speakers.

‖   indicates a caesural pause.

Shakespeare's Metrics

CHAPTER I

INTRODUCTION

One of the most striking features of Shakespeare's verse is his
extensive use of "syllabic variants": synonymous, etymologically related
words differing in the number of syllables which they contain. Sometimes
these variants are juxtaposed, as in M 1.2.56, "Point against Point,
rebellious Arme 'gainst Arme."[1] Often they are widely separated. But
every reader of Shakespeare tacitly recognizes the existence of such
form variation when he interprets comes as = becomes in AC 1.4.41-44,

> It hath bin taught us from the primall state
> That he which is was wisht, untill he were:
> And the ebb'd man, ne're lov'd, till ne're worth love,
> Comes [d]ear'd, by being lack'd,

and when he accepts Theobald's emendation dear'd (= endeared) in the same
line for the Ff reading fear'd.

Against, gainst, comes, and becomes are only a few of the almost two
thousand words functioning as syllabic variants in Shakespeare's plays;
about ten per cent of these were apparently formed by the poet himself
and were used only once or twice. Sometimes we find two, three, or even
four forms expressing the same lexical meaning. What accounts for this
extraordinary abundance of synonyms?

1

Shakespeare's incomparable brilliance as a stylist provides one explanation. Let us consider four of his nonce-words: <u>Duff</u> (= <u>Macduff</u>), <u>Dansker</u> (= <u>Dane</u>), *<u>an-hungry</u> (= <u>hungry</u>), and *<u>carlot</u> (= <u>carl</u> 'peasant'). All of these words are more colloquial than their more common syllabic variants, though they are not colloquial in precisely the same way.

Banquo uses the aphetic form <u>Duff</u>, for example, after Macduff has told him of Duncan's murder: "Deare <u>Duff</u>, I prythee contradict thy selfe" (M 2.3.94). The word is not only an affectionate shortening of <u>Macduff</u>, as suggested by the adjective <u>dear</u>, but also a compressed form conveying Banquo's haste and excitement in a moment of extreme shock.

Contextual evidence also provides a clue to the form <u>Dansker</u>, once found (in H 2.1.7) instead of the common synonym <u>Dane</u>. Polonius adopts an intimate and persuasive tone when giving Reynaldo instructions to "enquire . . . what <u>Danskers</u> are in Paris" in order to spy on Laertes. As a direct adoption of the Danish word for 'a Dane,' <u>Dansker</u> presumably would have had more "local flavor" than <u>Dane</u>.[2] It may even have been a slang term in Shakespeare's time,[3] for it is never found in formal oratory in the play, even where it would have been as acceptable metrically as <u>Dane</u>, e.g. in H 1.2.44, "You cannot speake of Reason to the Dane." Therefore, it seems likely that <u>Dansker</u> too is a colloquialism, adopted by Polonius on this occasion in an effort to create an atmosphere of camaraderie with his servant.

The nonce-word *<u>an-hungry</u> is used by Coriolanus in indirect quotation of plebeian speech ("They said they were <u>an hungry</u>, sigh'd forth Proverbes," C 1.1.209). The form is a variant of *<u>a-hungry</u>, used only by Slender and Aguecheek (in prose), the prefix apparently having been expanded in the belief that <u>a</u>- represented OE <u>on</u>-, whereas in fact it represented OE <u>of</u>-.[4] Both <u>an</u>- and the <u>a</u>- which represented OE <u>of</u>- tend to

be associated with low speech in Shakespeare. We have, in addition to
*a-hungry, the Host's as yet unexplained form An-heires in MW 2.1.228
and Mrs. Quickly's adowne'a in MW 1.4.44, both prose. Dogberry's mala-
propism aspitious in MA 3.5.50 (for auspicious) may also be mentioned.
Thus, Coriolanus is almost certainly meant to be depicted as scornfully
mimicking the speech of the populace.[5]

A somewhat similar case is *carlot, once used to mean carl 'peasant':

And he hath bought the Cottage and the bounds

That the old Carlot once was Master of.   AYLI 3.5.108

Though one might at first classify this as a legitimate derivative in -ot
like Cypriot or patriot, it does not express the meaning 'one belonging
to, native to [the root word]' which characterizes such derivatives. In
addition, the shepherd Silvius is the speaker, and F prints the word in
italics as if it were an unfamiliar foreign term. All of this evidence
strongly suggests that Shakespeare intended *carlot as an ignorant per-
version of carl (possibly by confusion with harlot, then often masculine
as in WT 2.3.4) for purposes of characterization.[6]

It is not difficult to find words of this type in which stylistic
considerations seem to have had major importance in determining form.
Possibly this is one explanation for the fact that so much critical attention has been given to Shakespeare as a supreme verbal stylist, and so
little to Shakespeare as a metrist. Yet when we look again at the syllabic variants discussed above, we see that in each case the iambic pentameter line would have been irregular had he used the more common word:

Deare Duff, I prythee contradict thy selfe

Enquire me first what Danskers are in Paris

They said they were <u>an</u> <u>hungry</u>, sigh'd forth Proverbes

That the old <u>Carlot</u> once was Master of.[7]

In view of this, I believe we are justified in asking whether metrical as well as stylistic considerations may have influenced Shakespeare's choice; and, further, whether in some cases desire for metrical regularity may have been the <u>prime</u> factor involved.

For example, in Shakespeare's plays the verbs <u>quite</u>, <u>quittance</u>, and <u>requite</u> all mean 'to repay,' as in the following lines:

Farewell, be trustie and Ile <u>quite</u> thy paines   RJ 2.4.204

As fitting best to <u>quittance</u> their deceite   1H6 2.1.14

And will with Deeds <u>requite</u> thy gentlenesse.   TA 1.1.237

Here the suffix <u>-ance</u> and the prefix <u>re-</u> seem to have no discernible meaning or stylistic effect. It is true that <u>re-</u> sometimes carries reiterative force, but since this idea is already contained in the simple verb <u>quite</u>, it is redundant here; <u>-ance</u> is a formative of nouns of action and has no force when it is found in a verb. Therefore, if Shakespeare uses <u>quite</u> when a monosyllabic word is desirable for the meter, and the stress variants <u>quittance</u> and <u>requite</u> when a disyllabic word is desirable, as in the examples I have given, then meter must have been the factor governing his choice.

Virtually every other Renaissance poet also uses syllabic variants of this type, though not so extensively as Shakespeare. Spenser, for instance, has <u>gainst</u> and <u>against</u> juxtaposed in <u>Faerie</u> <u>Queene</u> V.7.10.8-9 (" . . . her sonnes, which <u>gainst</u> them did rebell, / With inward griefe and malice did <u>against</u> them swell"). And he has <u>less</u> along with <u>lesser</u> in a typically Spenserian pronouncement (<u>Faerie</u> <u>Queene</u> II.5.15.6-8):

>Losse is no shame, nor to be _lesse_ than foe,
>
>But to be _lesser_, then himselfe, doth marre
>
>Both loosers lot, and victours prayse alsoe.

Obviously, meter **was** the determinant of form in these cases. Spenser's name variants also alternate in accordance with metrical requirements: occasionally he has _Archimage_ for _Archimago_, _Duess'_ for _Duessa_, _Glorian_ for _Gloriana_, and even the full form _Britomartis_ for _Britomart_. The poet George Gascoigne, too, must have had meter in mind when he wrote that the nightingale sings in the dark

>To _wray_ the woo that makes hir weepe.
>
>So sing I now for to _bewray_
>
>The lothsome life I lead alway.[8]

(Both _wray_ and _bewray_ meant 'disclose, reveal, betray' at the time.) And both Ben Jonson and John Webster use many syllabic variants in their plays. All of this evidence from the poetry of Shakespeare's contemporaries suggests a probable correlation between meter and word choice in his verse as well.

Purpose of the study

In this study, therefore, I have investigated Shakespeare's metrical or unmetrical use of syllabic variants such as _quite_ vs. _quittance_ and _requite_. From his vast number of etymologically related words, those have been chosen which differ in number of syllables (henceforth referred to as their "syllabic value") but not in lexical meaning or stylistic connotations.[9] When I find that these variants are used metrically in the line, and not haphazardly so as to create irregularities such as

trisyllabic or monosyllabic feet, then I will say that they "alternate
metrically" or are "metrical variants." The amount of such metrical
alternation will enable us to see that Shakespeare was in fact greatly
concerned about preserving the regularity of his verse.[10]

By "regularity," I mean conformity to the metrical pattern regarded
as regularly iambic in his time. Though the basic iambic scheme requires a strict alternation of unstressed and stressed syllables in disyllabic feet, a few deviations from this norm were sanctioned by
Renaissance critical authority and poetic practice. Among these permissible "licenses," which are discussed in full on p. 32 ff. below, are
initial truncation, initial or postcaesural inversion, feminine endings,
and extra unaccented syllables in the caesura.

It should be mentioned also that not all of Shakespeare's lines are
pentameter, though the great majority are, and that he occasionally has
stray trimeters, tetrameters, or alexandrines even in the middle of
blank verse passages. These variations in line length are not considered "irregular" in the present study, since only the presence or
absence of an _iambic_ prosody--as opposed to a purely accentual prosody--
is in question here. In a purely accentual prosody, the lines are composed of a fixed number of stressed syllables separated by a widely varying number of unstressed syllables, and typically contain many trisyllabic
feet.

That Shakespeare's poetry, when read in a modern edition, does not
always appear to be iambic is to some extent attributable to the dili-
gence of modern editors in expanding Renaissance forms. For example,
Hardin Craig renders F _boystrous_ in H 3.3.22, quoted below, as
boisterous, thus creating a trisyllabic foot. In addition, scholars have
long recognized that the old editions themselves are often corrupt.

Contractions may not always have been orthographically indicated; a full
form such as he is, for instance, may have been carelessly substituted
for an intended he's by a Renaissance typesetter or even by the poet
himself. But despite such corruptions, it is not difficult to find
F passages in which Shakespeare clearly has chosen to avoid trisyllabic
or monosyllabic substitutions.

Consider the memorable lines on kingship in Hamlet (3.3.15-22):

> . . . the cease of Majestie
> Dies not alone; but like a Gulfe doth draw
> What's neere it, with it. It is a massie wheele
> Fixt on the Somnet of the highest Mount,
> To whose huge Spoakes, ten thousand lesser things
> Are mortiz'd and adjoyn'd: which when it falles,
> Each small annexment, pettie consequence
> Attends the boystrous Ruine.

Had Shakespeare been unconcerned about metrical regularity, he could have
written surcease instead of cease, *confixed instead of fixed, less instead of lesser, and joined instead of adjoined; all of these alternate
forms are found elsewhere in his plays. Moreover, he could have used the
common Elizabethan word annex instead of *annexment--a form which he apparently created for the occasion, not recorded elsewhere by OED except
in Coleridge's writings over two hundred years later.

That Shakespeare did none of these things strongly suggests that he
intended his lines to be iambic and regular rather than studded with trisyllabic feet. But in a study of metrics, it is desirable to be thorough
rather than selective in admitting evidence--to consider all of the uses
of such variants rather than selected ones which seem persuasive. There-

fore I have carried out a complete statistical analysis of the internal evidence provided by Shakespeare's verse.

In interpreting the results, the reader should keep in mind the widespread textual corruption and inconsistent orthography in Elizabethan verse generally. As mentioned above, an irregularity may appear to have been created by haphazard use of an inappropriate syllabic variant when in fact it is due to an error made by a careless compositor. Then, too, Renaissance orthography was no more consistent than our own, and considerably less consistent than that of the eighteenth century, when elisions were usually indicated by an apostrophe. For example, in the line "Of what your reverence shall incite us to" (H5 1.2.20), hypermetrical as printed, it might appear that cite 'impel, urge' should have been used instead of incite to eliminate an anapestic third foot. However, surely it is more probable that then, as now, reverence was often pronounced rev'rence, though written here as a trisyllable (cf. the Elizabethan spelling diffrence in 2H4 4.1.181, Q). This study will demonstrate that if the two factors mentioned above--human error and illogical orthography--are taken into account, no evidence remains to show that Shakespeare was attempting to write anything but an iambic line.

Summary of previous scholarship

It may seem peculiar that modern-day critics should have to battle for the principle that Shakespeare was a careful metrist as well as a stunningly original thinker. And yet, perhaps as a carryover from Romantic appreciations of his "rugged" vitality, we still find those who apparently believe that he did not write regular iambic poetry. As recently as 1953, a scholar attempting to demonstrate that Milton's verse was iambic said that Shakespeare's, in contrast, was written "on accentual rather than syllabic principles." (Opposing "accentual" to "syllabic" poetry, he defines the former as "that type in which the number of strong accents, and therefore the number of feet, must be five, but the number of weak syllables may vary within broad limits"; in the latter type, there are still five feet, but "the number of syllables in each foot is two.")[11]

It will be recognized, also, that modern editors who gratuitously expand metrically exact forms like boystrous in H 3.3.22 must do so in the belief that Shakespeare freely indulged in trisyllabic substitution. And many scholars support this editorial practice. A. C. Partridge, for example, accuses Helge Kökeritz of "insensibility to Shakespeare's skill in modulating the later poetry" because of his statement in Shakespeare's Pronunciation (p. 28) that such tampering violates Shakespearean prosodic rules. In fact, it seems to have become quite usual for critics to deny that Shakespeare's later verse was iambic at all: Partridge comments further that "the editing of the First Folio was niggling in its attempt to fit Shakespeare's subtly modulated accentual rhythms to the old Marlovian pattern of iambic pentameter."[12]

But let us take a close look at two of the lines quoted by critics to demonstrate the poet's alleged evolution toward purely accentual verse. F. E. Halliday remarks that "all the feet are irregular" in T 1.2.129, which he reproduces and scans as follows:

$$/ \ x \qquad x \ x \qquad / \ x \qquad x \ x / \qquad xx \ / \qquad x$$
Fated   to the   purpose   did Anton   io op   en.[13]

It must be said at the outset that although Halliday does not reveal his textual authority, it is apparently modern, for the F reading is "Fated to th' purpose, did Anthonio open." Here we have clear orthographic indication that the in the form th' was meant to be joined to the preceding

preposition and the combination pronounced as a monosyllable, a usage
common in Shakespeare (e.g. ith' T 1.2.130, the very next line, bith'
L 5.3.19, Q) as well as in other writers of the period (e.g. o'th' in
Jonson's Sejanus 2.370). And as for Anthonio, Halliday has failed to
recognize that i in a Romance ending of the -io type could (then as now)
become consonantal [j] when metrically necessary,[14] allowing the word to
be trisyllabic. When the facts are taken into consideration, then, we
can see that this line,

```
   / x       x    /     x   /     x  /     x /     x
Fated     to th' pur   pose did   Anthon  io o   pen,
```

supposedly full of rhythmic eccentricities, including two anapestic feet,
is actually perfectly regular blank verse with the "permissible" variations (to be discussed in full in the following chapter) of an initial
inversion and a feminine ending.

If it seems strange that a critic should attempt to talk about Renaissance metrics without consulting the original texts, we must remember
that even a careful scholar such as Partridge is occasionally carried
away by his belief that Shakespeare's blank verse shows increasing liber-
ation from an iambic pattern. He recognizes that an extra unaccented
syllable in the caesura was a common variation in the Shakespearean line.
And he mentions with approval Evelyn Scholl's study of musical settings
of Elizabethan poetry--a study which suggests, among other things, that
the word patience had a trisyllabic variant pronunciation at the time.
Nevertheless, he scans TC 1.2.5 as follows,

```
   x  /     x   /     x    /     x   x      / x
To see    the bat   tell: Hec   tor whose  pacience,
```

remarking that such inversion of stress in the last foot was "another
daring innovation which Shakespeare began to practise."[15] It is clear

from his own comments outlined above, however, that the line is regular
and should be scanned

```
  x   /     x   /     x      / x     x    /     x /
To see    the bat   tell: ‖ Hector   whose pa   cience,
```

with an extra syllable before the caesura and an (allowable) inverted
foot immediately following it. Even if we wish to be extremely cautious
and regard _patience_ as a disyllable here, as in Modern English, the line
is still regularly iambic by Renaissance standards (though short, with
a feminine ending). Certainly there is no possibility of inversion in
the fifth foot.

Though such errors in scansion are relatively minor, they proceed
from the important assumption that Shakespeare's blank verse, or at least
his later blank verse, was not consistently intended to be iambic. And
this assumption is responsible for many serious "blind spots" in Shakespeare criticism. When commentators praise Shakespeare for his bold use
of functional shift, when they say that he "risks all for meaning, and
rather than be stopped or impeded in his course dares everything that the
flux of forms made possible,"[16] and when they plaintively ask why there
are so many nonce-words in the plays ("jewels . . . never shown but
once"),[17] any possible effect of meter on form is being overlooked. Con-
versely, important stylistic, phonological, and lexical implications (summarized in the final chapter of this study) emerge when it can be proved
that Shakespeare consistently chose forms desirable for iambic verse.

Certain scholars, lacking the evidence collected in the following
pages, have nevertheless intuitively recognized this Shakespearean preference. Unfortunately, however, most of them have done more harm than
good by their extremism and lack of phonological training. Pope's
extensive regularizing (and rewriting) of the F text is well known.

William S. Walker followed in the nineteenth century with A Critical Examination of the Text of Shakespeare (London, 1860), which, though basically sound, includes many alarmingly rash emendations; and his frequent admission that he does not have the F reading "at hand" does not add to the reader's confidence.

E. A. Abbott, also writing in the 1860s, vacillates between an extreme syllabist and an accentualist position. He recognizes that Renaissance spellings indicate that Elizabethan pronunciation differed from our own, and that written anapests might be spoken iambs, and he compiles a body of pronunciation rules based on his findings. But he adds to these rules others which are purely conjectural, with the result that some of his relentlessly "iambic" readings are eccentric indeed. On the other hand, his accentualist leanings can be seen in a statement that "there may be more than two syllables in any foot" providing that only one is accented and that the supernumerary ones are "slurred."[18] Caught between two opposed theories of versification, Abbott takes a time-honored middle course by advocating "half" pronunciation of syllables.

He had a zealous follower in George H. Browne, whose strained readings are usually taken directly from Abbott's work. In a strange little pamphlet (Notes on Shakspere's Versification) written in semiphonetic spelling, Browne laudably stresses that we must "realize something of the changd [sic] conditions of accent, pronunciation, etc. of Elizabethan English before we can approach the subject of rythmic [sic] versification intelligently." Yet he does not live up to this ambitious manifesto, for he wishes to read the italicized particles as quasi syllables in the following lines:

Co-me good Fellow, put thine Iron on.   AC 4.4.3

Yea, look'st thou pa-_le_? Let me see the Writing.   R2 5.2.57

Go-_od_ my Lord, give me thy favour stil.[19]   T 4.1.204

Such rigorous attempts to regularize Shakespeare's verse betray an ignor-

ance of the freedoms allowed by the prosodic tradition of the Renaissance,

for not one of these three lines is irregular as it stands in the F text.

It is to be hoped that Helge Kökeritz' definitive study, Shake-

speare's Pronunciation, will prevent such grotesque misreadings in the

future. Drawing on an extensive knowledge of historical phonology,

Kökeritz defines the main differences between Elizabethan pronunciation

and our own. By thus establishing that Shakespeare had at his disposal

various types of syncopation or expansion which are not viable in modern

usage, Kökeritz lays the groundwork for a major reassessment of Eliza-

bethan metrical practice. In a further article, "Elizabethan Prosody and

Historical Phonology," he examines the metrical or unmetrical use of

certain Shakespearean synonyms to provide additional support for the pro-

vocative theories set forth in his larger work. I am indebted to this

article for the general method followed in my study, but I have refined

the technique and increased the scope of the investigation to include more

than 1,500 syllabic variants occurring in approximately 13,000 lines of

verse.

External evidence

It is necessary to argue primarily from internal evidence because

the external evidence, such as the writings of Renaissance theorists on

meter, can never be conclusive in reference to specifically Shakespearean

practice, or, indeed, to Renaissance poetic practice in general. But it

is difficult to believe that poets such as Samuel Daniel and George

Gascoigne would expound a theory far removed from actuality when they sat down to write about their craft. And, without exception, the Renaissance theorists indicate that a basically iambic line was the norm. Although they are willing to permit occasional slight variations such as feminine endings and initial inversion (see below, p. 34 f.), their comments clearly show that the standard blank verse foot was to consist of two, and only two, syllables: the first unstressed, the second stressed.

Daniel, for example, refers (ca. 1603) to "the plaine ancient verse, consisting of ten sillables or five feete, which hath ever beene used amongest us time out of minde."[20] And Gascoigne sets up a contrast between Chaucer's verse, which he thought was accentual, and the Elizabethan "playne and simple manner of wryting, that there is none other foote used but one . . . this playne foote of two syllables." He laments the fact that Renaissance versification thus lacks Chaucer's poetic variety! Although he does not speak specifically of blank verse, he does say that sonnets have "fouretene lynes, every line conteyning tenne syllables."[21]

Then there is George Puttenham's statement (1589) that "meeter and measure is all one, for what the Greekes called metron, the Latines call Mensura, and is but the quantitie of a verse, either long or short. This quantitie with them consisteth in the number of their feete: & with us in the number of sillables, which are comprehended in every verse, not regarding his feete, otherwise then that we allow, in scanning our verse, two sillables to make one short portion (suppose it a foote) in every verse."[22] Puttenham is unwilling to use the term foot because he thinks it suggests motion and relative speed, and hence quantity (which is, of course, not fixed in English as it was in the classical languages). But his meaning is clear.

Further, two theorists offer evidence that a specifically iambic

foot was normative. King James VI comments that "the form of placeing
syllabes in verse is this. That your first syllabe in the lyne be short,
the second lang, the thrid short, the fourt lang, the fyft short, the sixt
lang, and sa furth to the end of the lyne."[23] If this seems unconvincing
because the terminology suggests a preoccupation with quantity rather than
stress, we can compare William Webbe's statement (1586): "The naturall
course of most English verses seemeth to run uppon the olde Iambicke
stroake, and I may well thinke by all likelihoode it had the beginning
thereof."[24]

There are, in contrast, very few Renaissance allusions to specifically Shakespearean versification. In <u>Palladis</u> <u>Tamia</u> (1598), Francis
Meres refers to Shakespeare's "fine filed phrase,"[25] and Ben Jonson's
complimentary couplet in F is well known:

> the race
Of Shakespeares minde, and manners brightly shines
In his well tornèd, and true-filèd lines.

Both of these references are inconclusive, however, because we have no assurance that Meres and Jonson reserved their praise of well "filed" verse
for what we would call regular iambic pentameter. Thus we are again
thrown back on internal evidence such as Shakespeare's metrical or unmetrical use of syllabic variants.

Internal evidence

I have stated above that a consistently <u>metrical</u> use of such variants
would indicate that Shakespeare was in fact adhering to an iambic rather
than a purely accentual prosody and wished to preserve the basically deca-

syllabic line. It may be objected that such reasoning is circular, because there is nothing to prevent us from assuming that Shakespeare wanted
to use a specific variant in each specific context for stylistic reasons
having nothing to do with meter. If so, he would have arranged the rest
of the line around the variant, thus creating metrical lines, perhaps, but
metrical lines which prove nothing. But there _is_ something to prevent us
from assuming this. There would have been no motive for a specific
Shakespearean preference among the variants which I discuss--no motive,
that is, except a desire for metrical regularity.

Those who disagree would say that no two words are ever identical in
stylistic connotations, because one word will always be more colloquial,
elevated, rare, poetic, etc. than the other, no matter how infinitesimal
the difference may be. And this is probably true. But I have excluded
from my study all words which are obviously appropriate only in certain
contexts, e.g. the nonce-word *an-hungry as opposed to hungry, or sirrah
as opposed to sir. The question to be decided here, then, is whether,
among the remaining variants, any possible connotative differences would
have been sufficiently marked to have influenced Shakespeare's word choice.

Investigation of the matter clearly shows that these differences were
not sufficiently marked--that even the neologistic variants, which we
would expect to have very strong connotations of rarity, etc., were not
used according to a rigid idea of stylistic appropriateness, but simply
in accordance with the demands of the meter. In carrying out my investigation, I first isolated those variants which seemed likely to have the
strongest stylistic connotations; then considered any external evidence
surrounding them (historical data and standard Elizabethan usage); and
finally surveyed the internal evidence--whether or not they tended to appear only in certain contexts in Shakespeare. My findings about related

groups of variants are summarized below.

Distribution of selected affixes

Several authors have attempted to assign specific connotations to individual prefixes and suffixes. George Gordon, for example, suggests on p. 274 of his study that the adjectival -y suffix (as in *plumpy 'plump') is rustic or archaic; and John Crowe Ransom feels that it produces a "homely" effect.[26] But this opinion is not justified either on historical grounds or on the basis of Shakespearean usage. The widespread popularity of the -y adjectives among other Elizabethan poets indicates that the -y probably functioned as a convenient "filler" syllable for metrical purposes. The mere fact that a forerunner of the suffix existed in Old English, and that Spenser was fond of -y adjectives, does not mean that these words necessarily had a rustic or archaic flavor.[27] Similarly, the fact that they occur several times in the fairytale atmosphere of A Midsummer Night's Dream does not mean that they are found only in "rustic" contexts; on the contrary, the evidence from Shakespeare points in the other direction. The -y variants which are statistically significant in this study occur twenty-two times in the plays. A breakdown shows that Henry V and Henry VI, Part 2 each have four of these -y adjectives; that Henry IV, Part 1, Henry VI, Part 1, and Romeo and Juliet each have two; and that Henry VI, Part 3, Richard III, Titus Andronicus, Antony and Cleopatra, Timon of Athens, The Two Gentlemen of Verona, The Merchant of Venice, and A Midsummer Night's Dream each have one.

B. Ifor Evans feels that there is a "harsh" quality inherent in certain suffixes. Speaking of the abstract nonce-words in Troilus and Cressida, he says that "they seem endowed with a deliberate harshness to which the frequent ending of -ive as in persistive and -ure as in soilure

give [sic] emphasis."[28] One wonders what he would have thought of Shake-

speare's permissive and pleasure, both of which occur in dark comedies.

Surely this is a case of the sound appearing to echo the sense, when in

reality the sense is prompting a subjective interpretation of the sound.

OED's designation of the en- prefix as frequently intensive, sec-

onded by Var. Ed.,[29] is more difficult to refute. But the mere fact that

Shakespeare seems to have created so many en- or in- forms (see Appendix,

Table III) leads one to question whether he really could have needed an

"intensive" word quite so often. In the following lines, also, the en-

form does not seem to differ in meaning from the simple verb without en-:

> Your breath first kindled the dead coale of warres,
>
> Betweene this chastiz'd kingdome and my selfe,
>
> And brought in matter that should feed this fire;
>
> And now 'tis farre too huge to be blowne out
>
> With that same weake winde, which enkindled it.   J 5.2.83-87

Unfortunately, in this and a similar case, the prefix be-, it is impos-

sible to cite every line for the reader's judgment. But the evidence in-

dicates that if there is any intensifying force in such prefixes, it is

due merely to the minute amount of emphasis that is furnished by an addi-

tional syllable. The difference in emphasis between a long word and a

short one is, I believe, so small as to be for practical purposes non-

existent.

However, lines such as "To emblaze the Honor that thy Master got"

(2H6 4.10.76) and "To enforce the painèd impotent to smile" (LLL 5.2.864)

present a special problem. In these lines, to must be read as proclitic

t' to make the meter regularly iambic, giving t'emblaze and t'enforce

with loss of the o̤ vowel. Thus it could be argued that Shakespeare must
have had a stylistic preference for the derivative here--emblaze rather
than blaze, enforce rather than force--since by use of the simple verb he
would have eliminated the need for a contraction. But other explanations
are possible. First, the compositor may have erroneously substituted
derivatives for intended short forms. Or, if Shakespeare himself was indeed responsible, it may be that contractions such as t'emblaze and
t'enforce were so usual in speech, and so erratically reproduced in the
orthography (as indicated by Kökeritz' discussion in Shakespeare's Pronunciation, pp. 275-276), that the poet felt no compunction about writing
the full forms. He knew that his readers would make the necessary adjust-
ment. Thus it would have been a matter of indifference to him whether he
used the simple verb or the derivative in these instances.[30]

Since it is well known that a Latinate style usually gives an impression of elevation, Romanic prefixes and suffixes have been thought to
add an elevated quality to root words. This opinion is supported[31] by
Hamlet's studied use of *concernancy, *definement, *extolment, and *inven-
torially in the prose exchange with Osric (H 5.2.117-128; Qq only; om.
Ff), by Armado's pedantic couplement and *infamonize, and by Mrs. Quickly's malapropisms familiarity (for familiar) and *temperality (for
temper). But there is a twofold difficulty involved in making such a
generalization. First, with very few exceptions, only wholly Romanic
words function as syllabic variants of words with Romanic prefixes or suffixes. Thus, for example, *control vs. controlment would be the rule,
blast vs. *blastment the exception. It does not seem logical to say that
the elevation is inherent only in the Romanic affix and not in the Romanic root-word, and therefore, in such cases, all that could possibly be
added by an affix would be the slight amount of additional elevation

furnished by the extra syllable.

And there is a second difficulty. In some instances it is actually the shorter word which seems more elevated, simply because it is rarer than the longer one. For example, Shakespeare apparently created the short forms *effuse (= effusion), *illume (= illuminate), *import (= importance), *impose (= imposition), *lament (= lamentation), *leagued (= colleagued), and *ostent (= ostentation). Surely if all Shakespearean neologisms[32] and all forms with Romanic prefixes or suffixes were compared, it would be the neologisms (unless they were jocular formations) that we would expect to be more consistently correlated with certain types of characters or plays.[33] It would seem likely that the nonjocular neologisms, being rare, elevated, or arcane, would tend to be associated with the more sophisticated dramatic contexts.

If this proved to be true, the case for saying that Shakespeare could have had no stylistic preference for one variant over another would be greatly weakened. It would be possible to argue, for example, that when he had a choice between a neologism and its non-neologistic synonym in a late tragedy (or in a speech by Hamlet), he would naturally prefer to use the neologism, whereas in an early comedy or history play he would prefer the non-neologistic variant. Thus, in this case and possibly in others, word choice would be dependent on Shakespeare's stylistic development and/or his desire to characterize particular speakers, rather than on metrical considerations.

Distribution of neologisms

In order to examine the validity of such an argument, I listed all of the lines in which statistically significant neologisms or their non-

neologistic synonyms occurred: a total of approximately 1,000 lines.[34]
Then I constructed two tables showing the distribution of both groups of
variants, first among the plays (see Appendix, Table I), then among the
major characters (Table II). Complete data will be found in the Appendix, including a list of words surveyed (Table III), but the results may
be summarized as follows.

The seven plays which had the largest number of neologistic variants were Troilus and Cressida, Hamlet, Othello, Henry V, King Lear,
Richard III, and (surprisingly) Henry VI, Part 1.[35] Of these seven plays,
all except Lear were among the nine plays which had the largest number of
non-neologistic variants. Though Lear does rank higher on the neologistic
scale than on the non-neologistic one, other late tragedies do not, e.g.
Antony and Cleopatra and Coriolanus, which one would suppose to be characteristic of Shakespeare's later manner. Similarly, although the play
highest in number of non-neologisms, Richard III, is early, its three
closest competitors are all late: Coriolanus, Hamlet, and Othello. And
the early comedies The Two Gentlemen of Verona, A Midsummer Night's Dream,
and The Taming of the Shrew actually rank lower on the non-neologistic
scale than on the neologistic one.

Most important of all, the order of the plays on each list correlates
fairly well, at least at the extremes of the scale, with the order of the
plays in terms of number of verse lines. Thus, though our expectation
that the late tragedies tend to have a large number of neologisms is cor-
roborated, we see that this is largely due to the fact that Troilus and
Cressida, Hamlet, Othello, and Lear are long plays. Since these same
tragedies also have many non-neologistic synonyms, it is evident that
Shakespeare did not show a consistent preference for neologisms in one
kind of play, and for their more common syllabic variants in another. And

since his word choice in these cases was not determined by stylistic considerations, it must have been determined by something else--namely, as we shall see, by meter.

If we turn to examine the distribution of these variants among individual characters, a similar pattern emerges. Though the figures are too small to be conclusive, the characters who use neologisms most frequently (Henry V, Macbeth, Troilus, and Richard III) also use a relatively large number of non-neologistic synonyms. Hamlet actually ranks much higher on the non-neologistic scale than on the neologistic one. Therefore, I conclude that when Shakespeare had to choose between a neologism and a non-neologism in writing a line of verse, he did not consistently choose one or the other on the basis of its stylistic suitability for the play or character. That he consistently chose one or the other on the basis of its _metrical_ suitability--that, in other words, he was more interested in having Hamlet's speeches be metrically exact than in filling them with as many unusual formations as possible--will be demonstrated in this study.

CHAPTER II

METHOD

Using John Bartlett's <u>Concordance</u> in conjunction with Schmidt's

<u>Shakespeare-Lexicon</u> (to provide a general idea of meaning and the more

important quarto variants), I listed all of the syllabic variants which

occur in Shakespeare. Each occurrence of each listed word was then

checked against the Globe text[1] to determine whether or not it was used

in such a way as to create an irregular line. Any lines which were not

perfectly regular, as well as all lines specifically cited in this study,

were then rechecked against the F text[2] and the variant readings given by

Var. Ed. when necessary. Then I compared the meanings assigned by

Schmidt with those in OED, making sure that variants were truly synony-

mous and, except a few of the analogical ones, could be traced to the

same root. The words were classified according to the principles out-

lined below, and a list was made of cases in which the printed form

created an unmetrical line.

Although the procedure was thus fairly simple in essence, the sub-

sidiary problems involved in a study of this type are complex. The F

text frequently is marred by mislineation and erroneous printing of lines

as prose which are obviously meant to be verse.[3] And even when there is

no conspicuous textual corruption, many forms remain which have not yet

been satisfactorily explained. My practice has been either to omit such words, or to indicate clearly the tenuous nature of the proposed reading.

Incompleteness of primary and secondary sources is another difficulty. F omits <u>Pericles</u>, the poems, and many passages in the plays, most
notably in <u>Hamlet</u> and <u>Lear</u>. Therefore I have sometimes relied on readings supplied by other sources.[4] The <u>Concordance</u> too is incomplete, but
as a practical necessity, for if all of the common "function words" and
proper names had been included, it would probably have been doubled or
tripled in length. For similar reasons, Schmidt also does not give a
full listing of such words. Therefore, in several cases my figures are
undoubtedly smaller than those which a thorough rereading of Shakespeare
would reveal. Despite these obstacles, however, it is possible to carry
out a reasonably complete investigation of Shakespeare's metrical practice if normal precautions are taken. The following discussion deals
more fully with such precautions, summarizing the organization of this
study and the lexical and metrical assumptions on which it rests.

Terminology and classification

Because there is no one standard reference work on morphology, the
terminology used by various authors is inconsistent. For this reason, I
give below a list of the major terms which are used in my discussions,
together with brief definitions.

A <u>simplex</u> is the smallest indivisible linguistic unit capable of independent existence. Thus a <u>compound</u> is not a simplex, though one or
more simplexes may be contained within a compound.[5] A <u>prefix</u> or <u>suffix</u>
is a particle that can be affixed to a simplex but itself cannot exist
independently. A <u>derivative</u> is a word composed of a simplex plus a prefix, a suffix, or any combination of the two. Derivatives which are also

syllabic variants have been called <u>derivational</u> <u>variants</u>.

Some syllabic variants are not composed of a simplex plus a living prefix or suffix, but of a simplex plus some other kind of prepositive or postpositive particle. If this particle is traceable to an ancient etymological element in English or a foreign language, I have classified the variant as <u>etymological</u>. If, on the other hand, this particle is ultimately derived from an oblique case ending (e.g. <u>-ow</u> in <u>meadow</u>) or a conjugational sign (<u>-ate</u> in <u>ruinate</u>), I have classified the variant as <u>morphological</u>. If this particle has been added to the simplex on the analogy of a derivational, etymological, or morphological particle in another word--with no historical justification for its being there--I have classified the variant as <u>analogical</u>.[6]

Thus far I have spoken primarily of variants which represent a lengthening of the simplex. But there are many which are shorter than the word from which they arose. These I have called <u>clipped</u> <u>forms</u>, and have subdivided them according to the part of the word that has been removed. If an initial syllable has been dropped, I have called the variant <u>aphetic</u>;[7] if a medial syllable has been dropped, <u>syncopated</u>; if a final syllable or two has been dropped, <u>apocopated</u>. Occasionally I have deviated from perfect consistency of classification in order to discuss related variants together.

The basic classification in this study is historical: derivational variants, etymological variants, morphological variants, analogical variants, clipped forms. But the largest group, that involving derivational processes, has been subdivided according to the general <u>function</u> of the prefix or suffix (negation, reiteration, diminution, etc.). I have chosen to organize the variants in this way in order to create an interesting and meaningful grouping in which I could contrast synonymous prefixes and suffixes of different syllabic value, e.g. -ance and -ation. A small amount of etymological information has been included to help explain why two or more etymologically related words could have been used synonymously.[8]

Limitation of the subject

I have previously defined syllabic variants as words which are etymologically related, and which differ in syllabic value but not in lexical meaning or stylistic connotations. Not all such variants could be included in a study of this length. The following large groups have been omitted:

1. All variant forms of the past participle,[9] whether involving a weakening of an originally strong form (e.g. shaked vs. shaken, weaved vs. woven), a shortening of a strong form (spoke vs. spoken, untrod vs. untrodden), a shortening of a weak form (acquit vs. acquitted, blent vs. blended), or an anglicizing of an adopted L form (consecrated vs. consecrate, created vs. create).

2. All forms involving the alternation of the simplex with a derivative consisting of the simplex plus -ly. Examples are the adverbs bright and brightly, representing OE beorhte and beorhtlíce, respectively:

The moone shines bright. In such a night as this   MV 5.1.1
A substitute shines brightly as a King.   MV 5.1.94

These double adverbial forms are ultimately due to the fact that Old English had an adjectival -líc ending to which the adverbial -e was added.

But even when there was only an adverb in simple -e in Old English (e.g.

fǽȝere 'fairly,' giving ModE fair), an adverb in -ly usually appears

later.[10] Thus Shakespeare had at his disposal the word fairly as a con-

venient syllabic variant of fair, as we see in J 4.1.37-38:

> Hubert.   Can you not reade it? Is it not faire writ?

> Arthur.   Too fairely Hubert, for so foule effect.

Some of the OE -líc adjectives survived into Modern English (e.g.

hláfordlic, giving ModE lordly), and after the analogy of these, new ad-

jectives in -ly were formed even when a simple adjective was already in

existence. As a result, we occasionally find alternation between a

simplex and a form with -ly in adjectives also. Compare the use of sick

and sickly by two dying men:

> My blood, my want of strength, my sicke heart shewes,
>
> That I must yeeld my body to the Earth.   3H6 5.2.8

> A pleasing Cordiall, Princely Buckingham,
>
> Is this thy Vow, unto my sickely heart.   R3 2.1.42

To some extent, such variants are made possible by meanings now obsolete:

note the King's startling comment (in AW 2.3.118) that Helena has raised

him from his "sickly bed."

These two groups of variants have been excluded partly to keep the

study from becoming unwieldy, and partly to avoid duplicating the evi-

dence collected by Kökeritz in "Elizabethan Prosody and Historical

Phonology." Investigating over 1,100 lines containing such forms, he

found that only three showed possible trisyllabic substitution caused by

the variant itself.[11] There is no reason to suppose that a full-scale
study would reveal any greater proportion of possible irregularity.

With the exceptions noted above, all significant syllabic variants
have been included in this study. But the word "significant" demands
further definition. Words can be identical in lexical meaning, and (in
Modern English) different in syllabic value, and yet not function as
statistically significant variants in Shakespeare. To do this, they must
fulfill certain additional requirements which are outlined below.

Lexical, stylistic, and syntactical criteria

Lexical identity in itself is sometimes quite difficult to determine. I have taken great care to insure that the variants I include
would be admitted to be synonymous by most readers--first, by surveying
only etymologically related words and not those of the city vs. town
variety; second, by devoting much attention to the question of the interchangeability of the words in context. Even so, it is possible that
there may be differences of opinion, especially when one's interpretation
of the entire thematic content of a play is involved. For example, OED
defines the nonce-word *recomforture in R3 4.4.425,

But in your daughters wombe I bury them.
Where in that Nest of Spicery they will breed
Selves of themselves, to your recomforture,

as 'consolation, comfort.' Thus it would be a syllabic variant of
comfort. However, since Richard is here persuading the widowed Queen
Elizabeth to woo her daughter for him, the word might well mean 'new comfort' or 'restored comfort' in the larger structure of the play.

Usually, I have relied on the OED definition of any given word, as-
signing the listed meaning which to me seemed most appropriate if the
specific line was not cited. In a few instances, where I disagreed
strongly with OED, I have included both the dictionary definition and my
own, in order to let the reader judge for himself. And a few definitions
proposed by Schmidt or the standard editions of Shakespeare (Yale, New
Arden, etc.) have been mentioned. But if a definition is given without
comment, it may be assumed that it represents an abridged version of a
meaning assigned in OED.

Once it has been decided that two variants are lexically identical,
one would think that they would be interchangeable--that, were it not for
the difference in syllabic value, one could just as easily have been used
in a specific context as the other. But this is not always the case;
and, indeed, extreme caution is necessary in determining interchangeability.

As my initial discussion of _Duff_, _Dansker_, *_an-hungry_, and *_carlot_
indicated, stylistic overtones can often be so strong that only one of
two variants could have been used in _one_ context, though either variant
might have been possible in another. For example, _Kate_ is much more colloquial than either _Katharine_ or _Katharina_ (in addition to the fact that
it carries within itself the possibility of a pun on _cate_, as in TS
2.1.189-190), and would not have been appropriate in formal address:

Petruchio. Good morrow _Kate_, for thats your name I heare.
Katerina. Well have you heard, but something hard of hearing:
They call me _Katerine_, that do talke of me. TS 2.1.183-185

All such variants have been excluded, as indicated in Chapter I.[12]

The syntactical environment required by a specific variant can also affect interchangeability. Let me illustrate with a comparison of the apocopated variant coz and the full form cousin. Coz and cousin are both used of blood relatives and in the wider sense 'friend, acquaintance'; they are both used on formal as well as on intimate occasions; and they are both used by kings and nobles as well as by "lower" characters, so that coz is not a "low" form, as is sometimes supposed. However, coz is subject to the following limitations:

1. It is never used in the plural (and even if it were, its syllabic value would not differ from that of cousins).

2. It is never used in conjunction with proper names, so that we do not find, for example, Coz of Exeter or Coz Beatrice.

3. It is never used except in direct address, except for one occurrence in prose (not relevant to this metrical study).

Therefore I feel that if, in listing the occurrences of cousin, we include plural examples, examples used with proper names, and examples not in direct address, the resulting figures will misrepresent the facts of the situation. Shakespeare would not have said cozzes, Coz of Exeter, or (probably) here comes my coz in verse, so that we cannot legitimately say that these were actual possible alternate forms in the specific context. Whenever there were such restrictions placed on the use of a variant, I have placed similar restrictions on all words with which I compare it, and as a result my figures are in many cases smaller than the actual number of occurrences listed in the Concordance. All of the important limitations of this kind have been noted in the text.

Coz is an extreme case, and usually it is not necessary to be so careful that the usage of the variants is precisely the same. Still, we have several words like right, which is a syllabic variant of rightful 'just, equitable' but could not have been used in H5 1.2.293 (" . . . to put forth / My rightfull hand in a wel-hallow'd cause") because of ambiguity arising from context; shipping 'ships collectively,' which alternates metrically with ships but could not possibly have been used with adjectives of quantity, e.g. many shipping; and stony, which is a synonym of stone but could not have been substituted for it in the proverbial Hunger broke stone walls (C 1.1.210).[13]

Some variants lack not only syntactical parallelism but synonymity as well. For example, if one verbal variant is used transitively (e.g. engender 'to beget'), another intransitively (gender 'to copulate'), the two forms are not really synonymous, though both could be glossed 'to breed.' All variants of this type have been omitted.

For similar lexical and syntactical reasons, I have felt it important to compare only parallel verb forms and not, for example, the present tense of one verb with the past tense of another. In this study, the following morphological categories have been recognized: the present tense and infinitive considered together, excluding -eth forms; -eth forms; the past tense; the past participle; the past participial adjective; the present participle; the present participial adjective; and the verbal substantive in -ing. This practice has occasionally involved me in minor absurdities; for instance, when one verb is used only in the past tense and its variant only in the past participle, it seems overly subtle to exclude both on the grounds of lack of parallelism. Therefore, a few cases of this type have been mentioned in my discussion but not counted in the final reckoning. They have been placed in footnotes for ease of identification, as have all interesting forms which are relevant to the variants being considered but themselves lack statistical significance.

Metrical criteria

In judging whether a line is or is not "metrical," I have followed Kökeritz, Jakob Schipper,[14] and the Renaissance theorists in regarding the following variations on a basically decasyllabic iambic pentameter line as permissible:

1. Initial truncation, or omission of the first unaccented syllable in the line.

2. Inversions of stress in the first foot and/or the foot immediately following a caesura, provided that the inversions do not result in wrenching of the stress. For example, two feet in succession could not be inverted; and weak endings or "function words" could not be stressed at the expense of important words in the line.

3. Feminine endings.

4. Substitution of trimeter, tetrameter, and hexameter lines for the usual pentameter.[15]

5. Irregularity in the (marked or unmarked) caesura. Such irregularity is of three types, all involving the addition of an unaccented syllable.

a) Addition of a syllable before the caesura:

A forted res<u>idence</u> || 'gainst the tooth of time   MM 5.1.12[16]

b) Addition of a syllable after the caesura:

Then say if they be true: || <u>This</u> misshapen knave T 5.1.268

c) Addition of a syllable which could be regarded as being
either before or after the caesura:

Lest I Revenge. <u>What?</u> || <u>my</u> Selfe upon my Selfe? R3 5.3.186

This type is known as the "feminine epic" caesura, most
commonly found in lines broken between or among speakers
where the break is so strongly felt that the first part of
the line has almost independent status. (Notice how the
feminine epic caesura resembles an internal feminine ending.)

In addition to these variations, I have allowed two standard poetic
devices: the use of the syllabic inflectional ending -<u>ed</u>; and the variation between monosyllabic and disyllabic forms of the Romanic suffixes
-<u>ia</u>, -<u>iage</u>, -<u>ial</u>, -<u>iance</u> (-<u>ience</u>), -<u>iant</u> (-<u>ient</u>), -<u>iate</u>, -<u>ier</u>, -<u>io</u>, -<u>ion</u>,
-<u>iour</u>, -<u>ious</u> (-<u>eous</u>), -<u>ius</u>, etc.[17] <u>Erudition</u>, for example, could have
either four syllables or five. Finally, any pronunciation which is indi-
cated typographically in F has been accepted.

These "licenses" are found in almost all of the heroic and blank
verse of Shakespeare's time, and must have been accepted as a matter of
course, if, indeed, they were not cultivated as metrical beauties. I
rely not only on the evidence cited by Schipper, but also on the statements of the Renaissance theorists themselves, though, as we have seen

before, such statements can never furnish conclusive proof.

Puttenham is apparently willing to admit initial truncation and caesural irregularity,[18] and we have clear indication that he allowed feminine endings. Commenting on Surrey's decasyllabic pentameter line "What holy grave? alas, what sepulcher?" (from "Of the Death of Sir Thomas Wyatt"), he says, " . . . if I had the making of him, he should have bene of eleven sillables and kept his measure of five still, and would so have runne more pleasantly a great deale; for as he is now, though he be even, he seemes odde and defective, for not well observing the natural accent of every word." Puttenham was obviously an advocate of the alternate Elizabethan stressing of _sepulcher_ (x / x ; both accentuations are found in Shakespeare), for he gives as his revision of the line

$$\overset{/}{\text{What ho}} \quad \overset{x \quad x}{\text{ly grave?}} \overset{/}{} \quad \overset{x}{\text{alas,}}\overset{/}{} \quad \overset{x}{\text{what fit}} \overset{/}{} \quad \overset{x}{\text{sepul}}\overset{/}{} \quad \overset{x}{\text{cher,}}^{19}$$

thus adding a feminine ending.

Thomas Campion is even more definite in sanctioning extra unaccented syllables in the caesura and at the end of the line. Speaking of the English "Iambick licentiate," which he feels is appropriate for tragic and heroic poems and worthy of imitation, he says that in the first, second, and fourth foot " . . . we may use . . . sometime a _Tribrack_ or _Dactile_."[20] Later, he comments that even in the third and fifth foot "a _Tribrack_ may be very formally taken," and he gives these examples (italics mine):

Men that do fall to mis_ery_, _quickly_ fall.

Some trade in Barb_ary_, _some_ in Turky trade.

Renown'd in ev'ry art there lives _not any_.

Renaissance theorists who were still attuned to the classical quantitative system frequently classified feet as tribrachs (x x x) which would now be called anapests (x x /) or amphibrachs (x / x). Campion's terminology does not, however, obscure the fact that he is allowing an extra unaccented syllable in the caesura or at the end of the line. And he sees no reason to exclude trochees from the first foot, citing "Noble, ingenious, and discreetly wise" as acceptable.[21]

Taking into account all of this evidence, I have not considered that a line is made "irregular" by initial truncation, inversion, a feminine ending, caesural irregularity--or by being an alexandrine or a short line.

My concern is that of determining whether an individual _word_ is used metrically or unmetrically in the line: whether it _in itself_ creates an unmetrical line which could have been avoided had a syllabic variant been used instead. Therefore, in lines which would have been unmetrical in either case because of irregularity in some other part of the line, uses of a specific variant have not been counted as irregular. Two examples may be cited: baby in 2H6 1.3.148, "Shee'le hamper thee, and dandle thee like a Baby," where babe would merely remove a feminine ending; and against in T 1.2.158, "Against what should ensue. // How came we a shore," where gainst would merely make the line headless.

In neither of these lines would substitution of the alternate variant improve the meter. Sometimes, however, we find that the alternate form would make the line syllabically exact. But even such cases have not been counted as "irregular uses" if the alternate would result in stress-wrenching or inversions at odd places in the line. For example, if haught had been substituted for haughty in TA 1.1.302 ("Thee never: nor thy Trayterous haughty sonnes"), the unimportant weak ending -ous would have received the stress; and if hate were used instead of hatred in C 3.1.20 ("To oppose his hatred fully. Welcome home"), the line would have ten syllables, but his would be stressed at the expense of the noun that it modifies. And in M 5.1.86, "My mind she ha's mated, and amaz'd my sight," mazed would create a decasyllabic line, but then mated would be an inverted foot directly preceding the caesura--not a permissible position for inversion.

Variants must also be selected with caution so that only those which are actually of different syllabic value are included. Accordingly, I have omitted the following types in which syllabic identity is disguised:

1. Type even vs. evening. Both of these words mean 'the latter part of the day,' but since evening is always disyllabic in Shakespeare (as it usually is today), the words are not statistically significant. A similar case is hasting vs. hastening; the latter is syncopated to a disyllable in Shakespeare. If two words are ever syllabically identical in the plays, they have not been counted.[22] For example, *enthroned and throned have been excluded because throned is twice disyllabic, even though it also occurs four times as a monosyllable.[23]

2. Type *embraces vs. embracements. These plurals show no difference in syllabic value although the singular forms are significant variants. Sometimes, as in *villagery 'villages collectively,' the sense of a word requires a syllabically identical plural form (here, villages) as its synonym.

For the same reason--lack of statistical significance--words which occurred only at the end of the line where an alternate variant would have
been equally acceptable metrically were excluded. Thus Syracuse and
Syracusa were omitted because Syracuse appeared only once, in final position: "No sir, not I, I came from Siracuse" (CE 5.1.363). If, on the
other hand, it had ever been used within the line where the extra syllable would have been metrically significant, I would have included both
forms in my statistics.[24]

Method of listing variants

It has not been possible to cite all of the relevant line numbers.
However, citations have been given for all variants which occur fewer
than three times in the plays; and for others, citations have been given
as frequently as space allows. If different Renaissance texts show two
different variants in identical position in the same line, the line has
been counted under both words. Estimated figures have been given for the
few variants which occur more than 150 times in Shakespeare.

Forms found only in the poems are included whenever they are needed
to function as syllabic variants for words used in the plays. Otherwise,
the poems have been omitted from this study, since the regularity of
Shakespeare's verse is more often questioned in reference to the dramatic
works. The notation "poems" after a variant means that it occurs only
in the poems, at least in the relevant sense, and that it occurs at
least once there. Each of these citations has been counted as "one occurrence" in the final reckoning.

In listing the number of appearances of each variant in the plays,
I have used a shorthand method of reference. Thus, for example, the ex-

pression "<u>humility</u> 12x - <u>humbleness</u> 7x" means that <u>humility</u> is found twelve times in the plays, alternating metrically with its synonym <u>humbleness</u> which is found seven times--always, of course, in verse. The phrase "alternating metrically" is to be understood unless otherwise specified.

CHAPTER III

DERIVATIONAL VARIANTS: VERBS

Reiteration

-le,

representing OE -lian,[1] forms verbs which express repeated action or movement. When the simple verb itself carries these implications, synonymous variants become possible. Thus we find in Shakespeare prattle 5x - prate 9x in the intr. sense 'to talk idly or childishly.'

re-,

a prefix of L origin, forms verbs and verbal derivatives. Though its primary sense is 'again, anew,' even in Latin the precise meaning is not always clear, and in English its original force is often greatly obscured. For this reason, and because the simplex also frequently implies the senses of re-, we have many cases in which the derivative and simplex are synonymous.

These include recite in the poems - cite 2x TG 4.1.53, AW 1.3.216 'to mention, recount.' Also there is recollect 1x P 2.1.54 'to infer, deduce' ("And from their wat'ry empire recollect / All that may men approve, or men detect"), alternating metrically with collect 1x 2H6 3.1.35.[2]

Similarly, Shakespeare has <u>recommend</u> 2x C 2.2.155, M 1.6.2, a metrical variant of <u>commend</u> 21x in the two meanings 'to consign' and 'to make pleasing.' Examples in the latter sense are "Nimbly and sweetly <u>recommends</u> it selfe" (M 1.6.2; F mislineates) and "Whose vertue and obedience doth this instant / So much <u>commend</u> it selfe . . . " (L 2.1.116). And <u>recure</u> 1x R3 3.7.130 'to heal' is found along with <u>cure</u> 24x.

Trisyllabic or tetrasyllabic <u>redoubled</u> 2x R2 1.3.80, 1H4 3.2.144 alternates with disyllabic <u>doubled</u> 6x in the two senses 'made twice as great' and 'repeated' ("He kist the last of many <u>doubled</u> kisses," AC 1.5.40).[3] Another pair of p.ps. is *<u>reinforced</u> 1x H5 4.6.36 - <u>forced</u> 1x M 5.5.5 ("Were they not <u>forc'd</u> with those that should be ours"); the meaning is 'strengthened by additional troops.'

Toward the end of the sixteenth century, <u>re-</u> began to be considered as an ordinary English prefix, and was freely attached to native words: thus we find in Shakespeare <u>regreet</u> 2x R2 1.3.67, 1.3.186 along with <u>greet</u> 32x. The two meanings are 'to address, salute, meet' and 'to greet each other, meet' (intr.).[4] The p.p. *<u>remarked</u> 1x H8 5.1.33 'noticed' alternates with <u>marked</u> 3x.[5] And <u>represent</u> 3x 'to personate, symbolize' is found along with <u>present</u> 5x, as in MND 5.1.243 ("This Lanthorne doth the hornèd Moone <u>present</u>"; F prints as prose).

<u>Return</u> 123x is found along with <u>turn</u> 9x in the two meanings 'to give or send back' and (intr.) 'to come or go back'; it is true that <u>turn</u> is sometimes used with the advs. <u>again</u> and <u>back</u>, but so is <u>return</u>, e.g. in R2 1.3.120. Examples of <u>turn</u> in these two meanings are "And I will <u>turne</u> thy falshood to thy hart, / Where it was forged" (R2 4.1.39) and "Ere from this warre thou <u>turne</u> a Conqueror" (R3 4.4.184). In P 4.1.99,

There's no hope she will <u>return</u>. I'll swear she's dead, the one relevant line that is hypermetrical as printed, New Arden Ed. accepts Malone's emendation she'll for she will.[6] In the p.p., Shakespeare has returned 5x - turned 1x TmA 2.1.26 'given or sent back,' and in the pr.p. returning 1x JC 1.2.178 - turning 1x AYLI 2.7.162 in the intr. sense 'coming or going back.'

Some verbs also have related nouns which are statistically significant. For example, Shakespeare has both the p.ps. reguerdoned 1x 1H6 3.4.23 - guerdoned 2x 2H6 1.4.49, 3H6 3.3.191 'rewarded' and the related nouns reguerdon 1x 1H6 3.1.170 - guerdon 2x LLL 3.1.170, MA 5.3.5 'reward.' Similarly, requite (and its variant form requit) are used 24x along with quite (and quit) 18x and quittance 1x 1H6 2.1.14 'to repay.' If spelling is taken as a guide to the meter in O 4.2.16, requit creates a trisyllabic foot which could have been avoided by the use of quit:

Let Heaven requit it with the Serpents curse.

However, Kökeritz notes that Shakespeare, like his contemporaries, often pronounced heaven as a single syllable: orthographic indication of this is found in J 5.1.29 (heav'n, before a consonant) and elsewhere.[7] And, speaking of words like heaven and seven in a plea for a revised system of spelling, Gabriel Harvey says that he does not wish to " . . . either in the PROSODIE, or in the ORTHOGRAPHY either, allowe them two sillables in steade of one, but woulde as well in Writing as in Speaking, have them used as Monosyllaba, thus: heavn, seavn . . . But see what absurdities thys yl favoured ORTHOGRAPHYE, or rather PSEUDOGRAPHY, hathe ingendred, and howe one errour still breedeth and begetteth an other. Have wee not . . . even for evn, Divel for Divl . . . ?"[8] From the verb requite was formed the noun requital 4x 'repayment,' which alternates metrically with quittal in the poems.

Nouns derived from re- verbs include recognizance 1x O 5.2.214 'token, emblem' alternating with the simple cognizance 3x; recompense 2x MND 3.2.180 (rhyme), TmA 5.1.153 along with compensation 1x T 4.1.2 'restitution, amends'; and reprisal 1x 1H4 4.1.118 ("To heare this rich reprizall is so nigh") along with prize 18x 'anything seized; booty.'

Reciprocity and Partnership

As we saw in such variants as the intr. verb regreet, the prefix re- occasionally has the sense of reciprocal action, developing from the basic meaning of 'back, again.' The prefixes co- and inter- express this idea even more strongly, along with the idea of partnership. But in the words discussed in this section, co- and inter- are redundant additions to a verb which already carries senses of reciprocity and partnership.

co-,

together with its variant forms col-, com-, con-, and cor-, is ultimately derived from the L prefix com-, which in turn represents the prep. cum. The primary sense is 'together, together with' in verbs and adjs., and 'joint' in nouns. Co-, in Latin used only before vowels, h, and gn, is the spelling now assumed by the prefix as a living English formative; in Shakespeare, it is occasionally found in hybrids such as *co-mingled.

Other examples in the plays include trisyllabic *confixed 1x MM 5.1.232 'immovably fastened or placed'; it alternates with the monosyllabic or disyllabic p.p. fixed 21x. Also there is confront 2x H 3.3.47, 2H4 5.3.108 'to face, meet, oppose' along with the simple front 4x and the derivational variant affront 3x (in one of these instances, Cy 4.3.29, my definition of affront differs from OED's, which is 'to prepare to meet, look out for,' but is supported by New Arden Ed.). In the p.t. we have confronted 1x M 1.2.55 - fronted 1x AC 2.2.61 'faced, met, opposed.'

Conjoin 2x 2H4 4.5.64, R3 5.5.31 ("By Gods faire ordinance, conjoyne together"--notice the use of the adv. together even though the prefix already expresses this idea) and its variant cojoin 1x WT 1.2.143 both are used in the intr. meaning 'to unite, combine' along with join 35x. One possibly irregular use of join has turned up, "Why so brave Lords, when we joyne in league" (TA 4.2.136), but F2 substitutes we all for we to make the line scan, and thus the omission of all may well have been a compositor's error. New Arden Ed. suggests, also, that this could be a case of internal truncation, with a pause after the caesura supplying the place of a missing unaccented syllable.[9]

Another synonymous pair is trisyllabic colleagued 1x H 1.2.21 and *leagued 1x Cy 4.2.213, two p.ps. meaning 'joined.' And we also have the hybrid *co-mingled 1x H 3.2.74 (only in Ff; Qq comeddled) along with mingled 6x 'mixed together.' *Co-mingled was probably formed after the analogy of words like commix, which Shakespeare also uses 1x Cy 4.2.55 (with ellipsis of reflexive object) 'to blend,' alternating metrically with mix 1x 2H4 5.2.46. And a related pair of nouns is *commixture 2x LLL 5.2.296, 3H6 2.6.6 and mixture 3x 'a product of mixing.' Mixture is also found 1x (TC 1.3.95) meaning 'a mixed state,' in which sense its metrical variant is commixtion 1x TC 4.5.124 (Ff sp. commixion).

Another noun with this prefix is the nonce-word *co-mart 1x H 1.1.93 (only in Qq; Ff cov'nant) 'a bargain'; its variant is mart 1x TS 2.1.329,

And venture madly on a desperate Mart.

If spelling is taken as indicating pronunciation, this use of <u>mart</u> is irregular, for *<u>co-mart</u> would have created a regular alexandrine. But
then, as now, <u>desperate</u> could easily have been syncopated in speech, as
indicated orthographically (<u>desp'rate</u>) in AW 5.3.176, 1H6 4.6.54, etc.
Kökeritz notes (<u>Shakespeare's Pronunciation</u>, p. 284) that "a medial vowel
followed by <u>l</u>, <u>r</u>, or <u>n</u> is especially liable to syncopation, the reason
being, of course, that these consonants can be combined with almost any
other preceding consonant." In short, this line is probably another case
in which an inconsistent orthography is to be reckoned with.

The hybrid <u>co-mate</u> 1x AYLI 2.1.1 is found along with <u>mate</u> 9x 'a companion, fellow'; the occurrences of <u>mate</u> in nautical or contemptuous use
are omitted because <u>co-mate</u> is not used in this way. And we have <u>copart-
ner</u> in the poems meaning 'associate, fellow' as a metrical variant of
<u>partner</u> 6x (occurrences of the latter meaning 'colleague in business' are
omitted from the count). Also, <u>consort</u> 2x TG 4.1.64, L 2.1.99, stressed
on the second syllable, alternates metrically with <u>sort</u> 7x 'a group of
persons,' e.g. "Sent from a <u>sort</u> of Tinkers to the King" (2H6 3.2.277).
Finally, Shakespeare has <u>constrain</u> 2x C 5.3.100, L 2.2.103 and <u>strain</u> 2x
J 3.3.46, RJ 4.1.47 (F sp. <u>streames</u>) 'to compel,' along with their related p.ps. <u>constrained</u> 8x and <u>strained</u> 2x MV 4.1.184, RJ 2.3.19.

Use of the prefix in adjs. is seen in the obviously redundant <u>co-
equal</u> 1x 1H6 5.1.33 ("Hee'l make his cap <u>coequall</u> with the Crowne"),
which alternates with <u>equal</u> 22x, as in 2H6 5.1.89 ("And let thy tongue be
<u>equall</u> with thy heart").[10] And use in an adv. formed on an adj. is seen
in *<u>conjointly</u> 2x J 2.1.379, JC 1.3.29 'together,' a metrical variant of
<u>jointly</u> 4x.

<u>inter-</u>

represents the L prep. and adv. <u>inter</u> 'between, among.' When used
with verbs, this prefix has the sense 'mutually, reciprocally, together.'
As with <u>co</u>-, the synonymity of the variants is attributable to the fact
that the simplex also carries the idea of mutuality or reciprocity.

We find, in Shakespeare, the nonce-word *<u>interjoin</u> 1x C 4.4.22 along
with <u>join</u> 13x 'to connect with one another'; the occurrences of the
phrase <u>join</u> (. . .) <u>together</u> have been omitted because *<u>interjoin</u> is
not used with <u>together</u>. And, since <u>inter</u>- has remained a living prefix,
freely used to form new derivatives on native as well as Romanic simplexes, we have <u>intermingle</u> 1x O 3.3.25 'to mix together' along with <u>mingle</u>
2x C 1.9.3, L 2.4.237 (the occurrences of <u>mingle</u> with <u>together</u> have been
omitted). Finally, the p.p. <u>intermixed</u> 1x R2 5.5.12 alternates metrically
with <u>mixed</u> 4x 'blended.'

Direction or Position

The derivatives discussed in this section contain a sense of position or direction either within themselves (e.g. <u>afar</u>, representing <u>on</u> +
OE <u>feor</u>, '<u>in</u> [the] far') or in relation to an object (e.g. <u>bewail</u> 'to
wail <u>about</u>'). A few advs. have been included along with the verbs.

<u>a-</u>

sometimes represents the OE prep. <u>of</u>, which was combined with various words to mean 'off, from' or 'of.' Because the simplex adj. <u>new</u> had
two related advs.--<u>new</u> and the derivative <u>anew</u> (earlier <u>o-new</u>, probably
for <u>of</u> <u>new</u>)--synonymous adverbial variants became possible. <u>Anew</u> occurs

5x (once in the poems) along with new 30x; the latter is also a syllabic
variant of newly 3x, and all three words are used to mean 'afresh, again'
or 'in a new manner.'

a-

    can also represent the OE prep. on, which had as its original sense
'in, on, engaged in.' OE on was prefixed to various parts of speech in
combinations which were really two words, and was sometimes reduced to a-
even in Old English.

    In the adverbial group of variants, we have afar 2x 1H4 1.1.4,
WT 2.1.104 - far 73x 'at or to a great distance in space' or (fig.) 're-
motely, indirectly.' Synonyms were here made possible because the original simplex of afar (OE feor) was itself an adv., giving ModE far. We
also find the advs. aright 8x and right 16x; the latter is also a syllabic
variant of rightly 16x 'correctly.' If LLL 3.1.194,

    And never going a right, being a Watch,

is pronounced according to modern usage, aright creates an anapestic foot
where right would have been metrically exact. (F3-4 make the line an
alexandrine by substituting but a watch for a watch, but there is still
stress-wrenching on aright.) The solution seems to be a monosyllabic pronunciation of going by suppression of the second vowel, a feature of colloquial speech known as synaeresis. Kökeritz cites the inverted spelling
knowing for known (final -ing was often reduced to -in in speech) in
Cy 1.6.97 as evidence for this type of elision.[11] It is not out of the
question, either, that aright was simply an error for right, which appears
in the very next line. Here, synonymity was possible because the noun

simplex of aright, represented in Modern English by right, had an adv. of the same form.

In the prepositional group, we find amid 1x TS 4.1.206 (originally on middan 'in [the] middle,' from midde, adj. 'middle') and its variant form with genitival -s amidst 1x TC 1.3.91. Both alternate metrically with *midst 1x 1H6 1.2.24 and mean 'in the middle of.' Synonymous variants are possible because the superlative of the simple adj. midde developed into a monosyllabic prep., ModE *midst.

Finally, Shakespeare has the verb awake, in which a- probably represents OE on- (in onwǣcnan) but may perhaps be the OE intensive a- instead. Awake 56x alternates metrically with wake 43x in the two meanings 'to cease to sleep' (intr.) and 'to rouse from sleep.' In the second sense, both verbs alternate also with awaken 1x C 5.1.23 and with waken 4x; the -n represents an ancient OTeut suffix. Similarly, in the p.p. awaked 11x is found along with waked 8x in both meanings listed above. Awaked in 2H4 5.5.55 (Q; F awake) presents a minor difficulty: "But being awakt, I do despise my dreame." However, if we assume an unmarked caesura before being, setting off the participial phrase, the line would be regular with an extra unaccented syllable preceding the caesura.[12] Awaked and waked alternate also, in the meaning 'roused from sleep,' with the p.ps. awakened 1x TS 5.2.42 and wakened 2x O 2.1.188, Cy 2.2.13.

In the p.t., awaked 2x AYLI 4.3.133, R3 1.4.42 is a metrical variant of waked 6x 'ceased to sleep' (intr.); and in the pr.p. we find awaking 1x MND 4.1.71 - waking 3x 'ceasing to sleep.' Awaking also occurs 1x as a vbl. sb. (RJ 5.3.258; Q2 has *awakening, also metrically possible because in a caesura) meaning 'the act of ceasing to sleep,' along with waking 3x. And in the sense 'a state of wakefulness,' awaking is used 1x

(" . . . such as you / Nourish the cause of his <u>awaking</u>. I / Do come
with words," WT 2.3.36) as a metrical variant of <u>waking</u> 1x WT 3.3.19 and
the simple <u>wake</u> 3x (1x rhyme). OED defines <u>awaking</u> in the line quoted as
'rising or arousing from sleep,' but in context--the reference is to
Leontes' insomnia--I feel that the meaning I have supplied is preferable.

<u>ad-</u>,

together with its variant forms <u>a-</u>, <u>ac-</u>, <u>af-</u>, <u>ag-</u>, <u>ap-</u>, <u>as-</u>, and <u>at-</u>,
ultimately represents the L prep. <u>ad</u> 'to, at.' L <u>ad</u> was used in combina-
tion with various words to express motion or direction <u>to</u>, bringing <u>into</u>
a state, or addition or increase. In Old French, <u>ad-</u> was reduced to <u>a-</u>,
and although in the fourteenth century the written forms began to be refashioned after the L spellings, some words retained this <u>a-</u> (e.g. <u>avouch</u>
below). The other variant forms of <u>ad-</u> are assimilated spellings derived
from Late Latin.

In many words, the prefix lost its original force in the process of
transmission from Latin, so that derivative and simplex were synonymous
long before Shakespeare's day. Thus, in the verbal group, we find <u>accite</u>
1x 2H4 5.2.141, "Our Coronation done, we will <u>accite</u> / (As I before re-
membred) all our State," and <u>cite</u> 1x 3H6 2.1.34, "I thinke it <u>cites</u> us
(Brother) to the field," both meaning 'to summon.' The p.ps. <u>accited</u> 1x
TA 1.1.27 and <u>cited</u> 1x H8 4.1.29 also occur.

<u>Account</u> 12x is found along with <u>count</u> 11x in the two meanings 'to
esteem, think' and 'to make account, judge' [<u>of</u>], an intr. sense.
<u>Account</u> in Cy 1.6.80,

In you, which I <u>account</u> his beyond all Talents,

hypermetrical as printed, is probably a misprint for count. Shakespeare

also has the p.ps. accounted 3x and counted 8x 'esteemed, thought.'

The three variants acquit 4x, quit 8x, and acquittance 1x R3 3.7.233

all mean 'to release, absolve'; and address 5x is a synonym of dress 1x

H5 4.1.10, "That we should dresse us fairly for our end," 'to prepare.'

(Technical uses of dress in phrases such as dress meat, dress a chamber

are omitted.) In the p.p. we find addressed 6x - dressed 1x TC 1.3.166.

Appertain 2x MA 4.1.210, JC 2.1.282 is a metrical variant of pertain 6x

'to belong, relate' [to], an intr. sense; and in the pr.p., appertaining

2x RJ 3.1.66, T 3.1.96 and pertaining 1x H8 1.3.27 are synonymous.

Approve occurs 18x, prove 72x in the two senses 'to test, try' and

'to confirm' (in the first sense, approve may represent Fr éprouver, with

the prefix thus derived from L ex- rather than ad-). The p.ps. approved

14x and proved 14x also occur in both of these meanings. And Shakespeare

has the synonymous verbs attest 2x H5 Prol.16, 3.1.22 and testify 4x (1x

rhyme) 'to certify.' Finally, avouch 8x alternates metrically with vouch

7x in the two meanings 'to assert' and 'to answer for, acknowledge.' In

the p.ps., there is avouched 1x L 5.1.44 along with vouched 2x C 1.9.24,

M 3.4.34 'asserted.'

Some of these verbs also have related nouns which function as syl-

labic variants. Among these nouns are account (or accompt) 26x and count

(compt) 8x 'reckoning' or 'answer for conduct.' 2H4 1.1.167 is hyper-

metrical as printed, with accompt used where compt would have been metri-

cally preferable,

And summ'd the accompt of Chance, before you said;

but here, the vowel of the was undoubtedly meant to be elided before the

following vowel. Such an elision is indicated orthographically in
H8 3.2.210, th'Accompt. The and to are very frequently so shortened before a following vowel in Shakespeare, in accordance with the colloquial
usage of the day, although the shortening is not always represented in
the written form; see Kökeritz, Shakespeare's Pronunciation, pp. 275-276,
282.

The noun acquittance 2x H 4.7.1, LLL 2.1.161 is a syllabic variant
of quittance 1x AYLI 3.5.133, "But that's all one: omittance is no
quittance"; the meaning is 'release from an obligation.' It will be
noticed that quittance occurs in a proverb, but Tilley's evidence (s.v.
Forbearance, p. 235) indicates that it was not established there to the
exclusion of the acquittance form. Approbation occurs 1x in MM 1.2.183
meaning 'trial' (here, as a novitiate): "This day, my sister should the
Cloyster enter, / And there receive her approbation." Compare probation
1x MM 5.1.72: "I, (in probation of a Sisterhood)." And approof is used
2x AC 3.2.27, AW 1.2.50 along with proof 14x meaning 'the state of having
stood a test; trial.' (Occurrences of proof in reference to armor, e.g.
targets of proof, have been omitted.) Finally, the noun *avouch occurs
1x H 1.1.57 as a variant of *vouch 3x 'testimony, assurance.'

In the adjectival class, we find the past ppl. adjs. accustomed 4x
- customed 2x 2H6 5.1.188, J 3.4.155; a third synonym is customary 5x,
and all three mean 'habitual.' In J 3.4.155, "No common winde, no cus-
tomèd event," customed is trisyllabic and therefore differs only from
customary in syllabic value. *Admirable 2x MND 5.1.27, AW 2.1.26 alternates metrically with mirable 1x TC 4.5.142 'to be wondered at.' And
there is one adverbial pair: assuredly 4x 'certainly' as a syllabic variant of surely 25x.

In several words, the Fr prep. à 'to' was added even though there
was no corresponding ad- form in Latin. Such is the case with accompany
6x (a. Fr accompagner) - company 1x Cy 5.5.408 'to go along with'; and
Shakespeare also has appale 1x H 2.2.590 (F sp. apale; probably ad. Fr
appalir) - pale 1x H 1.5.90 'to make pale.' Similarly, we find avenge 1x
1H6 1.4.94 (a. OF avengier) along with the simple venge 7x and revenge
31x 'to exact retribution for; to uphold by retribution.' In R2 1.2.40,
revenge creates a trisyllabic foot if spelling is taken as indicating
pronunciation:

Let heaven revenge: for I may never lift.

But the case is parallel to that of Heaven requit discussed above on p.
41; heaven must be pronounced as a monosyllable. A final word of this
type, lacking a L ancestor, is await, which occurs 3x along with wait 2x
J 4.3.152, TG 4.2.134 in the two meanings 'to remain in readiness for'
[something] and--in the phrases await for, wait for--'to look forward to,'
an intr. sense. Compare, for example, 1H6 1.1.48, "Posteritie await for
wretched yeeres," and TG 4.2.134, "That wait for execution in the morne."

In the noun advantage, the prefix is due to the mistaken interpretation of initial a- in Fr avantage (really representing L ab) as a representative of L ad, when the a- forms were refashioned after L models.
The ad- spelling has been established in English as a permanent perver-
sion of the word. Shakespeare has advantage 51x and vantage 42x in the
three meanings 'a favorable condition,' 'profit,' and 'superiority.'[13]

be-

represents OE be-, the weak or stressless form of the prep. and adv.

bí, ModE <u>by</u>. It is sometimes used to make intr. verbs into trans. verbs

by adding a sense of direction toward an object. Usually, the meaning

added is 'about,' as in <u>beweep</u> 'to weep <u>about</u>' [something or someone];

as OED notes, this meaning can often be detected beneath the 'against,'

or other prep., required by modern idiom. Synonymous metrical variants

become possible when the root verb itself develops a trans. sense.[14]

In Shakespeare, we find <u>bestride</u> 5x in the two meanings 'to sit upon

with the legs astride' and 'to step across,' alternating with <u>stride</u> 2x

C 1.9.71 ("I meane to <u>stride</u> your Steed, and at all times") and Cy 3.3.35

("A Debtor, that not dares / To <u>stride</u> a limit"). <u>Bethink</u> occurs 2x

3H6 3.3.39, RJ 3.1.158 and <u>think</u> 24x (probably too small a figure; the

line listings in both the <u>Concordance</u> and Schmidt's <u>Lexicon</u> are incom-

plete). The two meanings are 'to devise' and 'to consider, recollect.'

<u>Think</u> may be irregular in AC 4.1.6, "Laugh at his Challenge. // Caesar

must <u>thinke</u>," but it was not counted as such because the line could be

short with an extra unaccented syllable in the caesura.[15] <u>Bewail</u> occurs

3x and <u>wail</u> 18x 'to lament': in the p.p. Shakespeare has <u>bewailed</u> in the

poems and <u>wailed</u> 1x CE 4.2.24, and in the pr.p. <u>bewailing</u> 1x H8 3.2.255

and <u>wailing</u> 1x RJ 3.2.128, both in the intr. sense 'lamenting.' <u>Beweep</u>

3x and <u>weep</u> 8x 'to weep about' conclude the verbal group of variants.

In advs., preps., and conjs., the original meaning 'about' was weak-

ened into a general expression of position 'at' or 'near.' Thus <u>before</u>,

f. OE <u>be-</u> + the adv. <u>foran</u>, originally meant '<u>at</u> or <u>near</u> the front.'

But since the OE root adv. <u>fore</u> also gave a ModE adv. (<u>fore</u>), we have the

synonymous metrical variants <u>before</u> 14x - <u>fore</u> in the poems 'previously.'

In addition, the compound adv. <u>beforehand</u> 'in advance' is once used ad-

jectivally (J 5.7.111; F prints as two words), "Since it hath beene

before hand with our greefes"; and it alternates metrically with forehand
in MA 4.1.51, "And so extenuate the forehand sinne."

The advs. before and fore later passed into preps. by addition of a
noun object, so that we find before 56x (probably incomplete) and fore
21x. The latter has another syllabic variant, afore 3x--used by such
characters as Prospero, Capulet, and York in Richard II, and thus not a
"low" form. In J 3.1.233, the first before creates a trisyllabic foot if
the words are read as printed:

And even before this truce, but new before.

However, even in this line probably was meant to be pronounced without
its v (cf. the parallel loss of v in o'er as contrasted with over). This
monosyllabic form of even is frequently represented orthographically in
the old editions; Kökeritz cites, for example, e'ene H 5.1.201 and e'ne
AC 1.2.50, both prose (Shakespeare's Pronunciation, p. 203). As conjs.,
before occurs 25x and fore 2x WT 5.1.226, J 5.1.7 'earlier than.'

In a final pair of conjs., because and cause, be- represents an
original prep. by (in the phrase by cause) which was spelled be- when it
became a stressless prefix. Because 14x (incomplete) alternates metrically with cause 2x TA 5.2.63, M 3.6.21, an elliptical use for because;
both variants mean 'for the reason that.'

ex-

developed from the L prep. ex; its primary force as a prefix is
'out, forth,' adding an adverbial qualification to a verbal simplex. But
when the simplex already had these implications, synonymous variants became possible.

Shakespeare has the verb exchange 9x along with change 18x and interchange 1x 3H6 4.7.3 'to give and take reciprocally.' In the p.ps. we find the parallel forms exchanged 2x 1H4 1.1.87, 1H6 1.4.29 - changed 1x T 1.2.441 - interchanged 2x MND 1.1.29, 2.2.49, and in the pr.ps. changing 2x 1H4 1.3.101, Cy 2.5.30 - interchanging 2x 1H6 4.6.19, RJ 1.1.120. The related noun, exchange, occurs 5x in the two meanings 'the act of giving and taking reciprocally' and 'alteration' (as in MV 2.6.35, where Jessica, disguised as a boy, says "For I am much asham'd of my exchange"). Its variant is change, which occurs 46x in the same two meanings; one line (AC 5.2.128) is hypermetrical if benefit is pronounced in the modern way:

A benefit in this change: but if you seeke.

Though loss of a medial vowel before f is relatively rare in Shakespeare, Kökeritz cites two lines (WT 2.1.113, 4.4.543) in which he believes that qualify should be read as so syncopated, and presents as evidence the ME form sorful (= sorrowful) listed by OED; see Shakespeare's Pronunciation, pp. 285, 390. Thus it seems likely that benefit was meant to be read as a disyllable here. Counterchange is also used 1x Cy 5.5.396 in the first meaning given above, 'the act of giving and taking reciprocally,' and two further synonyms, interchange and *interchangement, are discussed under -ment on p. 94 below.

Finally, we have one occurrence (M 5.2.5) of the verb excite in the sense 'to impel.' It is a metrical variant of the simple cite 1x TG 2.4.85, "For Valentine, I need not cite him to it," and the latter is also a syllabic variant of incite 5x. As noted above on p. 8, incite creates a trisyllabic foot in H5 1.2.20,

> Of what your reverence shall <u>incite</u> us to,

unless we assume a disyllabic pronunciation of <u>reverence</u>. Kökeritz' data (<u>Shakespeare's Pronunciation</u>, pp. 373-374) reveals that such a loss of medial unstressed <u>e</u> before <u>-rence</u> (<u>-rance</u>) is quite common in Shakespeare. It is shown orthographically in the forms <u>diffrence</u> LC 300, 2H4 4.1.181 (Q), <u>furth'rance</u> H5 1.2.301, P 2.1.160, <u>suffrance</u> H8 5.1.68 etc., <u>temp'rance</u> H8 1.1.124, M 4.3.92, and <u>uttrance</u> H 3.2.378 (Q2, prose), TA 5.3.91. But often, as here, it must be deduced from the scansion because of inconsistencies in the orthographical practice of the time.

<u>ob-</u>

represents the L prep. <u>ob</u>, which in combination with verbs was assimilated to <u>op-</u> before <u>p</u>. Its primary meaning was 'toward, against,' and in <u>oppress</u> it additionally implies the injurious or objectionable nature of the action. However, in some contexts <u>press</u> also has these implications. Thus Shakespeare has the synonymous metrical variants <u>oppressed</u> 7x - <u>pressed</u> 2x RJ 1.1.193, O 3.4.177, "I have this while with leaden thoughts beene <u>prest</u>." The meaning is 'weighed down' (said of the mind, etc.). The occurrence of <u>pressed</u> in the phrase <u>pressed</u> <u>down</u> has been omitted from the count because of lack of parallelism with <u>oppressed</u>.

<u>pro-</u>

is a prefix ultimately derived from the L prep. <u>pro</u>, whose original meaning was 'for.' <u>Proportion</u> occurs 3x in the plays, meaning 'an inheritance' or 'a part, share'; its syllabic variant is <u>portion</u> 5x. One relevant line, MM 5.1.219, is typographically irregular:

Partly for that her promis'd proportions.

(Portions could have been trisyllabic if necessary, and would thus have created a regular pentameter line.) Here, however, the apostrophe in promis'd is undoubtedly erroneous, and the ppl. ending -ed was meant to have secondary metrical stress: in Shakespeare's Pronunciation, p. 264, Kökeritz cites several parallel errors in the old editions.

sub-,

a development of the L prep. sub 'under, close to,' often indicates position when added to verbs and their derivatives. Thus, for example, subsequent etymologically means 'following close to.' It occurs once in the plays, in TC 1.3.344, alternating with sequent 4x; the meaning is 'following in time or serial order.' OED assigns the definition 'consequent; following as a result' to one of the four occurrences of sequent ("Immediate sentence then, and sequent death," MM 5.1.378), but the parallelism with immediate suggests that the word has a temporal sense.

sur-

is the Fr form of the L prefix super-, which in turn represents the prep. and adv. super 'over, above.' A common secondary sense was 'beyond,' as in surpass in the poems, alternating with pass 2x LLL 4.3.241, WT 2.2.20 'to excel, go beyond.' In the -eth form, surpasseth occurs 1x T 3.2.110 and passeth 1x H 1.2.85. Shakespeare also has the synonymous pair surrender 1x H8 1.4.81 and render 5x 'to give up, yield'; in four out of these five instances, render is used with up (whereas surrender is not), but I have counted these variants because as a noun, surrender is

once found with <u>up</u>. <u>Surrender</u> **2x** H 1.2.23, LLL 1.1.138 ("About <u>surrender</u>
up of Aquitaine") is used along with the related noun of action <u>render</u>
lx Cy 5.4.17 'the act of giving up.' In all of these variants, synonymity is possible because the shorter form also carries the sense of the
prefix.

-<u>ward</u>(s

represents OE -<u>weard</u>(es, and indicates direction or position. Although -<u>ward</u>(s sometimes does alter the meaning of the simplex (e.g. <u>go</u>
<u>backward</u> does not mean quite the same thing as <u>go</u> <u>back</u>), in the cases
listed below I have felt that the simplex and -<u>ward</u>(s form were synonymous. This is due to the fact that both variants are advs. and the idea
of relative position is included in the short form itself.

<u>Afterward</u> 6x and its genitival variant <u>afterwards</u> 6x alternate with
adverbial <u>after</u> 10x (incomplete) 'at a later time.' And in the meaning
'from this time forward,' <u>henceforward</u> 3x is a synonym of <u>henceforth</u> 30x,
not a simplex but a compound showing the nonsyllabic suffix -<u>th</u> of ancient
origin. Finally, <u>inwardly</u> 'internally' is used 2x MA 3.1.78, TmA 1.2.211
along with <u>inly</u> 2x T 5.1.200, H5 4.Prol.24.

Intensification

It will be noted that in many of the prefixes discussed below, the
intensive sense developed from an originally adverbial expression; this
is the case, for example, in <u>a</u>- representing OE <u>a</u>-, <u>be</u>-, <u>co</u>-, and <u>en</u>-.
In the variants themselves, however, any possible intensive quality is so
weak as to be, for all practical purposes, nonexistent.

a-

representing OE a- originally meant 'away, up, on, out' and thus added intensity in verbs of motion such as arise. But the intensive idea was so weak by Shakespeare's time that the a- derivative and the simplex are often synonymous. He uses alight 1x L 3.4.127 - light 3x in the intr. meaning 'to dismount,' and the related p.ps. alighted 2x MV 2.9.86, TmA 1.2.181 (F prints as prose) - lighted 1x 1H4 1.1.63. Arise 29x is found along with rise 59x in three intr. senses: 'to get up,' 'to ascend,' and 'to come into existence.' The variants alternate metrically in Caesar's speech to Cleopatra in AC 5.2.114-115: "Arise, you shall not kneele: / I pray you rise, rise Egypt." In the first sense listed above, ariseth is found in the poems and riseth 1x in MV 2.6.8; and in the same meaning in the p.t. we have arose 1x JC 2.1.239 and rose 6x. Finally, the intr. pr.p. arising in the poems 'ascending' is used with rising 5x.

In several a- variants, the idea of intensification was originally present even though the root verb was not a verb of motion. We can see this in Shakespeare's *aboded, related to OE abéodan, f. a- 'away, back' + béodan 'to announce.' The p.t. *aboded is found 1x H8 1.1.93 as a synonym of boded 1x 2H6 3.2.85 'portended.' From the verbs, we have the nouns *abodement 1x 3H6 4.7.13 and *bodement 2x M 4.1.96, TC 5.3.80; both are hybrid formations meaning 'a portent.' The a- prefix is probably also intensive in origin in amazed, though here again the simplex is not a verb of motion. Shakespeare has the p.ps. amazed 31x - mazed 3x 'stupefied.'

a-

representing OE ȝe- is here classified as intensive because its primary meaning in Gothic was 'together, altogether, completely.' However, it often had no discernible sense even in Old English. Thus if we look at the OE adjs. ӡewǽr and wǽr, we see that both mean 'wary' or 'informed,' although, strictly speaking, the prefix was supposed to be perfective or intensive. These two words gave ModE aware and ware, respectively, which in turn form the roots of Shakespeare's synonymous adverbial variants *unaware in the poems and unwares 1x 3H6 2.5.62 'unconsciously, inadvertently.' Compare also the related adverbial phrases at unawares 3x (1x only in Ff) and at unwares 1x TC 3.2.40 (Q only; Ff at unawares, which changes the line from tetrameter, with an extra syllable in the caesura, to pentameter). Both phrases are used to mean 'unexpectedly.'

be-,

as noted above, originally had an adverbial sense: 'around, about.' But OED states that in such words as bespatter, this meaning naturally intensified the sense of the verb, and thus be- developed the meaning 'thoroughly.' The intensive force of Shakespeare's be- words, like that of his en- words, is highly questionable. Abbott, for example, feels that at least in p.ps., the prefix is often redundant (p. 322). In the absence of conclusive evidence, the matter must be decided by individual interpretation; I list below the forms which I regard as synonymous.

Even OED does not claim that all of the be- derivatives show a strongly intensive sense. Rather, it divides them into three groups: (1) those words in which the sense of 'about' is expressed vaguely or figuratively, e.g. become = come about; (2) those in which the sense of 'about' is spatial, meaning 'all over the surface' or 'from side to side';

and (3) those in which an intensive sense may be present. I follow this
classification in listing my variants.

Group 1

Bechance 1x TG 1.1.61 'to occur,' an intr. meaning, is a variant of
chance 6x: phraseological use of the latter in how chance 'how chances
it' has been omitted. Shakespeare also has become 28x along with come
3x 'to grow to be, get to be' (intr., with noun or adj. complement), and
in the p.t. we find became 11x - came 7x; all of these figures are too
small because of incomplete listings. In this group also are beget 20x
and get 13x 'to produce (lit. or fig.).' One relevant line, TS 1.1.45,
is hypermetrical if pronounced according to modern usage:

Such friends (as time) in Padua shall beget.

Kökeritz, however, feels that Padua is disyllabic here; he cites the
spellings mutally (= mutually) in MW 4.6.10 (Q) and Covitha (= Cophetua)
in 2H4 5.3.106 as evidence suggesting that the u vowel was suppressed.[16]

In the p.t., we find begot 6x and got 8x in the two meanings 'pro-
cured to be' and 'produced'; compare, in the first meaning, " . . .
there's one / whom he begot with childe . . . " (MM 5.1.517) and "And at
that time he got his wife with childe" (AW 5.3.302). And in the p.p.
Shakespeare has begot 13x 'produced' along with got 13x. Once, in
LLL 5.2.869, begot creates a trisyllabic foot if modern pronunciation is
followed:

Whose influence is begot of that loose grace.

But influence was undoubtedly meant to be disyllabic. The case is parallel to that of <u>Padua</u> above, except that here, it is probably the vowel following the <u>u</u> which was suppressed (by synaeresis); see Kökeritz, <u>Shakespeare's Pronunciation</u>, pp. 287, 373. Shakespeare also has the vbl. sbs. <u>begetting</u> 1x Cy 5.5.331 'production' and <u>getting</u> 1x AC 3.13.107. And he has, finally, the related p.ps. *<u>unbegot</u> 1x R2 3.3.88 - <u>ungot</u> 1x MM 5.1.142 'not yet begotten,' and in the same meaning the strong p.ps. <u>unbegotten</u> 1x J 4.3.54 - <u>ungotten</u> 1x H5 1.2.287.

<u>Betake</u> 3x 'to make go,' a reflexive verb, is found along with <u>take</u> 3x; and <u>betoken</u> 1x H 5.1.242 'to signify' along with <u>token</u> 1x AW 4.2.63. One pair of nouns derived from verbs also belongs in this group. <u>Behest</u> occurs 2x RJ 4.2.19, Cy 5.4.122 as a synonym of <u>hest</u> 5x 'a command.'

Group 2

Shakespeare may have created *<u>bedabbled</u> 1x MND 3.2.443, which functions as a metrical variant of the p.p. <u>dabbled</u> 1x R3 1.4.54 'made wet.' He also has <u>bedeck</u> 1x RJ 3.3.125 - <u>deck</u> 8x 'to adorn,' and the pr.ps. <u>bedecking</u> 1x LLL 2.1.79 - <u>decking</u> 1x MND 1.1.211. <u>Begnaw</u> occurs 1x meaning 'to nibble' ("The Worme of Conscience still <u>begnaw</u> thy Soule," R3 1.3.222); its syllabic variant is <u>gnaw</u> 8x. O 4.2.136 is hypermetrical as printed:

A halter pardon him: And hell <u>gnaw</u> his bones.

(This is the Qq reading; F prints as two short lines, dividing at the colon.) Here, the unstressed particle <u>his</u> was probably meant to be reduced to an enclitic '<u>s</u>. Kökeritz (<u>Shakespeare's Pronunciation</u>, p. 272) cites many orthographically-represented parallels such as <u>make's</u> (= <u>make his</u>) in M 2.3.124, along with some that must be inferred from the meter.

Bepaint occurs 1x RJ 2.2.86 meaning 'to color, adorn' as a variant
of paint 9x; in the p.p. we find bepainted in the poems and painted 11x.
Shakespeare's p.p. *bescreened occurs 1x RJ 2.2.52 along with screened 1x
H 3.4.3 'sheltered or hidden as with a screen.' And besmear 1x JC 3.1.107
and smear 1x M 2.2.49 are metrical variants meaning 'to daub with a
sticky substance' (only the lit. occurrence of besmear has been counted).
Similarly, *besmirch 1x H 1.3.15 and smirch 1x AYLI 1.3.114 both mean 'to
stain'; and the trisyllabic p.p. bestained occurs 1x J 4.3.24 along with
monosyllabic or disyllabic stained 14x (lit. occurrences only are counted)
'discolored, defaced.'

Bestrew is used 2x T 4.1.20, TS Ind.2.42 to mean 'to cover with something scattered'; its variant is strew 9x. The related p.ps. also occur:
bestrewed 1x TS Ind.1.56 - strewed 5x. Finally, Shakespeare has the p.ps.
betossed 1x RJ 5.3.76 and tossed 5x 'disturbed, flung about,' and *betrim
1x T 4.1.65 as well as trim 2x RJ 4.4.24, P 1.4.27 'to adorn.'

Group 3

This group, by far the largest, includes variants occurring in lines
specifically cited by OED as showing "intensive" use of a be- derivative;
all of these lines have been quoted here for the reader's judgment. Thus
OED cites bedrench 1x R2 3.3.46 as an example of intensive use: " . . .
such Crimson Tempest should bedrench / The fresh greene Lap of faire King
Richards Land." However, drench is also used 3x in this sense of 'to
steep or soak,' e.g. in H5 4.7.80, "So do our vulgar drench their peasant
limbes / In blood of Princes."

We also find the verb befall 28x along with fall 11x in the intr.
meaning 'to happen' or (with personal indirect object) 'to happen to.'
Examples in the first sense are JC 5.1.97, "Let's reason with the worst

that may befall," and JC 5.1.105, "For feare of what might fall, so to
prevent." In the p.t. there is befell 1x AYLI 4.3.103 and fell in the
poems, both meaning 'happened' (intr.). Befit occurs 9x as a metrical
variant of fit 23x 'to suit'; and in the pr.p. we have befitting 1x
T 5.1.165 along with fitting 2x H 1.1.173, Cy 5.5.98. Compare also *unbefitting 1x LLL 5.2.770 and unfitting 1x O 4.1.78 (only in Q2-3; Q un-
suting; Ff resulting), two pr.ps. meaning 'unbecoming, unsuitable.'

Shakespeare uses befriend 5x along with friend 1x H5 4.5.17 'to
favor,' and in the p.p. befriended 2x TC 5.9.9, TA 3.1.52 as well as
friended 3x. OED cites the nonce-word *belocked in MM 5.1.210 as intensive: "This is the hand, which with a vowd contract / Was fast belockt in
thine." But surely it is fast, not be-, which here conveys intensity.
The simple locked occurs 7x in this fig. sense 'enclosed.'

Belong is found 20x in the intr. meaning 'to pertain' [to something
or someone]; its variant is the simple long 4x. In the other forms of
the verb we find the p.t. belonged 1x O 5.2.228 - longed 1x H8 2.3.48,
and the pr.p. belonging 3x - longing 2x AW 4.2.42, H8 1.2.32, all in the
same intr. sense. Then there are the pr.ps. beloving 1x AC 1.2.22 ("You
shall be more beloving, then beloved") and loving 3x, e.g. H8 2.1.92
("Ever belov'd and loving, may his Rule be"). Only the occurrences of
loving as a predicate adj. like beloving 'showing love' (intr.) have been
counted.

In the intr. meaning 'maddening,' we find Shakespeare's pr.p. *bemadding 1x L 3.1.38 (om. F); its syllabic variant is madding 1x AW 5.3.213.
Another word that Shakespeare may have formed is the p.p. *bemet, used 1x
(L 5.1.20) along with met 24x to mean 'met with' in salutations with conjoined adv., e.g. well met. And there is *bemete 1x TS 4.3.113 'to measure

(lit. or fig.)' as well as the simplex mete 1x 2H4 4.4.77.

Shakespeare uses *bemock 1x C 1.1.261 to mean mock 50x 'to deride, flout.' One relevant line, MA 3.1.75,

She would mocke me into ayre, O she would laugh me,

contains a trisyllabic first foot if pronounced as printed. Here, however, the initial she would was probably meant to be read she'd, though the contraction was not orthographically indicated.[17] In the p.p., we find *bemocked 1x T 3.3.63, "Wound the loud windes, or with bemockt-at-Stabs / Kill the still closing waters," and mocked 7x.

The vbl. sb. beseeming is used 1x Cy 5.5.409 along with seeming 11x 'external appearance'; the occurrences of seeming restricted to false appearance have been omitted. We also find beshrew 27x as a variant of shrew 2x WT 1.2.281, Cy 2.3.147 'to curse.' And the p.p. bestirred occurs 1x 1H4 2.3.60 meaning 'moved, disturbed'; its variant stirred occurs 6x with uses in the phrase stirred up deleted. Bestow is used 9x and stow in the poems 'to place,' and in the p.ps. we have bestowed 5x -stowed 2x T 1.2.230, O 1.2.62.

OED cites Shakespeare's use of *bethumped in J 2.1.466, "Zounds, I was never so bethumpt with words," as intensive; yet thumped 1x in R3 5.3.334, " . . . whom our Fathers / Have in their owne Land beaten, bobb'd, and thump'd," also carries the sense 'struck, drubbed,' and neither variant seems to me more "intense" than the other. Then there is betide 3x - tide 2x, both in MND 5.1.205, meaning 'to happen' (intr.). And finally, the p.p. bewet 1x TA 3.1.146, "His Napkin with her true teares all bewet" (specifically cited by OED as an intensive use), is a metrical variant of wet 2x R3 1.2.163, 1.2.216 'moistened.' The occurrences of <u>wet</u> preceding a noun are omitted.[18]

<u>co-</u>,

like <u>be-</u>, had an originally adverbial sense, but in Latin this primary meaning of <u>com-</u>, 'together,' shaded into 'altogether, completely'
and hence the intensive use of the prefix arose. Thus, in giving the
etymology of the verb <u>complain</u>, OED shows the components of its L ancestor <u>complangere</u> as <u>com-</u> intensive + <u>plangere</u> 'to lament.' However, even
in French the verb and its simplex <u>plaindre</u> were synonymous, and in
Shakespeare's England there was no difference between <u>complain</u> 4x and
<u>plain</u> 1x L 3.1.39 (om. F) in meaning; both meant 'to bewail.' The same
is true of the vbl. sbs. <u>complaining</u> 3x - <u>plaining</u> 2x R2 1.3.175,
CE 1.1.73 and <u>complaint</u> 17x - <u>plaint</u> 4x; all four have the identical
meaning, 'lamentation.'

Another case of the originally intensive use is in the noun <u>corrival</u>
(ultimately representing L <u>corrivalis</u>, a compound adding emphasis to the
relation expressed by <u>rivalis</u> 'rival'). <u>Corrival</u> occurs 2x 1H4 1.3.207,
4.4.31, alternating with <u>rival</u> 9x in the two meanings 'competitor' and
'companion.'

<u>de-</u>

in English words usually represents the L adv. and prep. <u>de</u>, whose
primary meaning was 'down, down from.' Through intermediary senses such
as 'down to the bottom,' <u>de-</u> in combination also developed an intensive
meaning: 'completely, thoroughly.' There are two derivational variants
in the plays, either adapted from Latin or formed in French on L models,

which originally had this intensive de-; however, for various reasons, it had become obscured or meaningless by Shakespeare's time.

First, we find default, a noun ultimately derived from Fr defaillir, f. de- 'thoroughly' + faillir 'to be wanting.' Default occurs 3x along with fault over 200x meaning 'transgression, imperfection' or (with possessive) 'failure in duty.' C 1.1.271 is typographically irregular:

Shall be the Generals fault, though he performe;

but Generals was almost certainly meant to be syncopated to Gen'rals by loss of medial unstressed e. Such a syncopation is indicated orthographically in gen'rall TmA 4.3.445 and sev'rall MW 5.5.65.[19]

In the noun demerit, the original meaning was 'that for which a person deserves honor'; the word is ultimately from L demereri, f. de- 'thoroughly' + mereri 'to deserve.' But in Romanic the prefix was apparently taken in a privative sense, so that a second meaning, 'a fault,' developed. Then, because merit was used in an indifferent sense to mean 'that for which a person deserves something,' we find both demerit 3x and merit 10x in the two meanings 'that for which a person deserves honor' and 'that for which a person deserves blame.' One example of demerit in the first sense is in C 1.1.276, where the people's preference for Caius Marcius (Coriolanus) over his commanding general Cominius is summarized: "Opinion that so stickes on Martius, shall / Of his demerits rob Cominius."

dis-,

like de-, is a prefix of L origin. When added to verbs, it had as its primary sense 'two ways, in twain, apart,' as we see in disrupt, lit. 'to break apart.' From this a privative sense developed naturally (dis-

join), but when dis- was prefixed to verbs which already contained the
notion of division, separation, or privation, the addition of dis- was
intensive: 'utterly, completely.' However, in several words this intensive idea was so weak that the derivative and simplex were synonymous.
Thus dissever 2x AW 2.1.125, J 2.1.388 and sever 3x are synonyms meaning
'to separate'; their p.ps. dissevered 1x WT 5.3.155 and severed 9x also
occur.

In depart and devoid, the de- really represents L dis-, which in
French was often altered to de-. Thus we find depart 48x along with part
56x in the intr. meanings 'go away,' 'die,' and 'separate,' as well as in
the trans. meaning 'leave.' The two words could be used synonymously because part, like sever, already implied the notion of separation, and because the intensive force of de- in depart was practically nonexistent.
Depart means 'to separate' in Cy 1.1.108, where Posthumus says to Imogen,

> . . . Should we be taking leave
> As long a terme as yet we have to live,
> The loathnesse to depart, would grow: Adieu;

and metrical alternation can clearly be seen as she answers,

> Nay, stay a little:
> Were you but riding forth to ayre your selfe,
> Such parting were too petty.

In the p.t., departed 3x alternates metrically with parted 4x 'went away'
(intr.), and in the pr.p. departing is used 1x 2H4 1.1.103 along with
parting 1x H6 2.5.115 'dying.' Finally, the vbl. sbs. departing 3x and
parting 14x are metrical variants meaning 'a separation' or 'the act of

going away.' In the latter sense, compare also the synonymous variants
departure and depart, discussed under -ure below, p. 99.

The adj. devoid 1x TA 5.3.199, "Her life was Beast-like, and devoid
of pitty," was originally the p.p. of a verb devoid. Since it also has
a simplex which already is privative--void 3x as in "Which makes me hope
you are not void of pitty" (2H6 4.7.69)--the two words are synonyms in
the meaning 'free' [of or from something].

en- and in-

are variant forms of the L prepositional prefix in-, whose primary
sense was 'into, in, within.' En-, the Fr form, is by far the more common: the em- (im-) spellings are assumed before b, p, and m. In my discussion of these variants, the form preferred by OED has been used.

Here I will be dealing primarily with trans. verbs formed by prefix-
ing en- to a verb. OED says that, in this combination, the prefix has
one of three effects: (1) it gives the additional sense of 'in,' i.e. has
the effect of an adv.; (2) it intensifies the simple verb; or (3) it
merely furnishes an additional syllable for metrical purposes. I have
found very few cases in which the first effect seems to be operative; one
is the nonce-word *endart (= dart in) in RJ 1.3.98, "But no more deepe
will I endart mine eye." Such cases are quite rare, however, and Shakespeare's frequent use of the prep. (not the adv.) in with an en- form
further indicates that he himself felt no difference in meaning between
the en- form and the simplex.

En- (Em-) Forms

Shakespeare has enact 2x R3 5.4.2, T 4.1.121 'to carry out in action'

or 'to perform as a dramatic actor' along with act 16x. In the first
sense, we find also the p.t. enacted 1x 1H6 1.1.122 along with acted 1x
RJ 3.2.16, and the p.p. enacted 1x 1H6 3.1.116 along with acted 2x
M 3.4.140, AC 5.2.45. Emblaze, used 1x in 2H6 4.10.76, creates a trisyllabic foot if spelling is taken as a guide to the meter:

> To emblaze the Honor that thy Master got.

However, to was probably meant to be read as a proclitic here, giving
t'emblaze with loss of the o vowel; compare the parallel t'enjoy, represented orthographically in Cy 2.1.70. This was a standard poetic device
well into the eighteenth century, and according to Kökeritz (Shakespeare's
Pronunciation, pp. 275-276), it was a feature of colloquial speech as well.
The syllabic variant of emblaze is blaze 'to set forth conspicuously,'
used 2x RJ 3.3.151, JC 2.2.31; and blaze is also a syllabic variant of
blazon 1x RJ 2.6.26 in the same meaning. (Though blaze and blazon are not
etymologically related, the two verbs acted and reacted on each other in
the sixteenth century.)

The nonce-word *enclog occurs 1x in O 2.1.70 (only in Ff; Qq clog),
where, however, it may be a compositor's error ("Traitors ensteep'd, to
enclogge the guiltlesse Keele"), its en- having been acquired by attrac-
tion from *ensteeped rather than intended by Shakespeare. In any case,
the irregularity would occur in the caesura. Its metrical variant is
clog 2x M 3.6.43, O 2.1.70 (Qq only) 'to encumber.'[20]

We also find engild 1x MND 3.2.187 as a variant of gild 4x 'to make
bright and shining like gold.' And engirt 1x 2H6 5.1.99 is used along
with girt 2x 1H6 3.1.171, 2H6 1.1.65 meaning 'to surround'; the latter is
also a syllabic variant of girdle 1x J 2.1.217. Englut 1x O 1.3.57 and

glut lx T 1.1.63 are synonymous in the sense 'to swallow.' And the p.p. engrafted occurs lx JC 2.1.184, in a line misprinted in all of the old editions: "Yet I feare him, / For in the ingrafted love he beares to Caesar." The sense shows that in should be omitted; Var. Ed. comments that the compositor may have anticipated the first syllable of ingrafted.[21] In any case, engrafted has two syllabic variants--grafted 3x and engraft lx O 2.3.145 (F sp. with in-); all mean 'firmly rooted.'

Shakespeare has engrave lx R3 4.4.272 (F sp. with in-) - grave in the poems 'to carve, imprint,' together with the corresponding p.ps. engraved 2x TG 2.7.4, 1H6 2.2.15 - graved lx MV 2.7.36; the latter alternates also with the strong form graven lx R3 4.4.141 (only in Qq; Ff branded). *Enguard occurs lx L 1.4.349 along with guard 33x 'to protect.' And enkindle 2x M 1.3.121, L 3.7.86 is a metrical variant of kindle 6x 'to cause to blaze up (lit. or fig.)'; in the same meaning, we also find the p.ts. enkindled lx J 5.2.87 - kindled lx J 5.2.83 and the p.ps. enkindled 2x TC 2.2.63, JC 2.1.249 - kindled 3x.

Other p.ps. are the nonce-words *ensteeped lx O 2.1.70 and *insteeped lx H5 4.6.12, functioning as metrical variants of steeped 11x 'immersed.' And finally there is entreat lx 2H6 4.4.9, "Ile send some holy Bishop to intreat," as well as treat lx J 1.1.101, "To treat of high affaires touching that time," meaning 'to negotiate' (intr.).

Nouns related to these verbs are entreatment lx H 1.3.122, "Set your entreatments at a higher rate, / Then a command to parley," and treaty lx H8 1.1.165, "To this last costly Treaty: Th'enterview," both in the sense of 'conversation, conference.' Though not derived from a verb, ensign (ultimately from L in- + signum 'sign') may show an originally intensive prefix. It occurs 6x along with sign 11x in the two meanings 'a banner'

and 'an emblem'; an example of sign in the first meaning is in JC 5.1.14,
"Their bloody signe of Battell is hung out."

In- (Im-) Forms

Shakespeare has *inclip 1x AC 2.7.74, "What ere the Ocean pales, or
skie inclippes" (notice the lack of parallelism with the simple pales);
its variant is clip 2x AC 5.2.362, O 3.3.464 'to enclose.' And the p.p.
incorporate 6x occurs along with disyllabic corporate 1x TmA 2.2.213,
"They answer in a joynt and corporate voice," in the meaning 'united into
one body, closely united.' OED says that the TmA use means rather 'belonging to a body politic, or to a body of persons,' but the nonpolitical
sense seems better in context.

*Impaint occurs 1x 1H4 5.1.80 along with paint 2x TC 1.1.94 and once
in the poems, meaning 'to depict' or 'to color (fig.).' We also have
*impawn 1x H5 1.2.21 and pawn 5x 'to pledge,' and in the same sense the
p.ps. *impawned 2x WT 1.2.436, 1H4 4.3.108 and pawned 4x. The p.p. *impleached 'intertwined' occurs 1x in the poems (LC 205) in a line hypermetrical as printed, where pleached 2x AC 4.14.73, H5 5.2.42 would be exact:

With twisted mettle amorously empleacht.

Here, however, amorously was almost certainly meant to be syncopated to a
trisyllable, with loss of the vowel preceding r.[22] Also in the p.p., we
find *impressed 2x 1H4 1.1.21, L 5.3.50 'forced into military service' as
well as pressed 5x. And the p.p. imprinted 1x MND 1.1.50 is a variant of
printed 1x 2H6 3.2.343 'stamped.'[23]

Among nouns derived from verbs, we find the nonce-word *immure 1x
TC Prol.8 (F sp. with em-) along with mure 1x 2H4 4.4.119 'something that

divides; a wall.' Also there is <u>inheritance</u> 9x as well as <u>heritage</u> 1x
P 2.1.129 'that which is inherited.' In 3H6 1.1.78, <u>inheritance</u> is used
where <u>heritage</u> would have been metrically preferable:

It was my <u>Inheritance</u>, as the Earledome was.

Cambridge Ed., however, states that <u>The True Tragedie of Richard Duke of
Yorke</u> (commonly regarded as the 1595 Q) has '<u>Twas</u> for <u>It was</u>, which would
regularize the meter and was probably the form intended by Shakespeare.
In either case, there would be an extra syllable in the caesura or loss
of the vowel of <u>the</u> before <u>Earledome</u>.

Shakespeare also has *<u>impressure</u> 2x AYLI 3.5.23, TC 4.5.131 along
with <u>pressure</u> 1x H 1.5.100, "All sawes of Bookes, all formes, all <u>presures</u>
past," in the sense 'an indentation made by pressure.' <u>Pressure</u> is also
a syllabic variant of <u>impression</u> 3x in the same meaning. Another pair of
nouns is <u>imprint</u> in the poems 'a stamp (lit. or fig.)' and <u>print</u> 5x. One
statistically significant line, MM 2.4.130, is typographically irregular:

And credulous to false <u>prints</u>. // I thinke it well.

However, <u>credulous</u> was no doubt meant to be syncopated, since its medial
<u>u</u> was probably at that time pronounced [ə], and therfore could easily have
been eliminated before <u>l</u>.[24] A related case is <u>marv'llous</u> in C 4.5.30,
R3 1.2.254, where the syncopation is orthographically represented; cf.
also the development of <u>parlous</u> as a syncopated form of <u>perilous</u>. Two
final nouns, both used only in the plural, are *<u>investments</u> 2x H 1.3.128,
2H4 4.1.45 and <u>vestments</u> 2x CE 2.1.94, TmA 4.3.125 'clothing.'

<u>In-</u> in the adj. *<u>inexecrable</u> 1x MV 4.1.128 may be intensive if the
form is not a misprint (F3-4 have <u>inexorable</u>): "O be thou damn'd, <u>inexe-</u>

crable dogge." However, since there is no related verb <u>inexecrate</u> to carry a possible intensive sense, and since <u>in</u>- here does not seem to be the negative <u>in</u>- as in <u>invaluable</u> (the speaker goes on to "execrate" the person addressed), I feel that this form does not differ in meaning from the simple <u>execrable</u> 1x TA 5.3.177, "Give sentence on this <u>execrable</u> Wretch."

Change of State

<u>be</u>-,

as noted above, originally meant 'around, about,' but in the verbal variants discussed below it was added to a noun or adj. with the sense 'to affect with' or 'to make (into).' Thus it here implies that the direct object of the verb is being <u>changed</u> in some way. Synonymous variants arise because the root noun or adj. has a related verb of the same form which carries within itself the senses of <u>be</u>-.

The prefix was added to a noun-stem in <u>bedew</u> 3x, alternating with <u>dew</u> 4x 'to affect with dew.' Also formed on a noun is Shakespeare's *<u>be</u>-<u>monster</u> 1x L 4.2.63 (om. F) in which the meaning is rather 'to make into a monster,' found along with *<u>monster</u> 1x L 1.1.223. Formed on adj.-stems are the p.ps. <u>bedimmed</u> 1x T 5.1.41 alternating with <u>dimmed</u> 2x R3 4.4.16, TA 4.4.82 'made dim,' and <u>benumbed</u> 1x TC 2.2.179 alternating with <u>numbed</u> 1x L 2.3.15 'made numb.'

<u>en</u>- and <u>in</u>-

are variant forms of the L prepositional prefix <u>in</u>-.[25] The meaning of the prefix in the words discussed in this section is varied, but it always implies a change of state. The en- and in- variants have been divided into two groups (corresponding to OED's En-[1] 1 and En-[1] 2) according to the sense carried by the prefix.

Whereas in the derivatives included in the preceding section, the prefix was added to verb-stems (see above, p. 59 ff.), here the root word is a noun or adj. The original locative sense of the prefix--'into, in, within'--is perceptible; nevertheless, synonymity is possible because the syllabic variants of the en- words contain within themselves the senses of the prefix. Abbott contends, for example, that there is "little or no difference" between the verbs free and enfree in terms of lexical meaning (p. 323).[26]

Group 1

In this group, en- is added to nouns, either with the sense 'to put into' [what is denoted by the noun], as in imprison, or with the sense 'to put [what is denoted by the noun] into,' as in envenom. Synonymous variants arise because the root noun has a related verb of the same form.

Shakespeare uses embalm 1x TmA 4.3.40 along with balm 1x TS Ind.1.48 'to anoint with something fragrant,' and embar 1x H5 1.2.94 (F sp. with im-) along with bar 15x 'to exclude, refuse to permit.' And he has *embounded 1x J 4.3.137 as well as bounded 2x 1H6 4.2.45, TC 1.3.111, two p.ps. meaning 'confined.' Trisyllabic encaged 2x R2 2.1.102, 3H6 4.6.12 (F sp. with in-) alternates metrically with disyllabic caged 1x TS Ind.2.38 'confined in or as in a cage.' Then there is encamp 3x - camp 1x AC 4.8.33 'to place in camp,' and encircle 1x MW 4.4.56 ("Then let them all encircle him about") along with circle 1x TA 3.1.277 ("You

heavie people, <u>circle</u> me about") 'to surround.' Similarly, the p.ps.
<u>encompassed</u> 5x (4x sp. with <u>in-</u> in F) and <u>compassed</u> 1x M 5.8.56 both mean
'surrounded.'

<u>Endamage</u> 2x TG 3.2.43, 1H6 2.1.77 is a metrical variant of <u>damage</u> 1x
R3 4.2.60 'to injure'; and <u>endanger</u> 1x TG 5.4.133 is used along with
<u>danger</u> 1x AC 1.2.199 'to imperil.' The p.p. <u>endowed</u>, which occurs once
in TmA 1.1.139, alternates metrically with monosyllabic *<u>dowered</u> 1x
L 1.1.207 (F sp. <u>dow'rd</u>); both words mean 'furnished with a dowry.' And
<u>endue</u> 2x C 2.3.147, J 4.2.43 (F sp. with <u>in-</u>) 'to endow, furnish' is a
synonym of <u>due</u> 1x 1H6 4.2.34, "This is the latest Glorie of thy praise, /
That I thy enemy <u>dew</u> thee withall."

Other relevant forms include *<u>enfettered</u> 1x O 2.3.351 'bound with
fetters' with its variant p.p. <u>fettered</u> 3x. And <u>enfold</u> 3x (F sp. with
<u>in-</u>) 'to enclose, cover' is used as a synonym of <u>fold</u> 3x (the occurrences
in the phrases <u>fold in</u>, <u>fold up</u> are excluded). Also, trisyllabic *<u>en-
hearsed</u> 1x 1H6 4.7.45 ("See where he lyes <u>inhercèd</u> in the armes / Of the
most bloody Nursser of his harmes") alternates with disyllabic <u>hearsed</u> 1x
H 1.4.47 'placed as in a coffin.'

In the meaning 'to fatten,' <u>enlard</u> is used 1x in TC 2.3.205, creating
a trisyllabic foot if the orthography is accepted as a guide to pronunciation:

That were to <u>enlard</u> his fat already, pride.

However, <u>to</u> was probably meant to be reduced to a proclitic <u>t'</u> before <u>en-
lard</u>; see the discussion of <u>t'emblaze</u> above, p. 69. <u>Lard</u> is found 2x
1H4 2.2.116 (F prints as prose), TmA 4.3.12. <u>Enlinked</u> 1x H5 3.3.18 meaning 'connected closely' also occurs along with the synonymous p.p. <u>linked</u> 5x.

OED defines <u>enring</u> in MND 4.1.49, "the female Ivy so / <u>Enrings</u> the barky fingers of the Elme," as meaning 'to put rings on'; I prefer the definition 'encircle'; but in any case the word alternates metrically with <u>ring</u> 1x J 3.4.31, "And <u>ring</u> these fingers with thy houshold wormes." And <u>enrounded</u> 1x H5 4.Prol.36 means the same as <u>rounded</u> 1x MND 4.1.56 'surrounded': "For she his hairy temples then had <u>rounded</u>, / With coronet of fresh and fragrant flowers." The occurrence of <u>rounded</u> with adverbial <u>in</u> is omitted from the count.

*<u>Ensnare</u> in the poems is a metrical variant of <u>snare</u> 2x T 2.2.174 (F prints as prose), 2H6 3.1.227; both words mean 'to catch in a snare'; and the p.ps. *<u>ensnared</u> 1x O 5.2.302 and <u>snared</u> 2x 2H6 2.2.73, 2.4.56 also occur. Similarly, we find <u>entangle</u> 1x AC 4.14.48 along with <u>tangle</u> 4x 'to ensnare,' and the related p.ps. <u>entangled</u> 1x AC 1.3.30 and <u>tangled</u> 1x H8 3.2.35. Shakespeare also has <u>enthralled</u> 4x as well as <u>thralled</u> 2x TS 1.1.225, H 3.4.74 (om. F) 'enslaved (lit. or fig.).' <u>Entombed</u> 1x TmA 5.4.66 and <u>tombed</u> in the poems 'buried' alternate metrically; and in the meaning 'insensible,' the p.p. <u>entranced</u> is used 1x P 3.2.94 along with <u>tranced</u> 1x L 5.3.218 (om. F).

We find <u>entrap</u> used 4x (F sp. with <u>in</u>-) to mean 'to ensnare'; its variant is <u>trap</u> 1x 2H6 3.1.340. In one statistically relevant line, MV 3.2.101,

To <u>intrap</u> the wisest. Therefore then thou gaudie gold,

<u>to</u> was probably intended to be read as proclitic <u>t</u>' before the following vowel.[27] The identical elision is represented orthographically a few lines further on in the play (MV 3.2.122): "A golden mesh <u>t'intrap</u> the hearts of men." Finally, <u>envenomed</u> occurs 4x (1x F sp. with <u>in</u>-) in the sense

of 'charged with venom,' along with <u>venomed</u> 2x R2 1.1.171, H 4.7.162.

Forms with <u>in</u>- or <u>im</u>-, still belonging to Group 1, include <u>impale</u> 2x 3H6 3.3.189, TC 5.7.5 (1x F sp. with <u>em</u>-) 'to surround, encircle,' alternating metrically with <u>pale</u> 2x 3H6 1.4.103, AC 2.7.74; the occurrences of <u>pale</u> followed by adverbial <u>in</u> have been omitted. The 3H6 lines may be compared: "Did I <u>impale</u> him with the Regall Crowne" and "And will you <u>pale</u> your head in Henries Glory, / And rob his Temples of the Diademe." <u>Impoison</u> occurs once in MA 3.1.86, "How much an ill word may <u>impoison</u> liking," as a metrical variant of <u>poison</u> 4x 'to affect adversely.' And Shakespeare also has the p.ps. <u>impoisoned</u> 1x C 5.6.11 (F prints as prose) and <u>poisoned</u> 4x.

Similarly, <u>imprison</u> 3x 'to put in prison, confine' occurs along with <u>prison</u>, found in the poems, and in the p.ps. we have <u>imprisoned</u> 9x as well as <u>prisoned</u> 1x Cy 3.3.43. In this case, there are also related nouns: <u>imprisonment</u> 11x and <u>prisonment</u> 1x J 3.4.161 'the condition of being confined.' If 3H6 4.6.11,

For that it made my <u>imprisonment</u>, a pleasure,

is read as printed, <u>imprisonment</u> is used where <u>prisonment</u> would be preferable for the meter. But Kökeritz suggests that since <u>my</u> had a variant pronunciation [mɪ], its vowel could have coalesced with the [I] of the following prefix; he cites <u>my</u> <u>invention</u> in O 2.1.126 as a parallel case (<u>Shakespeare's</u> <u>Pronunciation</u>, p. 274). The words <u>imprisonment</u> and <u>prisonment</u> have two other metrical variants in the same meaning: the simple <u>prison</u> 1x WT 2.1.120 ("When you shall know your Mistris / Ha's deserv'd Prison, then abound in Teares") and the vbl. sb. <u>imprisoning</u> 1x 1H4 3.1.30.

Finally, we find *<u>inshipped</u> used 1x 1H6 5.1.49 (only in F4, <u>where</u>,

inshipp'd, which is preferable for the sense; Fl-3 have wherein ship'd)
meaning 'put on board a ship':

> And so my Lord Protector see them guarded,
>
> And safely brought to Dover, where, inshipp'd,   (F wherein ship'd)
>
> Commit them to the fortune of the sea.

Its metrical variant, shipped, occurs 6x.

Group 2

In this group, the prefix is added to an adj. or (less frequently) a
noun, with the sense 'to bring into' [the condition or state denoted by
the root word]. Because some of these root words had related verbs of
the same form, synonymous variants were made possible.

Shakespeare uses *encrimsoned in the poems as well as *crimsoned 1x
JC 3.1.206, two p.ps. meaning 'made crimson'; and he has enfeebled 2x
H5 3.6.154, 1H6 1.4.69 along with feebled 1x J 5.2.146, both p.ps. in the
sense 'made feeble.' Enforce occurs 27x (F sometimes sp. with in-) along
with force 23x. Twice, the vowel of to must be elided before enforce
although this is not typographically indicated:

> To enforce the painèd impotent to smile.   LLL 5.2.864

> To inforce these rights, so forcibly with-held.   J 1.1.18

Enforce and force are relevant in three meanings: 'to constrain,' 'to emphasize,' and 'to compel the observance of.' In the p.t., enforced is
used 6x (e.g. in 3H6 1.1.230, juxtaposed with the simplex in the p.p.--
"Enforc't thee? Art thou King, and wilt be forc't?") and forced 5x; the
meaning is 'constrained.'

Similarly, the p.ps. <u>enfranchised</u> 4x and <u>franchised</u> 1x M 2.1.28 are both used to mean 'made free,' and the p.p. <u>enfreed</u> 1x TC 4.1.38 in the same meaning has a variant <u>freed</u> 3x. Shakespeare uses <u>enjoy</u> 34x in the sense 'to possess or experience with pleasure' (etymologically, <u>enjoy</u> = 'to bring into a condition of joy'; cf. modern <u>I</u> <u>enjoyed</u> <u>myself</u>). Its syllabic and metrical variant, <u>joy</u>, occurs 4x, as in 2H6 3.2.365, "I can no more: Live thou to <u>joy</u> thy life." In the p.t., <u>enjoyed</u> 3x is used as well as <u>joyed</u> 1x 2H6 4.9.1.

<u>Enraged</u> 10x alternates metrically with <u>raged</u> 2x R2 2.1.70, 2.1.173 in the ppl. sense 'made furious'; and the p.p. *<u>enrapt</u> occurs once in TC 5.3.65 as a variant of <u>rapt</u> 4x 'enraptured.' Similarly, <u>enriched</u> 6x, e.g. in R3 2.3.19, "For then this Land was famously <u>enrich'd</u>," is used as well as <u>riched</u>, which occurs 1x in L 1.1.65, "With shadowie Forrests, and with Champains <u>rich'd</u>." The meaning is 'made rich, adorned.' And, finally, *<u>entame</u> 1x AYLI 3.5.48 alternates with <u>tame</u> 7x 'to make tame.'

There are two variants which show not only the <u>en-</u> prefix but also the <u>-en</u> suffix which will be discussed in the following section. These words are <u>emboldened</u> 1x P 1.1.4, a p.p. alternating metrically with <u>boldened</u> 2x AYLI 2.7.91, H8 1.2.55 'made bold,' and <u>enlighten</u> in the poems 'to make bright,' alternating not only with <u>lighten</u> 2x H8 2.3.79, TA 2.3.227 ("A precious Ring, that <u>lightens</u> all the Hole") but also with the simple <u>light</u> 1x R2 3.2.38 ("Behind the Globe, that <u>lights</u> the lower World").

<u>-en</u>,

representing an ancient Teutonic suffix, forms verbs from adjs.,[28] adding much the same sense as the Romanic prefix <u>en-</u> discussed above.

That is, its primary meaning is 'to bring into' [the condition denoted by the adj.]. There is a second sense, 'to become' [the condition denoted], which occurs when an intr. verb is involved. In all of the verb-pairs listed below, the shorter form was the earlier, but is now rare or obsolete.

Shakespeare has darken 5x along with dark 1x P 4.Gower.35 'to dim, sully,' and he uses *deafened 1x P 5.1.47 as well as deafed 1x LLL 5.2.874, two p.ps. meaning 'made deaf.' Also, there is ripen 6x as a synonym of ripe 5x in the two senses 'to make ripe' and (intr.) 'to grow or become ripe.' And shorten occurs 7x along with short 2x (once in the poems) meaning either 'to make shorter' or 'to make ineffectual.' Examples in the second sense are "Yet to be knowne shortens my made intent" (L 4.7.9) and, in Cy 1.6.200, "Yes I beseech: or I shall short my word / By length'ning my returne," where the lack of parallelism with length'ning was probably metrically-inspired. In one line, WT 4.4.433, shorten creates a trisyllabic foot if the F text is accepted: " . . . by hanging thee, I can / but shorten thy life one weeke. And thou, fresh peece." But this is clearly a case of mislineation (note that the line begins with a lower-case letter); unfortunately, we have no quarto for comparison. According to Var. Ed., most modern editors print but with the preceding line, where it adds a feminine ending.

In all of these verbs, synonymous variants were made possible because the root adj. of the -en form already had given rise to a simple verb by functional shift. But in the pair hardened - hard, the latter is not the p.p. of a verb hard but the adj. itself, and sometimes it lacks the sense of past action carried by hardened. To insure synonymity, I give figures for hard only when it modifies heart, as hardened does in its one occur-

rence as an attributive adj. in Shakespeare. Thus, in the meaning 'un-
feeling, cruel,' we have <u>hardened</u> in the poems and <u>hard</u> 3x.

-<u>fy</u>

is a verbal suffix representing L -<u>ficare</u>, from the L verb <u>facere</u>
'to make, do.' When appended to nouns or adjs., it has the sense 'to in-
vest with the attributes of' [the root word] or 'to bring into' [the condition described by the root word]. And when the noun or adj. root has a
verb of the same form, synonymous metrical variants are possible. Thus
Shakespeare can use both <u>beautified</u> 1x TG 4.1.55 and <u>beautied</u> 1x H 3.1.51
as p.ps. meaning 'made beautiful'; and he has <u>fortified</u> 3x 'protected with
a fortification' (etymologically = 'made strong') and <u>forted</u> 1x MM 5.1.12.

-<u>ize</u>

is also a suffix forming verbs on nouns and adjs. It represents the
Greek verbal suffix -<u>izein</u>, which was adapted in Latin as -<u>izare</u>, and its
primary senses are the same as those of -<u>fy</u>. Shakespeare has two statistically significant examples, alternating with a simple verb formally
identical with the root of the -<u>ize</u> derivative. First, <u>moralize</u> occurs
in the poems (rhyme) as a metrical variant of the verb *<u>moral</u> 1x
AYLI 2.7.29 'to indulge in moral reflection,' an intr. sense. And we
also find the p.p. <u>scandalized</u> 2x 1H4 1.3.154, TG 2.7.61 ("I feare me it
will make me <u>scandaliz'd</u>") meaning 'reviled,' along with <u>scandaled</u> 1x
T 4.1.90 ("Her, and her blind-Boyes <u>scandald</u> company / I have forsworne").

CHAPTER IV

DERIVATIONAL VARIANTS: NOUNS

Action and the Result of Action

The derivational variants discussed in this section are partly verbal and partly substantival in nature. They are predominantly nouns of action, though some have developed a concrete sense.

-age

represents OF -age :- late L -aticum; when added to verbs, it usually forms nouns of action. Shakespeare has several variants in -age which alternate metrically with a noun formally identical to the root verb of the -age word. These include *guardage 1x O 1.2.70 as a synonym of guard 8x 'guardianship,' and passage 13x as a synonym of pass 3x 'the act of moving from one place to another' or 'permission to pass.' And Shakespeare uses tillage in the poems to mean 'cultivation of the soil' in a transferred application (S 3.6: "For where is she so faire whose un-eard wombe / Disdaines the tillage of thy husbandry?"). Its variant, showing the nonsyllabic suffix -th, is tilth 2x T 2.1.152, MM 1.4.44 (" . . . her plenteous wombe / Expresseth his full Tilth, and husbandry").

-<u>ance</u> and -<u>ence</u>

show a difference in initial vowel because, in Latin, the suffix of
the pr.p. had two forms (-<u>antem</u> and -<u>entem</u>), depending on the conjugation
of the verb. When nouns of action or quality were formed in Latin by
adding -<u>tia</u> to the present ppl. stem, the resulting suffixes were -<u>antia</u>
and -<u>entia</u>. These came down in French as -<u>ance</u> and -<u>ence</u>, with only the
-<u>ance</u> form subsequently used as a living formative to create nouns of
action on verb-stems. When the stem had a related noun, and when the
derivative lacked a strong sense of action, synonymous variants became
possible.

Thus Shakespeare has *<u>aidance</u> 1x 2H6 3.2.165 'assistance' along with
<u>aid</u> 46x. <u>Grievance</u> occurs 11x and <u>grief</u> over 250x in the three meanings
'sorrow, suffering,' 'a cause of grief,' and 'a hardship which is the
subject of formal complaint'; in the first sense, <u>grief</u> is also a metrical variant of the vbl. sb. <u>grieving</u> 2x MV 2.1.38, O 2.3.177. And <u>port-
ance</u>, used twice by Shakespeare (C 2.3.232, O 1.3.139) to mean 'deportment, bearing,' is a variant of <u>port</u> 3x.

Further, trisyllabic <u>tarriance</u> 1x TG 2.7.90 happens to differ in
syllabic value from disyllabic <u>tarrying</u> 3x 'the act of remaining in a
place.' And <u>usance</u> 2x MV 1.3.46, 1.3.142 occurs along with the simple
<u>use</u> 1x MM 1.1.41 'interest on money lent.' In the ppl. adjs. <u>affianced</u>
1x MM 5.1.227 ("I am <u>affianced</u> this mans wife, as strongly / As words
could make up vowes") and <u>affied</u> 1x TS 4.4.49 ("We be <u>affied</u> and such
assurance tane") 'betrothed,' a verb has been formed on the noun of
action, and it alternates with the simple verb.

In words which came into French at a relatively late date, the suffix with L -<u>e</u> vowel was usually retained, and even early borrowings were

sometimes refashioned after L models. There is one relevant case: occurrences 1x H5 5.Prol.40 'events' along with occurrents 1x H 5.2.368. Here, syllabic variation is due to the fact that occurrence ends in a sibilant.

-ance (-ence) vs. -ancy (-ency)

The suffixes -ancy and -ency are ModE differentiated forms of the earlier -ance and -ence: the -y represents L -ia. We still have many words which appear in both the French-influenced and the Latinate form, e.g. coherence vs. coherency, relevance vs. relevancy. Shakespeare makes extensive use of such double forms in his verse. Though OED says that the -y words are often used to express quality, state, or condition, whereas the simple -ance and -ence forms convey the idea of action or process, there is no such lexical distinction among the variants which are listed below.

Shakespeare has arrogance 6x (1x rhyme) along with arrogancy 1x H8 2.4.110, and convenience 1x AW 3.2.75 along with conveniency 1x MV 4.1.82 'propriety, fitness.' Excellence 10x and excellency 2x MA 2.3.48, O 2.1.65 (Qq only) are both used to mean 'surpassing merit.' And expectance 1x TC 4.5.146 is found as well as expectancy 1x O 2.1.41 (cf. also expectation 11x and the simple expect 1x TC 1.3.70, which is at the end of the line but the line is already an alexandrine); the meaning of all four variants is 'the state of waiting.' Similarly, importance 1x WT 2.1.181 'the fact of being important' alternates metrically both with importancy 1x O 1.3.20 and with *import 5x, a noun formed from the root verb by functional shift.

We also find innocence 21x (2x rhyme) used along with innocency 4x to mean 'freedom from guilt or cunning.' There are two uses which at

first seem irregular: <u>innocency</u> in R3 3.5.20 ("God and our <u>Innocencie</u>
defend, and guard us"), where, however, Q has <u>innocence</u> and thus <u>inno-
cencie</u> was almost certainly a misprint; and <u>innocence</u> in R2 1.3.84 ("Mine
<u>innocence</u>, and S. George to thrive"). Here again, the terminal <u>-e</u> and
<u>-ie</u> were undoubtedly confused; this error is frequent in the old editions.[1]
The line could also be regarded as tetrameter with an extra unaccented
syllable in the caesura (see p. 52, note 15). Finally, <u>observance</u> 5x is
used along with <u>observancy</u> 1x O 3.4.149 (only in F; Qq <u>observances</u>; F2-4
<u>observance</u>, which makes the line short); the meaning is 'respectful or
obsequious attention.'[2]

<u>-ance</u> vs. <u>-ation</u>

The compound suffix <u>-ation</u>, representing L <u>-ionem</u> added to the <u>-at-</u>
of a past ppl. stem, was also used as a formative of nouns of action.
Shakespeare seems to have taken advantage of the situation by choosing
the suffix preferable for the meter.

He has <u>considerance</u> 1x 2H4 5.2.98 - <u>consideration</u> 6x 'reflection'
as well as *<u>iterance</u> 1x O 5.2.150 (only in Ff; either disyllabic or in a
hypermetrical caesura) - <u>iteration</u> 2x O 5.2.150 (only in Qq), TC 3.2.183
'repetition.' And he uses <u>observance</u> 7x (1x poems) - <u>observation</u> 5x in
the three meanings 'the action of adhering' [to a law, custom, etc.],
'the action of paying attention,' and 'care, heed.'

<u>-ing</u>

representing OE <u>-ung</u>, <u>-ing</u> forms nouns of action (some with a concrete sense) on verbal roots. When there exists in English a noun with
the same form as the root word, this noun and the <u>-ing</u> form are often

synonymous (e.g. clasp along with clasp-ing), and it is such variants
that I will discuss in this section.

However, it is sometimes extremely difficult to determine whether
or not the -ing word is really equivalent to the related noun. In the
following lines, for example, loving may be a synonym of love, or it may
express too strongly the idea of action:

> So shall all the couples three,
>
> Ever true in loving be. MND 5.1.415

> If it prove so, then loving goes by haps
>
> Some Cupid kills with arrowes, some with traps. MA 3.1.105

In general, I have excluded such doubtful cases. The most reliable
examples of dominantly substantival -ing forms are those which are preceded by an article or an adj., or which occur in the plural; such uses
have been noted in the listing below.

*Acting 2x JC 2.1.63, H 3.4.108 (both with the definite article) is
a metrical variant of act 2x J 3.1.274, H 1.3.60 'execution'; compare
JC 2.1.63, "Betweene the acting of a dreadfull thing, / And the first
motion," and J 3.1.274, "The better Act of purposes mistooke, / Is to
mistake again." Act is also a syllabic variant of the nonce-word *acture
in the poems. And claspings 1x P 1.1.128, with adj., "By your untimely
claspings with your child," is found along with clasps 1x O 1.1.127, "To
the grosse claspes of a Lascivious Moore"; both mean 'embraces' (with
sexual connotations).

Also there is descending 1x P 5.1.129 'lineage': " . . . thou cam'st
/ From good descending? // So indeed I did" (Q1-3 only; the other old
editions have descent, which makes the line short with an extra syllable

in the caesura). <u>Descent</u> occurs 14x (1x Q4-6, F3-4 only). <u>Deserving</u> 10x

is similarly a metrical variant of <u>desert</u> 40x in the three meanings 'that

which is due to a person,' 'that for which a person deserves something,'

and 'meritoriousness.' And <u>ending</u> 4x (1x rhyme) is found along with <u>end</u>

82x meaning 'close, termination,' as in "From this day to the <u>ending</u> of

the World" (H5 4.3.58) and "A brand to th'<u>end</u> a'th World" (C 3.1.304).

The occurrences of <u>end</u> in concrete application and in phraseological use

(e.g. <u>there's an end, in the end</u>) have been omitted. Shakespeare also

has <u>excusing</u> 1x J 4.2.30 - <u>excuse</u> 2x P 2.3.96, 2H4 4.5.181 'the act of

apologizing.

The vbl. sb. <u>growing</u> 4x (1x rhyme) is used as a synonym of <u>growth</u> 8x

'the action of growing'; and <u>heaving</u> 1x WT 2.3.35 (pl.) means the same as

<u>heave</u> 'a deep sigh,' found 1x H 4.1.1. Shakespeare similarly has <u>howling</u>

1x RJ 3.3.48 (also pl.) along with *<u>howl</u> 1x H5 3.3.39 'a wailing cry of

humans.' And he uses <u>hunting</u> 3x (twice with article) as a synonym for

<u>hunt</u> 3x 'the act of hunting wild animals.'

<u>Loading</u> 1x O 5.2.363, "Looke on the Tragicke <u>Loading</u> of this bed,"

'that which is carried, burden' alternates metrically with <u>load</u> 14x. And

another vbl. sb. used with an adj. is <u>looking</u> 1x T 2.1.309, "Wherefore

this ghastly <u>looking</u>? // What's the matter?"; used to mean 'expression of

countenance, appearance,' it alternates with <u>look</u> 84x (4x rhyme). <u>Losing</u>

3x 'the fact of losing' (constructed with <u>of</u> followed by an object) oc-

curs along with <u>loss</u> 17x.

<u>Quarrelling</u> 2x MA 5.1.51, TmA 3.5.27 is found as a variant of <u>quar-</u>

<u>rel</u> 1x O 2.3.52, "He'l be as full of <u>Quarrell</u>, and offence / As my yong

Mistris dogge," meaning 'quarrelsomeness.' And *<u>questioning</u> 1x rhyme

AYLI 5.4.144 (in a tetrameter passage; therefore <u>question</u> would not have been metrically desirable) is used as a synonym of question 10x 'the action of interrogating; hence, discourse,' as in MV 4.1.346, "Ile stay no longer question. // Tarry Jew." Shakespeare has relieving 1x 1H6 2.1.70 'release of a sentinel from duty' along with relief 1x H 1.1.8. And resting 'repose' occurs once in R2 5.1.6 ("Here let us rest, if this rebellious Earth / Have any resting for her true Kings Queene") along with rest 30x (3x rhyme).[3]

Rising 1x TA 5.2.56 and rise 1x H5 4.1.289 both mean 'sunrise'; the latter is also a syllabic variant of uprise 2x TA 3.1.159, AC 4.12.18. And a parallel case is setting, found once in H8 3.2.225 as a synonym of set 3x 'the apparent descent of a heavenly body. Shipping 3x alternates metrically with ships 21x 'ships collectively'; occurrences of ships with adjs. of quantity, and shipping in the phrase shipping and lading, are omitted. The phrase take shipping 'to embark' also occurs 1x 1H6 5.5.87 as an interesting parallel of take ship 1x H5 2.Prol.30. In addition, Shakespeare once uses shouting in JC 1.2.79 as an equivalent of shout 12x (1x rhyme) 'a loud outcry of a large body of people.'

As a collective sg., sighing 1x TA 3.2.15, "Wound it with sighing girle, kil it with grones" (notice the lack of parallelism with groans), is found as well as sighs 38x (1x rhyme). And smelling 1x H 3.4.79 (om. F) 'the sense of smell' is a metrical variant of smell 1x TmA 1.2.132 (also om. F). Smiling occurs 1x with the indefinite article, along with smile 30x (1x rhyme); both are used in Cy 4.2.52-53, "Nobly he yoakes / A smiling, with a sigh; as if the sighe / Was that it was, for not being suche a Smile." And soliciting 2x M 1.3.130, H 2.2.126 'an entreaty' is a variant of *solicit 1x Cy 2.3.52 (F2-4 only; F has the form solicity, probably a printer's error).

Speeding 2x TS 2.1.303, P 2.3.116 is a metrical variant of speed 2x
TS 2.1.139, WT 3.2.146 'fortune, in a neutral or good sense.' And staying occurs 2x TG 3.1.245, AC 1.3.33 meaning 'continuance in a place'; we
find stay 15x (6x rhyme), as in O 1.3.277, where it occurs in the non-
parallel construction "her stay, or going." Twice, in AC 2.1.36 and in
the poems, stirring is used as a synonym of stir 3x 'movement'; and talking 2x 1H4 5.2.92, H8 1.4.40 is equivalent to talk 8x (1x rhyme) 'the act
of speaking, speech.'

We also find thanking 4x - thanks 116x - thankfulness 5x, all in the
sense 'expressions or feelings of gratitude.' Disyllabic threatening
occurs 1x H5 2.4.110 'a menace'; its variant is threat 11x. In TmA 3.5.43,
threats would be irregular if the words were pronounced according to modern usage:

> Why do fond men expose themselves to Battell,
>
> And not endure all threats? Sleepe upon't.

Here, however, endure was undoubtedly meant to be trisyllabic. This would
have been phonetically possible, since it contains a long vowel followed
by r,[4] and the resulting stress on all would be ideally suited to the meaning of the lines in context.

With the definite article preceding, touching occurs 1x P 5.3.42 as
a variant of touch 17x 'contact'; and wanting 'need' occurs 1x AYLI 2.7.126
along with want 8x. Washing 1x T 1.1.61 (F prints as prose) and wash 1x
H 3.2.166 both mean 'surging' (of waves). And Shakespeare has winking 2x
H 2.2.137, J 4.2.211 as well as wink 4x in the two senses 'a closing of
the eyes, as in sleep (lit. or fig.)' and 'a significant movement of the
eye.' Finally, there is wounding 1x L 1.4.322 (pl.), "Th'untented wound-

ings of a Fathers curse," where the meaning has to be 'injuries' because of the preceding adj.; the variant wound occurs 94x (2x rhyme). In one line, TmA 3.5.111,

> Powres into Captaines wounds? Banishment,

wounds is irregularly used unless we grant the possibility of internal truncation.[5]

Related to the above variants is the vbl. sb. bloodshedding 1x 2H6 4.7.108, but it has been formed after the analogy of shedding; there is no root verb bloodshed meaning 'to shed blood.' The noun bloodshed occurs 2x 2H4 4.5.195, J 4.3.55.

-ing vs. -ation (-ition)

The vbl. sb. in -ing has another type of metrical variant: a word in which -ation (rarely -ition) is, or seems to be, merely added to the verb, forming a noun of action. Since the two suffixes -ing and -ation have different syllabic values, useful syllabic variants are made possible.

Thus Shakespeare has imagining 1x M 1.3.138 (pl.) along with imagination 4x and the simple image 5x 'a mental image, idea.' Lamenting occurs 1x M 2.3.61 (pl.) as a synonym of lamentation 3x and *lament 5x 'an expression of grief.' And opposing is used 1x H 3.1.60 to mean 'antagonism'; its syllabic variant is opposition 6x, occurring in one typographically hypermetrical line (LLL 5.2.743),

> The liberall opposition of our spirits.

Here, however, liberall was almost certainly meant to be syncopated to a disyllable; it could easily have lost its medial unstressed vowel before

r, like desperate, amorously, Generals, and reverence previously discussed.
Kökeritz cites sev'rall MW 5.5.65 as a case in which a similar syncopation
is orthographically indicated. (See Shakespeare's Pronunciation, p. 372.)
Finally, usurping 1x J 2.1.119, "Excuse it is to beat usurping downe," is
a metrical variant of usurpation 3x 'unlawful encroachment' as in J 2.1.9,
"And to rebuke the usurpation," which shows how the -ation suffix could
add not one but two extra syllables if metrically necessary.

-ing

representing OE -ende is the suffix of the pr.p. and of adjs. derived
from the pr.p. In the ME period, OE -ende in its weakened form -inde was
confused phonetically and scribally with the -inge ending of the vbl. sb.;
hence our modern form -ing arose. Forms showing the present ppl. -ing
alternate metrically with other words which either have a suffix of verbal
nature, or intrinsically carry the idea of action.

In sunrising 1x R3 5.3.61, the ending -rising originated as a pr.p.
but later became identified with the vbl. sb. of the same form. Sunrising
is a metrical variant of the later form sunrise 1x MM 2.2.153 (F prints
as two words), which probably developed from the ambiguous use of the sub-
junctive verb rise in such phrases as before the sun rise, according to
OED.

An -ing variant similarly alternates with an originally verbal form
in the preps. excepting 3x and except 7x, where the latter was at first a
p.p. used before a noun and did not take the objective case until the fifteenth or sixteenth century. A parallel case is saving 4x (the pr.p. of
the verb save), which, in such phrases as saving your reverence, is a
metrical variant of save 27x. Save developed from the adj. safe but was

later identified with the imperative <u>save</u>; both <u>saving</u> and <u>save</u> are used to mean either 'without offense to' or 'except.'

The pr.p. is used adjectivally in two final variants: <u>intelligencing</u> and <u>living</u>. Intelligencing 1x WT 2.3.68 ("A most <u>intelligencing</u> bawd . . . ") 'conveying information' is a syllabic variant of <u>intelligent</u> 2x WT 1.2.378, L 3.1.25. The L line contains a trisyllabic foot if spelling is taken as an indication of the meter:

<u>Intelligent</u> of our State. What hath bin seene;

but the line is easily regularized by reading <u>our</u> as disyllabic.[6]

In the group <u>living</u> 14x, <u>live</u> 1x MND 2.1.172, and <u>lively</u> 1x TA 3.1.105 ("Now I behold thy <u>lively</u> body so"), <u>live</u> and <u>lively</u> carry an intrinsic sense of action or process. All mean 'alive'; <u>alive</u> could not be counted, however, because (unlike the other three variants) it always occurs in the predicate. If we pronounce C 5.3.97 as it is printed, <u>living</u> creates a trisyllabic foot where <u>live</u> would have been regular:

How more unfortunate then all <u>living</u> women.

F2-4 omit <u>all</u>, which regularizes the meter but is undesirable for the sense. Unless we wish to admit the presence of an unmarked caesura after <u>unfortunate</u>, then, we must read <u>unfortunate</u> as syncopated through loss of medial unstressed <u>u</u>; see p. 72, note 24 for some phonetic spellings indicating that this <u>u</u> was pronounced [ə] and therefore could have been elided.

-<u>ment</u>,

a suffix ultimately representing L -<u>mentum</u> through Fr -<u>ment</u>, is added to verb-stems to form nouns of action or the result of action.

Sometimes these nouns also developed concrete senses. When there was a noun formally identical with the verbal simplex of the -ment form, synonymous variants became possible.

Shakespeare has *blastment 1x H 1.3.42, "Contagious blastments are most imminent," meaning 'a cold gust of wind' (often symbolizing a pernicious influence) and the simple blast 10x. (OED defines blastment in the H line as = blasting 'a withering or shrivelling up,' but the adj. contagious, together with the use of blast in similar constructions in RL 869 and P 5.3.89, tends to support the meaning I have assigned.) We also find commandment 7x (phraseological use in ten commandments deleted) and its tetrasyllabic variant commandement 2x MV 4.1.451, 1H6 1.3.20 alternating metrically with command 28x 'an order.' And controlment 3x, e.g. in TA 2.1.68 ("Without controulement, Justice, or revenge") is used along with *control 2x J 1.1.17, R3 3.5.84 ("Without controll, lusted to make a prey") to mean 'restraint.'

Designment 2x O 2.1.22, C 5.6.35 is a metrical variant of *design 19x 'enterprise, purpose'; and we also find divorcement 1x O 4.2.158, "And ever will, (though he do shake me off / To beggerly divorcement) Love him deerely," along with divorce 10x in the combined meanings 'separation' and 'dissolution of matrimony'; it is difficult to tell which Desdemona means in the O line quoted. Embracement 3x is used as well as *embrace 2x 1H6 3.3.82, RJ 5.3.113 to mean 'an enfolding in the arms'; pl. occurrences of both variants are omitted because of syllabic identity.[7] And in the meaning 'reception, treatment,' Shakespeare usually has entertainment (6x) but once entertain (P 1.1.119): "And until then your entertain shall be / As doth befit our honour and your worth."

Impeachment 1x TG 1.3.15 (the pl. occurrence is om.) occurs as a

synonym of impeach 2x CE 5.1.269, 3H6 1.4.60 'accusation.' And Shakespeare may have created *interchangement as a metrical variant of interchange 3x; it occurs 1x TN 5.1.162 meaning 'the act of giving and taking
reciprocally.' Languishment 1x TA 2.1.110 means 'mental distress,' the
same as languor 1x TA 3.1.13, "My harts deepe languor, and my soules sad
teares." And lineament 7x (1x rhyme) 'contour of the body' is a synonym
of line 4x, as in Cy 4.2.104 in a description of Cloten's face: "Long is
it since I saw him, / But Time hath nothing blurr'd those lines of
Favour."

Payment 11x is similarly a variant of pay 14x (1x rhyme) in the two
senses 'the action of paying' and 'that which is paid.' *Retirement 3x
and retire 12x (1x rhyme) are both used to mean 'the act of withdrawing
to or from a place'; and revengement 1x 1H4 3.2.7 is a metrical variant
of revenge 78x and vengeance 40x 'retaliation.' (The pl. occurrences of
all three variants have been excluded, along with Revenge as the name of
the character in TA and the use of vengeance in imprecations.) Finally,
supplyment 1x Cy 3.4.182 is found along with supply 3x (1x rhyme) 'the
action of supplying something needed.'[8]

-ment vs. -ation

In two cases, a form in -ment alternates metrically with a synonym
in -ation. Shakespeare has *distilment 1x H 1.5.64 along with distilla-
tion in the poems 'a substance extracted by distilling'; and he uses both
presentment 1x H 3.4.54, "The counterfet presentment of two Brothers,"
and presentation 1x R3 4.4.84, "The presentation of but what I was," to
mean 'representation, image.'

In two further pairs of variants, syllabic variation is more or less

accidental. Admonishment 2x 1H6 2.5.98, TC 5.3.2 'warning, reproof' happens to vary with admonition 1x R2 2.1.117 because the -ion is disyllabic.
And *amazement 4x alternates metrically with amazedness 1x MW 4.4.55
'loss of self-possession through fear' because the ppl. root of amazedness was trisyllabic.

-sion and -tion

are compound suffixes representing, respectively, L -sionem and
-tionem, which consist of -ionem added to the -s- or -t- of a past ppl.
stem. Since L p.ps. in -atus are quite numerous, -ation was the usual
form that came down through French, and it became a living formative in
English as well. The usual sense is that of a noun of action, though
sometimes (as with -ing and -ment) a concrete sense has developed. When
the ppl. stem of the derivative had a related noun of the same or similar
form, synonymous metrical variants became possible.

Shakespeare has accusation 13x, as in WT 3.2.32 ("Innocence shall
make / False Accusation blush, and Tyrannie / Tremble at Patience") meaning 'the act of charging with crime, or the charge made'; its variant is
*accuse 1x 2H6 3.1.160 ("And dogged Yorke . . . / By false accuse doth
levell at my Life"). Similarly, action 50x is found along with act 86x
(1x rhyme) in the two senses 'the state of being active' and 'deed.' Act
is irregularly used in H8 1.2.85,

For our best Act: if we shall stand still,

if modern pronunciation is followed. But it is probable that this is
simply another case of disyllabic our, for the stressing of best would be
admirably consistent with the parallel stressing of worst two lines above.

Affection 79x and affect 3x occur in the two senses 'inclination' and 'kind feeling'; and in the meaning 'a quality ascribed,' attribution is used 1x 1H4 4.1.3 ("Such attribution should the Dowglas have") along with attribute 6x. Also, commendation 11x is a metrical variant of commend 4x meaning either 'recommendation, praise' or 'greeting.' And Hamlet uses contraction 1x 'betrothal' (H 3.4.46); the simple contract is found 16x. Conversation 3x and *converse 2x LLL 5.2.745, O 3.1.40 both mean 'contact, intercourse.' Shakespeare also has disposition 9x - *dispose 1x TC 2.3.174 'mood, inclination.'

Other variants include effusion 2x J 5.2.49, 1H6 5.1.9 along with *effuse 1x 3H6 2.6.28 ("And much effuse of blood, doth make me faint") meaning 'a pouring out'; and there is estimation 9x as well as estimate 5x in the two senses 'estimated value' and 'reputation, honor.' In the meaning 'outcry, reproach,' exclamation occurs 3x, e.g. in R3 4.4.153, "Thus will I drowne your exclamations," and exclaim 5x, e.g. in R3 4.4.135, "The Trumpet sounds, be copious in exclaimes." The variant imposition is similarly used 3x 'charge, injunction'; its synonym is *impose 1x TG 4.3.6. And intention 1x WT 1.2.138 'purpose' alternates with intent 62x (1x rhyme). The latter is also a syllabic variant of intendment 1x H5 1.2.144.

Limitation 2x C 2.3.146, JC 2.1.283 is used along with limit 6x in the two senses 'the condition of being limited' and 'an allotted time'; cf. in the latter sense C 2.3.146 (with initial truncation), "You have stood your Limitation," and R3 3.3.8, "Dispatch, the limit of your Lives is out." OED defines limit in this R3 line as 'boundary, bound,' but the word out seems to demand the meaning I have assigned. As far as we know, Shakespeare created *neglection 3x to go along with *neglect 7x (the latter is also a syllabic variant of negligence 11x) in the two meanings 'disregard' (the primary modern sense of neglect) and 'lack of proper care' (modern negligence). And he has ostentation 5x and *ostent 3x meaning 'display, exhibition.'

Preparation 14x, e.g. in MV 2.4.4, "We have not made good preparation," is a variant of prepare 1x 3H6 4.1.131, "Goe levie men, and make prepare for Warre"; the sense is 'preparatory action.' And in H8 1.1.151, Shakespeare has prescription 'that which is prescribed' (occurrences referring to medical prescriptions are omitted) as a synonym of prescript 2x H 2.2.142 (only in Qq; Ff precepts), AC 3.8.5. The derivative protestation similarly occurs 5x as well as the simple protest 2x TC 3.2.182, 1H4 3.1.260 'a solemn declaration.' In TC 5.2.116, recordation is used to mean 'mental notation': "To make a recordation to my soule"; its variant, stressed on the second syllable, is record 2x TC 1.3.14, TN 5.1.253, "O that record is lively in my soule."

Further variants are replication in the poems, alternating with reply 9x in the sense 'an answer,' and reputation 19x along with repute 1x TC 1.3.337 meaning 'the common estimate of a person.' Sequestration 2x H5 1.1.58, 1H6 2.5.25 'seclusion' and sequester 1x O 3.4.40, a nonce-use, are also metrical variants. And station 5x occurs as well as state 28x (2x rhyme) to mean either 'mode of standing' or 'rank, position.' It should be noted that OED does not list 'mode of standing' as a possible meaning of state. But in the line in which I think it occurs, LLL 4.3.185 (F prints as prose), " . . . I / Will praise a hand, a foot, a face, an eye: / A gate, a state, a brow, a brest, a waste," gate and state seem to be used antithetically; and also, L status (the word's ultimate source) was used to mean 'mode of standing.'[9]

Shakespeare also has succession 5x and success 2x 2H4 4.2.47,

WT 1.2.394 in the sense 'transmission of an inheritance, or the principle
by which this occurs.' In one relevant line, WT 1.2.394,

In whose <u>successe</u> we are gentle: I beseech you,

<u>we are</u> must be read <u>we're</u> or <u>w'are</u> for the meter. As previously noted,
such contractions were a feature of the colloquial language then as now;
Kökeritz cites <u>w'are</u> in H8 Epil.8 as an instance which was orthographi-
cally indicated.[10] <u>Supposition</u> is found 2x CE 3.2.50, MA 4.1.240 'a con-
jecture or opinion,' and its syllabic variants are <u>suppose</u> 3x and
<u>supposal</u> 1x H 1.2.18. Compare the following: "The <u>supposition</u> of the
Ladies death" (MA 4.1.240); "That we come short of our <u>suppose</u> so farre"
(TC 1.3.11); and "Holding a weake <u>supposall</u> of our worth" (H 1.2.18).
Two final examples are <u>valuation</u> 2x 2H4 4.1.189, Cy 4.4.49 - <u>value</u> 1x
C 2.2.63 (F prints as prose) 'evaluation,' and <u>variation</u> 1x 1H4 1.1.64 -
<u>vary</u> 1x L 2.2.85 ("With every gall, and <u>varry</u> of their Masters") meaning
'alteration.'[11]

The word <u>comparison</u> shows the ModE -<u>ison</u> ending which developed from
OF -<u>aison</u>, the form by which L -<u>ationem</u> was represented in colloquial
French. <u>Comparison</u> is used 7x in the two meanings 'the capacity of being
likened' and 'the similitude itself (concrete),' alternating with <u>compare</u>
6x. Finally, in the pair <u>executioner</u> 11x and <u>executor</u> 1x H5 1.2.203
'one who carries out a death sentence,' agent-nouns have been formed both
on the noun of action and on the ppl. root. For -<u>ation</u> alternating with
monosyllabic suffixes, see the discussions of -<u>ance</u>, -<u>ing</u>, and -<u>ment</u> above.

-<u>ure</u>

represents L -<u>ura</u>, which formed nouns, primarily nouns of action, on

past ppl. stems. Some of the words listed below actually had L ancestors;
some were formed by analogy. The presence of synonymous variants here is
attributable to the fact that the stem of the -ure derivative often was
also, or was used as, a noun.

We find *composture 1x TmA 4.3.444 along with compost 1x H 3.4.151
'manure'; and Shakespeare has coverture 2x MA 3.1.30, 3H6 4.2.13 along
with cover 5x and the disyllabic vbl. sb. covering 3x 'anything that cov-
ers.' Departure 16x is a metrical variant of depart 4x in the meaning
'the act of going away' (also, fig., 'death,' as in 1H6 4.2.41,
3H6 2.1.110). Tetrasyllabic distemperature occurs 5x (once, in P 5.1.27,
only in Q1-2; the other old editions have distemperance instead) as a
synonym of distemper 6x 'disorder of the body or mind.'

The nonce-word *enacture occurs 1x H 3.2.207 (F sp. ennactors; Qq
have ennactures, F2-4 enactors):

> What to our selves in passion we propose,
>
> The passion ending, doth the purpose lose.
>
> The violence of other Greefe or Joy,
>
> Their owne ennactors with themselves destroy.

OED tentatively defines the word as 'carrying into act,' but I feel that
it means 'purposes, resolutions,' like enact 1x TA 4.2.118, "The close
enacts and counsels of the hart."

Forfeiture 9x is a metrical variant of forfeit 15x in the two senses
'the loss of something as a result of breach of obligation' and (concrete) 'that which is lost.' In the meaning 'a rounded form,' *roundure
occurs 1x J 2.1.259 (F sp. rounder) and *rondure in the poems. The latter is an adaptation of Fr rondeur and does not have precisely the same

suffix as *roundure; compare soilure on p. 231, note 12 below. Both

*roundure and *rondure alternate metrically with the simple round 4x.

Shakespeare has tainture 1x 2H6 2.1.188 as well as taint 2x

LLL 1.1.224, H8 5.3.28 'condition of decay; infection'; the latter is

probably also a metrical variant of attaint 1x H5 4.Prol.39, "But

freshly lookes, and over-beares Attaint," though OED tentatively defines

this occurrence as 'stain upon freshness.' If attaint is in fact a syn-

onym of taint here, then taint in H8 5.3.28 must be regarded as a typo-

graphically unmetrical use:

Commotions, uprores, with a generall Taint.

However, though attaint would create a regular alexandrine, the line can

be made metrically exact by reading general as a disyllable. Finally,

we find tincture used once in WT 3.2.206 as an equivalent for tinct 2x

H 3.4.91, Cy 2.2.23; the meaning is 'color, coloring.'[12]

In the verb pleasure, the suffix does not represent L -ura but has

been assimilated to the -ure form in English. The word developed by

functional shift from the noun pleasure, in which the suffix really rep-

resents the OF infinitive ending -ir. Pleasure occurs 1x meaning 'to be

agreeable to' ("And if what pleases him, shall pleasure you," 3H6 3.2.22);

and in this sense we also find the simple verb please 49x (2x rhyme).

Occurrences of please in stock impersonal constructions such as may it

please you have not been counted; the occurrences of the third person sg.

pleases have also been excluded, as there is no syllabic variation with

pleasures. The use of pleasure in the 3H6 line quoted above was evi-

dently not motivated solely by the desire to avoid repetition, for Shake-

speare uses please twice in a similar line (R2 2.2.5).

Condition or State

-<u>ity</u>

is the usual form in which the suffix -<u>ty</u> (representing L -<u>tas</u>,
-<u>tatem</u>) appears, and is also the form assumed by -<u>ty</u> as a living suffix.
In Latin, -<u>tas</u> was added to adjs. to create nouns of state or condition,
many of which later developed a concrete sense. When the adj. simplex
has a related noun of the same or similar form, synonymous variants are
possible.

In Shakespeare we find, for example, trisyllabic or tetrasyllabic
<u>extremity</u> 20x along with <u>extreme</u> 14x in the three concrete meanings 'the
utmost spatial point,' 'the highest degree,' and 'anything in its highest degree.' Other variants include the phrase <u>in</u> *<u>futurity</u> 1x O 3.4.117
- <u>in future</u> 1x TmA 1.1.141 'in future time,' and <u>nobility</u> 12x along with
<u>nobles</u> 23x 'noblemen collectively.' (All occurrences of <u>nobles</u> in con-
texts requiring a pl. word are omitted.) If we use modern pronunciation
in C 2.1.255, <u>nobles</u> is irregular where <u>nobility</u> would have been metrically exact:

And the desire of the <u>Nobles</u>.

However, if <u>desire</u> is read as a trisyllabic word (like <u>endure</u> discussed
above, p. 89), the result is an acceptable short line.[13]

<u>Particularity</u> 1x 2H6 5.2.44, "<u>Particularities</u>, and pettie sounds,"
alternates metrically with <u>particular</u> in the poems 'a particular case.'
And the originally abstract noun <u>superfluity</u> 1x C 1.1.230 is a synonym
of *<u>superflux</u> 1x L 3.4.35 'a surplus.'

After the connective vowel -<u>i</u>-, the suffix -<u>ity</u> takes the form -<u>ety</u>,

as in <u>contrariety</u> 1x C 4.6.73, which occurs along with <u>contrary</u> 1x
T 1.2.95 ("A falsehood in it's <u>contrarie</u>, as great / As my trust was").
The meaning is 'the state of being contrary.' In the sense 'things that
are the opposite of each other,' we find <u>contrarieties</u> 1x 1H6 2.3.59 -
<u>contraries</u> 3x. In <u>commonalty</u> 1x H8 1.2.170, the -<u>ty</u> suffix was added to
adjectival -<u>al</u>-. Used to mean 'the common people,' it is a metrical variant of another derivative, <u>commoners</u> 1x C 2.1.243, and of its own root
noun, represented in English by <u>common</u> 2x C 1.1.155, 3.1.29 and <u>commons</u>
24x. The suffix has been added to adjectival -<u>bili</u>- 'tending to' in
<u>mutability</u> 1x Cy 2.5.26 'alteration,' a synonym of the abstract noun of
action <u>mutation</u> 1x Cy 4.2.133.

-<u>ity</u> vs. -<u>ness</u>

Many nouns in -<u>ity</u> have alternate forms in -<u>ness</u>, a Germanic suffix
which also forms nouns of state or condition on adjectival roots. Examples in Shakespeare include <u>austerity</u> 3x - <u>austereness</u> 1x MM 2.4.155
'sternness, strictness'; <u>equality</u> 2x AC 1.3.47, J 2.1.327 - <u>equalness</u> 1x
AC 5.1.48 'the condition of being equal'; <u>gentility</u> 1x rhyme LLL 1.1.129
(Q has the form <u>gentletie</u>, which wrenches the stress) - <u>gentleness</u> 15x -
<u>gentry</u> 1x H 2.2.22 ("To shew us so much <u>Gentrie</u>, and good will"), all
meaning 'courtesy, good breeding'; and <u>gravity</u> 9x - <u>graveness</u> 1x
H 4.7.82 (om. F) 'dignity, solemnity.'

Also there is <u>humility</u> 12x - <u>humbleness</u> 7x 'meekness.' And Shakespeare has <u>nobility</u> 17x as well as <u>nobleness</u> 16x in the two meanings
'dignity in respect of rank or birth' and 'dignity in respect of mind or
character.' In the second sense, the two words are also syllabic variants of <u>noblesse</u> 1x R2 4.1.119 (only in Q; the other old editions have

noblenesse, but noblesse is metrically preferable). Finally, we find rarity in the poems (rhyme) along with rareness 1x Cy 3.4.95 'unusually excellent character'; and simplicity 7x (3x rhyme) is a synonym of simpleness 4x meaning either 'plainness' or 'ignorance, folly.'

-ness

represents OE -nes, and is attached to root-words (usually adjs.) to form nouns expressing state or condition. These adjs. are themselves often related to nouns of approximately the same meaning as the -ness derivative; thus, synonymous metrical variants are made possible.

In Shakespeare, we find easiness 1x H 3.4.166 as well as ease 1x O 1.3.29 'freedom from difficulty' (ease is omitted when in fixed phrases such as with ease). Guiltiness 8x and guilt 26x both mean 'the fact of being guilty'; and mightiness 2x H5 2.4.64, H8 Prol.30 is a metrical variant of might 8x 'great power' (occurrences of the title your mightiness have been excluded). Finally, there is speediness 1x Cy 2.4.31 - speed 62x (2x rhyme) 'quickness,' and worthiness 12x - worth 65x (2x rhyme) 'high personal merit.'

Of the same general type are faithfulness 2x P 1.1.63, 1.1.154 'fidelity' along with faith 63x (occurrences in oaths are omitted from the count); and fearfulness 1x JC 1.1.80, "And keepe us all in servile fearefulnesse," along with fear over 200x (occurrences in the phrases for fear and for fear of are excluded). The meaning is 'dread, timidity,' as in Cy 3.5.158:

You must forget to be a Woman: change
Command, into obedience. Feare, and Nicenesse

(The Handmaides of all Women, or more truely

Woman it pretty selfe) into a waggish courage.

Note that <u>fear</u> is here parallel to <u>niceness</u> syntactically but not formally.[14]

In <u>wilderness</u>, the suffix is appended to a compound noun (in Old
English, <u>wilddéor</u> 'wild beast') rather than to a simple adj. <u>Wilderness</u>
occurs 6x meaning 'a wild place,' alternating metrically with the noun
<u>wild</u> 2x MV 2.7.14, 3.2.184. It also occurs 1x in MM 3.1.142, "For such
a warpèd slip of <u>wildernesse</u> / Nere issu'd from his blood," meaning 'wild-
ness of character'; this is a nonce-use, after the analogy of <u>wildness</u> 5x
formed on the simple adj. <u>wild</u>.

-red

represents OE <u>ráeden</u> 'condition,' which was freely attached to nouns
as a combining-form, creating nouns of state. Only three members of this
class survive, <u>gossipred</u>, <u>hatred</u>, and <u>kindred</u>, of which the last two are
found in Shakespeare as metrical variants of the simple noun. <u>Hatred</u>
occurs 16x, <u>hate</u> 70x (4x rhyme) in the meaning 'extreme dislike.' Alternation determined by the meter can clearly be seen in MND 4.1.148-149,
"That <u>hatred</u> is so farre from jealousie, / To sleepe by <u>hate</u>, and feare
no enmity."

<u>Kindred</u> occurs 19x along with <u>kin</u> 11x (2x rhyme) meaning 'relatives
collectively'; one statistically significant line, R3 1.1.95, is irregular if modern pronunciation is used:

And that the Queenes <u>Kindred</u> are made gentle Folkes.

However, the -es of Queenes may well be a survival of the old syllabic genitive, and if so, the line is a regular alexandrine (the preceding line has seven feet). Franz (p. 185) cites several parallels in the plays, including "To shew his teeth as white as Whales bone"--LLL 5.2.332, and "You sent me for a ropes end as soone"--CE 4.1.99. This syllabic genitive is quite frequent in Spenser, e.g. in Faerie Queene I.5.17.4, "In wine and oyle they wash his woundes wide."

-ship

found in Old English as -scipe, forms nouns on noun-stems. It usually denotes 'the state or condition of being' [what is expressed by the simplex]. In Shakespeare, the word companionship 2x C 3.2.49, TmA 1.1.251, found along with company 7x 'fellowship,' illustrates this use. And because the suffix was also used to mean 'the office or function of' [the simplex], we have the pair *attorneyship 1x 1H6 5.5.56 ("Marriage is a matter of more worth, / Then to be dealt in by Atturney-ship") and attorney 1x R3 5.3.83 ("I by Attourney, blesse thee from thy Mother"), both meaning 'proxy.'

-y

as it appears in company above is a suffix representing Fr -ie, which in turn represents L -ia. Sometimes these nouns in -y developed concrete meanings, and when this happened, they were often synonyms of their noun simplexes.

So in Shakespeare we find treasury 7x alternating metrically with treasure 44x (2x rhyme; once in the poems) in the two senses 'a place

where stores of wealth are kept' and 'riches.' An example of treasury
in the second meaning is in H5 1.2.165, " . . . the Owse, and bottome of
the Sea / With sunken Wrack, and sum-lesse Treasuries"; and S 136.5 has
treasure in the first meaning, "Will, will fulfill the treasure of thy
love." Shakespeare also uses warranty 3x 'authorization' as well as
warrant 14x and warrantise 1x H 5.1.250 (F only; the rest of the old editions have warranty). And warrantise is used once to mean 'surety'
("Breake up the Gates, Ile be your warrantize," 1H6 1.3.13), and in this
sense it alternates metrically with warrant 12x; the suffix -ise ultimately represents L -itia.

The -y suffix also appears as the final element in many compound
suffixes, such as -acy in lunacy. Lunacies 1x H 3.3.7 (Ff only; Qq
browes, making the line pentameter rather than an alexandrine) means
'fits of lunacy' and is a metrical variant of the shorter form *lunes 1x
WT 2.2.30. In the word secrecy (in the fifteenth and sixteenth centuries
sp. secretee), we probably have to do with an analogical alteration of
the -ty suffix after words like primacy. As a collective sg. meaning
'things kept secret,' secrecy occurs 1x AC 1.2.9 (F prints as prose)
along with secrets 17x. One line, TC 4.2.74,

> Good, good, my Lord, the secrets of nature
>
> Have not more gift in taciturnitie,

is metrically defective unless we allow the possibility of a trisyllabic
pronunciation of secrets, for according to Kökeritz, nature could not
have been stressed on the second syllable.[15] The phrase in secrecy also
occurs 2x H8 3.2.403, H 1.2.207 as a synonym of in secret 3x.

Personal and Material Agency

Almost all of the agent-nouns discussed in this section are of a type
consisting of an -er form vs. a shorter variant. The two major exceptions
will be discussed first below.

-ant

is the Fr present ppl. ending, representing L -antem, -entem. Sometimes original pr.ps. in -ant were used as nouns of personal agency, e.g.
appellant; Shakespeare's noun *guardant 'protector, keeper' seems to have
been introduced after the analogy of such words. And since the verbal
stem of *guardant had a related noun represented by ModE guard, it was
possible for Shakespeare to use the variants *guardant 1x 1H6 4.7.9, "But
when my angry Guardant stood alone," and guard 10x. The latter also alternates with disyllabic guardian 1x M 2.4.35, "The Sacred Store-house of
his Predecessors, / And Guardian of their bones"; the occurrences of
guardian meaning specifically 'protector of an orphan' have been omitted.

-ard

is a suffix adopted from OF -ard, which in turn was an adoption of
German -hard 'hardy.' The suffix was used in French as a formative of
masculine common nouns, often pejorative (e.g. bastard), and in English
it was sometimes added to verbs with the sense 'one who does [something
discreditable] to excess.' In Shakespeare we find sluggard 1x R3 5.3.225
(formed on a verb slug) along with the related noun slug 2x CE 2.2.196,
R3 3.1.22, "Fie, what a Slug is Hastings, that he comes not." Both words
mean 'a slow-moving or indolent person.'

-er

as a suffix denoting agency may be either of Germanic or of Romanic origin. The Germanic -er, representing OE -ere, forms agent-nouns on verbal bases. When these verbs have related nouns of the same form, synonymous variants become possible.

Shakespeare has causer 3x along with cause over 150x (phraseological use in without cause, have cause is omitted), both meaning 'one who, or that which, causes.' An example of causer denoting material agent is found in LLL 4.3.311: "You have in that forsworne the use of eyes: / And studie too, the causer of your vow." Guider similarly occurs 1x C 1.7.7 meaning 'one who guides': "Our Guider come, to th'Roman Campe conduct us." Its variant, guide, occurs 3x (uses denoting a material agent are omitted because of lack of parallelism). Helper 3x 'one who helps' alternates metrically with help 2x WT 2.1.46, P 1.1.22, and mutiner 1x C 1.1.254 'one who mutinies' with mutine 2x H 5.2.6, J 2.1.378 ("Do like the Mutines of Jerusalem").

In the meaning 'that which nourishes,' Shakespeare has disyllabic nourisher 1x M 2.2.40 and nourish 1x 1H6 1.1.50, "Our Ile be made a Nourish of salt Teares"; both are syllabic variants of the reduced form nurse 4x. And in the sense 'one who nourishes' (constructed with of), we find nurser 1x 1H6 4.7.46 along with nurse 4x. In addition, trumpeter 3x 'one who sounds a trumpet' is used as a synonym of trumpet 5x (fig. occurrences omitted); an example of trumpet in this sense is "Goe, Trumpet, to the Walls, and sound a Parle," 3H6 5.1.16.[16]

In exorcizer 1x Cy 4.2.276 along with exorcist 2x AW 5.3.305, JC 2.1.323 'one who calls up spirits,' the agent suffix -er has been added to an -ize form of the root verb, whereas the Greek suffix represented by ModE -ist has not.

Along with this -er of Germanic origin, there was also an -er suffix representing OF -ere or -e)or :- L -ator. Though this -er is morphologically and lexically indistinguishable from the Germanic one, the derivatives in this section differ from the ones previously discussed in that they were adapted from an agent-noun existing in Old French and were not created in English directly from the verb.

Among the examples in Shakespeare is the word augurer 3x 'a soothsayer' alternating metrically with augur, which is found in the poems. And we might also count the form auguries in AC 4.12.4,

> Swallowes have built
>
> In Cleopatra's Sailes their nests. The Auguries
>
> Say, they know not, they cannot tell, looke grimly,
>
> And dare not speake their knowledge,

under augur, for it is almost certainly a misprint for augures, pl. of augure (a variant form of augur), by virtue of the final -e/-ie confusion. Another example of this -er type is briber 1x TmA 3.5.61 'something given as a bribe,' a nonce-use of the word to denote a material agent: "His service done at Lacedemon, and Bizantium, / Were a sufficient briber for his life." Its metrical variant, bribe, occurs 6x.

Diminution

-cle

in receptacle represents L -culum, which was used to form diminutives on nouns or verb-stems. However, in this word as in the other original diminutives discussed in this study, the idea of "smallness" has become greatly weakened or nonexistent. Thus receptacle 4x is a synonym and metrical variant of receipt 1x M 1.7.66 (ultimately representing L recepta) in the meaning 'a place which contains something.' The M occurrence is part of Lady Macbeth's description of the drunken chamberlains: "Memorie, the Warder of the Braine, / Shall be a Fume, and the Receit of Reason / A Lymbeck onely."

-el and -le

can represent OE -ela, which was appended to noun-stems as in nafela (ModE navel), usually adding either a diminutive sense or the idea of an appliance or tool. If navel was originally a diminutive of nave, at least it does not have this meaning in Shakespeare, where both are used to mean 'the umbilicus, or (fig.) the center.' Navel is found 1x C 3.1.123, nave 1x M 1.2.22, "Till he unseam'd him from the Nave toth' Chops." Probably this occurrence of nave, a nonce-use according to OED, is really a case of apocope for the meter.

When added to verb-stems, as in the noun girdle (OE gyrdel, f. gyrdan), the -el suffix was often instrumental. Since gyrdan survived in Modern English as the verb gird, and since girdle also came to be used as a verb through functional shift, Shakespeare had at his disposal two synonymous verbs of different syllabic value. In the p.p., girdled 1x 1H6 4.3.20 'surrounded' alternates metrically with girt (the short form of girded), used 1x 3H6 4.8.20.

In the word middle (OE middel), the suffix has been added to an adj.-stem (midd-). The -le seems to have no discernible function, and thus, as adjs., middle 3x and mid 2x T 1.2.239, TC 2.2.104 are synonymous. Cf.

also the combinations mid-summer 1x 1H4 4.1.102 and middle summer 2x
MND 2.1.82, WT 4.4.107. As nouns, we find middle 6x along with mid 1x
R3 5.3.77, "Ratcliffe, about the mid of night come to my Tent," and the
extended form midst 7x.

-et

occurs in English chiefly in words which were adopted in Middle
English from Fr diminutives in -et, -ette. OED comments that most of
these soon became used without any consciousness of their original diminutive sense. Shakespeare has several words of this type: they include
helmet 8x, used along with helm 14x 'armor for the head'; target 7x,
along with targe 3x 'a shield'; and trumpet 68x (fig. occurrences
omitted) along with trump 5x, the wind instrument.

Coronet was in origin a diminutive of OF corone, the ancestor of the
ModE syncopated form crown, and meant 'an inferior crown worn by the nobility.' To a large extent, it is still so used in Shakespeare, but
coronet and crown are for all practical purposes synonymous in the spe-
cialized sense 'a garland of flowers.' We find coronet used in this way
1x MND 4.1.57, "With coronet of fresh and fragrant flowers," and crown
3x, e.g. in T 4.1.129, "You Nimphs cald Nayades of the windring brooks,
/ With your sedg'd crownes, and ever-harmlesse lookes."

-y

as a suffix used to form pet names and familiar diminutives dates
from about 1400. It is probably this suffix which appears in the common
noun baby, occurring 12x in Shakespeare along with babe 61x in the two

meanings 'infant' and 'doll.' Compare, in the second sense, M 3.4.106,
"If trembling I inhabit then, protest mee / The Baby of a Girle," and
J 3.4.58, "If I were mad, I should forget my sonne, / Or madly thinke a
babe of clowts were he."

Collectivity

-age

is a suffix found in words ultimately derived from, or formed on the
analogy of, L abstract nouns in -aticum. The variants in which the suffix is appended to action verbs have already been discussed on p. 82.
When affixed to the names of things, -age usually denotes 'all that belongs to' [the noun] or conveys the idea of the whole functional apparatus
collectively. But in only one pair of statistically significant variants, *plantage along with plant, have I felt that the -age form was
really collective as compared with the noun simplex.[17] I therefore count
*plantage 1x TC 3.2.184 ("As true as steele, as plantage to the Moone")
only as contrasted with the pl. plants 8x 'plants collectively.'

In the following pairs of variants, the collective force of -age is
much weakened or is also inherent in the root noun. Anchorage 1x
TA 1.1.73, "From whence at first she weigh'd her Anchorage," I define as
a synonym of anchor 7x, i.e. 'an appliance for holding a ship in place
(lit. or fig.)'; OED disagrees, defining anchorage here as 'a set of
anchors.'

But there can be no question about cottage 4x and cote 1x 'a small
house,' which are juxtaposed in AYLI: "Buy thou the Cottage, pasture, and
the flocke" (2.4.92); and "Besides his Coate, his Flockes, and bounds of

feede" (2.4.83). Similarly, _fraughtage_ occurs 2x TC Prol.13, CE 4.1.87

meaning the same as _fraught_ 3x 'freight, contents.' And _personage_ 2x,

both in MND 3.2.292, "And with her _personage_, her tall _personage_," is a

metrical variant of _person_ 11x 'the living human body.' (It is not

necessary to assume syncopation of _personage_, for there could have been

an extra unaccented syllable in the caesura.) Finally,*_vaultage_ 1x

H5 2.4.124 'an enclosed space with an arched roof' is a synonym of _vault_

14x.

-ry

is a reduced form of the Romanic suffix -_ery_, added to nouns with a

general collective sense, or to signify appurtenance ('all that is con-

nected with' [the noun]). In one case, *_pageantry_ 1x P 5.2.6 (an octo-

syllabic line), "What _pageantry_, what feats, what shows," the -_ry_ seems

to have full collective sense, and therefore I have counted only the pl.

pageants as its metrical variant. The latter occurs 4x, e.g. in

H8 4.1.11, "In Celebration of this day with Shewes, / _Pageants_, and

Sights of Honor."

Similarly, _revelry_ 1x AYLI 5.4.183 (rhyme) seems to be collective;

but I compare it with both the sg. and the pl. of _revel_ because the sg.

could also have this sense, e.g. in H 1.4.17, "This heavy-headed _revel_

east and west" (this is the Q reading; the line is om. by F). _Revel_

occurs 14x and is also a syllabic variant of the vbl. sb. _revelling_ 2x

MA 1.1.322, MND 1.1.19; all of these variants mean 'merry-making.'

Appurtenance

<u>-al</u>

is usually an adjectival suffix, representing L -<u>alis</u>, -<u>alem</u>. However, some -<u>alis</u> adjs. were used substantivally in Latin; and either as
representatives of these, or on the analogy of them, we have many -<u>al</u>
nouns in English. Shakespeare used them as metrical variants of nouns
which were related to, or identical with, the root of the -<u>al</u> derivative.

Thus he has <u>mineral</u> 1x H 4.1.26 (originally <u>mineralis</u> 'pertaining
to mines') as a synonym of <u>mine</u> 6x 'an excavation for digging out miner-
als': " . . . like some Oare / Among a <u>Minerall</u> of Mettels base." And he
uses <u>original</u> 1x MND 2.1.117, "We are their parents and <u>originall</u>," to
mean 'source'; its variant is <u>origin</u> 2x H 1.4.26, L 4.2.32 (both om. F).
Similarly, <u>portal</u> is found 2x R2 3.3.64, H 3.4.136 as a synonym of <u>port</u>
8x 'gateway, doorway.' And, finally, <u>signal</u> 11x alternates with <u>sign</u> 32x
in the three meanings 'token, indication,' 'omen, portent,'[18] and 'something understood as the occasion of action.' In the first sense, for example, we find the variants juxtaposed in 2H6 3.3.28-29,

Hold up thy hand, make <u>signall</u> of thy hope.

He dies and makes no <u>signe</u>: Oh God forgive him,

where the reference is to Cardinal Beaufort's death.

<u>-ary</u>

is also primarily an adjectival suffix, representing L -<u>arius</u> 'connected with.' But sometimes in Latin the neuter of these -<u>arius</u> adjs.

was used as a noun, and the suffix -arium then had the sense 'a thing connected with' [the root noun]; cf. aquarium. Thus summary (L summarium)
was formed on the word which gave ModE sum, and these two words are used
synonymously in Shakespeare. Disyllabic or trisyllabic summary 2x
MV 3.2.131, 2H4 4.1.73 and sum 6x both mean 'an abridged account, essence.'

The suffix -arius itself sometimes appeared in L nouns referring to
persons, and gave the sense 'one connected with' [the root noun]. The
word officer contains this suffix in a disguised form. We find officer
22x 'office-holder' as a metrical variant of the simple noun office 2x
H 3.1.73, H8 1.1.44 (in this line, "Order gave each thing view. The
Office did / Distinctly his full function," used as a collective sg. meaning 'officers').

-ate

as a suffix in nouns ultimately represents L -atus, usually denoting
office or the persons performing it (e.g. medieval L curatus 'a curate;
one who holds a cura, or cure'). In Shakespeare, the word potentate 2x
TG 2.4.79, 1H6 3.2.136 'a person of independent power' belongs in this
class. It alternates metrically with potent 1x J 2.1.358, "You equall
Potents, fierie kindled spirits," which OED cites as the first occurrence
of potent in this meaning; we may in reality be dealing with an apocopated form of potentate here.

-ian

represents L -ianus, a suffix composed of an original or connective
vowel -i- plus -anus 'of or belonging to.' It is used to form both nouns

and adjs., and in present-day English as in Latin, it is most frequently found affixed to proper names to denote place of origin.

Nouns of this type in the plays are Ethiopian 1x WT 4.4.375 - Ethiop 7x 'an Ethiopian'; Grecian 14x - Greek 43x 'a Greek'; and Volscian 1x C 5.3.178 - Volsce 2x C 1.4.28, 1.10.5 'a Volscian.' The pl. occurrences of Volscian and Volsce are omitted because Volscian is frequently disyllabic, and therefore the pl. forms do not differ in syllabic value.

Adjs. of the same type include Dardanian 1x MV 3.2.58 - Dardan 1x TC Prol.13 'Trojan' and Grecian 13x - Greek 1x TC 4.5.127; the latter is also a syllabic variant of Greekish 8x. Hyrcanian occurs 2x MV 2.7.41, H 2.2.472 along with Hyrcan 1x M 3.4.101; in MV 2.7.41,

The Hircanion deserts, and the vaste wildes,

Hyrcanian creates a trisyllabic foot if the typography is taken as a guide to the meter. (Vaste is a misprint for Q vasty, Q2-3 vastie, due to the final -e/-ie confusion.) Here, the vowel of the was undoubtedly meant to be elided before Hircanion. F shows such an elision orthographically in H 2.2.472 ("The rugged Pyrrhus like th'Hyrcanian Beast," erroneously printed as prose), for which we also have the Q variants th'arganian (Q) and th'ircanian (Q2), clearly indicating that initial h was silent in this word. See Kökeritz, Shakespeare's Pronunciation, p. 308.

In all of the above cases, synonymous variants are possible because the -ian derivative alternates with a form representing a synonymous L noun or adj. in -u)s, an ending that was lost in English. But the pair musicians - music is of a different type. Here, synonymity depends on the fact that in Elizabethan English, music could be used to mean 'a company of musicians.' With all ambiguous occurrences omitted, including

one (LLL 5.2.216) which OED classifies as meaning 'musicians,' there are
still 5 uses of music in this sense, e.g. in H8 4.2.94, "Bid the Musicke
leave, / They are harsh and heavy to me." Its variant musicians (showing the compound suffix -ician) occurs 4x.

-ing

representing OE -ing forms nouns, usually on adjs. or other nouns,
with the sense 'one belonging to, or of the kind of' [the root word].
Shakespeare has lording 1x 2H6 1.1.145 meaning 'nobleman': "Lordings
farewell, and say when I am gone, / I prophesied, France will be lost ere
long." Its synonym, lord, is found 124x (incomplete; 2x rhyme); uses of
names or titles such as the Lord Aumerle, lord governor, and the stock
phrase my lord(s, are omitted from the count. There seems to have been
no stylistic reason for the lone use of lording in this sense. It might
at first be thought to be contemptuous (or diminutive, as in WT 1.2.62),
since the speaker is angry, but OED states that lordings in the pl. was
a frequent form of address in Shakespeare's time.[19]

Similarly, the word sweeting 4x (1x rhyme) 'darling, sweetheart'
(found only in direct address) might at first appear to be diminutive,
but I can find no evidence for this. It is used, for example, when
Charles speaks to La Pucelle in her warrior role (1H6 3.3.21). Its variant sweet--the root adj. used substantivally--occurs 29x in direct address (1x rhyme).

CHAPTER V

DERIVATIONAL VARIANTS: ADJECTIVES

Resemblance or Character

-able and -ible

are special forms of the suffix -ble representing L -bilem 'able to, tending to,' which was added to verbal stems to form adjs. In French, -ble was extended to verbs of all conjugations, and when -ant became the universal form of the Fr pr.p., -able became the universal form of the suffix as a living element, both in French and in English. The spelling -ible is essentially a fossil survival in words from Latin which were not directly attached to a living Fr verb, or were adopted in English in their more "Latinate" form.

As a living formative, -able can be used only with a passive sense, 'able to be.' But because it could be used in an active sense in Shakespeare's time, we find it alternating with many "active" suffixes of approximately the same meaning. When these suffixes are monosyllabic, syllabic variants become possible.

For example, Shakespeare has advantageable 1x H5 5.2.88 'profitable, furnishing advantages' along with advantageous 1x TC 5.4.22. He also has answerable 1x TS 2.1.361, "And all things answerable to this portion," as

118

well as the disyllabic pr.p. answering 1x AC 5.2.102 'corresponding' [to
something]. And we also find capable 1x O 3.3.459 used as a synonym of
captious 1x AW 1.3.208 'capacious'; and the amazing array of variants
deceivable 2x TN 4.3.21, R2 2.3.84 - deceitful 6x - deceiving in the poems
- *deceptious 1x TC 5.2.123, all meaning 'false, deceptive.'

In the same active sense, Shakespeare uses forcible 1x 3H6 1.2.3,
"But I have reasons strong and forceable," along with forceful 1x
WT 2.1.163 to mean 'powerful, characterized by force.'[1] And he has trisyllabic or tetrasyllabic variable 3x 'various' as in Cy 1.6.134, "Whiles
he is vaulting variable Rampes," alternating metrically with varied 2x
LLL 5.2.775, TA 3.1.86. Variable is also used 2x MV 2.8.13, RJ 2.2.111
to mean 'changing, full of mutations,' in which sense its synonym is the
disyllabic pr.p. varying 4x.

The active suffix -ible alternates with -ive in the words defensible
2x H5 3.3.50, 2H4 2.3.38 and defensive 2x R2 2.1.48, 1H5 2.1.49 'affording, or capable of affording, defense.'[2] And in the modern passive sense,
Shakespeare uses contemptible 1x 1H6 1.2.75 'despicable' as a synonym of
trisyllabic contemptuous 1x 2H6 1.3.86.[3]

-al

represents the L adjectival suffix -alis, -alem, which was added to
adjs. and nouns with the sense 'of the kind of, pertaining to.' On the
model of such L derivatives, or as representatives of them, we have many
-al adjs. in English. Shakespeare uses them as syllabic variants of
shorter adjs. related to the root of the -al form.

These variants include external 6x along with extern 1x O 1.1.63
'outward'; it is true that extern occurs following the noun ("In Comple-

ment externe") whereas external does not, but since the closely similar

adj. eternal follows the noun in WT 1.2.65 ("And to be Boy eternall") I

have not excluded this pair because of lack of syntactical parallelism.

Shakespeare also uses potential 2x to mean 'powerful' in O 1.2.13 and

L 2.1.78, " . . . the profits of my death / Were very pregnant and po-

tentiall spirits"; its variant is potent 18x.

Finally, Shakespeare has the adj. primal 2x H 3.3.37, AC 1.4.41

along with prime 1x R3 4.3.19 'primeval, belonging to the first age.'

And compare also bridal bed 3x - bride-bed 2x H 5.1.268, MND 5.1.410;

bridal, however, is not a true derivative but an original compound noun

(OE brýd-ealo, lit. 'wedding-ale') which came to be used attributively

by association with -al adjs. of L origin.[4]

-ical vs. -ic

In late Latin, the adjectival -alis, -alem was added to many nouns

of Greek origin which were really already adjs. used absolutely (e.g. L

clericalis 'clerical,' f. clericus 'a cleric'; clericus was properly an

adj. representing Greek klerikos 'pertaining to an inheritance'). Fol-

lowing the L analogy, many L adjs. in -icus were adopted in English as

-ical forms, even though the intervening -icalis adj. did not occur in

Latin. And because the simple -ic was also used to represent L -icus,

double forms such as historical and historic sometimes arose.

Shakespeare makes use of these double forms as convenient syllabic

variants: he has, for example, *critical 2x MND 5.1.54, O 2.1.120 as well

as critic 1x LLL 4.3.170 ("And Critticke Tymon laugh at idle toyes") in

the meaning 'censorious.' Both fantastical 3x and fantastic 4x are used

to mean 'imaginary' and 'capricious.'

Heroical 2x H5 2.4.59, TC 3.3.192 is found along with heroic 1x
1H6 2.5.78 'eminently brave'; H5 2.4.59 is irregular if pronounced according to modern usage:

Saw his Heroicall Seed, and smil'd to see him.

If heroical was not erroneously substituted for heroic here, its medial
i was probably meant to be suppressed as in the parallel case going discussed above on p. 46. Heroical would thus have been pronounced as a
trisyllable. Magical 1x AC 3.1.31,

That magicall word of Warre we have effected,

occurring as a synonym of magic 3x, also creates a trisyllabic foot. But
it is possible that the medial i of magical, too, could have been elided.
Kökeritz cites several words which he believes to have been similarly
syncopated after [dʒ]: these include dang'rous JC 2.1.78, fugitive
AC 3.1.7, regiment AC 4.6.95, R3 5.3.60, and vigilant C 1.1.119 (Shakespeare's Pronunciation, pp. 374-375, 387, 390). Since only dang'rous
shows orthographic evidence of syncopation, however, and since elision
before r is not precisely parallel to elision before c, it remains possible that magical was simply an error for magic.

Majestical 6x is used along with *majestic 3x; and the adjs. mechanical 2x 2H4 5.5.38 (F prints as prose), JC 1.1.3 and mechanic 3x are
metrical variants in the sense 'of the artisan class; hence, mean or
vulgar.' As nouns, *mechanical occurs 2x MND 3.2.9 (rhyme), 2H6 1.3.196
and mechanic 1x C 5.3.83 'a handicraftsman.' And Shakespeare has musical
3x 'harmonious' as a variant of the quasi-adj. *music 1x H 3.1.164 (Ff
only; Q2-4 have the interesting form musickt = *musicked, which is prob-

ably a formation in -ed :- OE -ede, meaning 'provided with music'). The
H line as it stands in F is "That suck'd the Honie of his Musicke Vowes."

Finally, we find tragical 5x along with tragic 8x 'calamitous, sad';
in MND 5.1.57,

And his love Thisby; very tragicall mirth,

tragical, like magical above, is used irregularly if pronounced as spelled.
The same comments apply, except that here, stylistic factors may have entered in. Lysander is reading the description of the play-within-a-play
as set forth by the "rude mechanicals" themselves, and Shakespeare may
have intended a hypermetrical line for characterization.

There are also two cases in which -ical or its adverbial form -ically
alternates metrically with the semi-suffix -like, which forms adjs. and
advs. Angelical 1x RJ 3.2.75 is used as well as angel-like 1x TG 2.4.66
'resembling an angel'; and Shakespeare has prophetically 1x 1H4 3.2.38 and
*prophet-like 1x M 3.1.59 as synonyms meaning 'in a prophetic manner.'

-ary,

in adjs., represents L -arius 'connected with, pertaining to.' Variants in -ary alternate with derivatives having monosyllabic adjectival
suffixes. Shakespeare uses imaginary 5x and imagined 3x in the two senses
'characteristic of the imagination' and 'produced by the imagination.'
OED does not list the first meaning as a possible sense of imagined; the
lines in which I think it occurs are "Bring them I pray thee with imagin'd
speed" (MV 3.4.52) and "Thus with imagin'd wing our swift Scene flyes"
(H5 3.Prol.1). And temporary is once used, in MM 5.1.145, "I know him

for a man divine and holy, / Not scurvy, nor a <u>temporary</u> medler," as a
synonym of <u>temporal</u> 6x 'worldly, earthly.'

<u>-ed</u>

as the suffix of past ppl. adjs. represents OE <u>-ed</u>. Since <u>-ed</u> derivatives of this type denote past action, they cannot ordinarily be
synonyms of other adjs. However, Shakespeare's <u>inclined</u> 14x 'disposed in
some direction' is for all practical purposes equivalent to <u>inclinable</u> 2x
C 2.2.60 (F prints as prose), TC 2.2.58, "And the will dotes that is
<u>inclineable</u> / To what infectiously it selfe affects" (in which Q has <u>at-</u>
<u>tributive</u> instead of <u>inclinable</u>). When used to mean 'produced by the
imagination,' <u>imagined</u> and <u>imaginary</u> discussed in the preceding section
are also synonyms of this type.[5]

<u>-ed</u>

in phrases such as <u>musicked vows</u>, mentioned above on p.121, raises
the question of the significance of the suffix. In some cases, Shakespeare's <u>-ed</u> seems to represent not the past ppl. ending but OE -ede (=
Old Saxon -ðdi), forming adjs. on nouns with the sense 'provided with,
characterized by' [what is denoted by the noun]. I suggest, therefore,
that <u>musicked vows</u> really means 'vows provided with, characterized by,
music'--with <u>music</u> taken, of course, in a fig. sense.

Adjs. of this type are of ancient formation, and Shakespeare makes
frequent use of them as convenient verbal short cuts. OED, however, is
conservative in the matter and nearly always prefers to classify them as
uses of the p.p. rather than as derivatives of the noun, whenever there

is in existence a verb formally identical with the noun. Thus, for example, since *musicked is not listed as a separate adj., the reader must assume that the OED editors regarded it as a p.p. (used adjectivally) derived from the verb music. But the first citation for the verb is dated 1713; and, in any case, there is no sense of the verb which corresponds to the meaning of *musicked in the H line.

Similarly, it is probable that the word ravined as used (perhaps not by Shakespeare) in M 4.1.24 in the witches' incantation,

Scale of Dragon, Tooth of Wolfe,

Witches Mummey, Maw, and Gulfe

Of the ravin'd salt Sea sharke,

means 'provided with spoil or prey' rather than, e.g., 'ravenous' as proposed by Malone and Schmidt. OED actually defines the word correctly, in my opinion ('glutted'), but classifies it as a form of the verb raven 'to eat voraciously' rather than as an adjectival derivative of the noun ravin. It will be noticed that the sense would preclude an interpretation of ravined as the p.p. of raven unless we wish to believe that it is the witches who are doing the "ravening."

Schmidt, Furness, and other commentators have suggested that there are many similar uses of this type of adj. which have gone unnoticed in Shakespeare. For example, disdained 1x 1H4 1.3.183, "Revenge the geering and disdain'd contempt / Of this proud King," is not the p.p. but an adj. meaning 'characterized by disdain, scornful'; its metrical variant is disdainful 7x. Similarly, dishonoured 2x C 3.1.60, L 1.1.231 means 'characterized by dishonor, shameful,' as in " . . . nor ha's Coriolanus / Deserv'd this so dishonor'd Rub, layd falsely" (C 3.1.60), and is thus

a synonym of <u>dishonourable</u> 5x. The parallel forms <u>honoured</u> 6x and <u>honour-</u>
<u>able</u> 75x also alternate metrically in the sense 'characterized by honor';
one example of <u>honoured</u> used in this way is in L 5.1.9, "Do you not love
my Sister? // In <u>honour'd</u> Love."

Some of the adjs. which OED does classify as <u>-ed</u> :- OE <u>-ede</u> derivatives, and which Shakespeare seems to have formed, are *<u>chaliced</u>, which
could not be from the verb since (according to OED's evidence) none
exists; *<u>childed</u>, which has no verb with a corresponding sense; and
*<u>daisied</u>, which appears before the verb is recorded. There are two words,
classified by OED as of this type, which have syllabic variants in Shakespeare. These are <u>shrewd</u> 5x, representing ME <u>schrewed(e</u> and alternating
with <u>shrewish</u> 1x CE 3.1.2 'ill-natured' (said of a woman); and <u>unmannered</u>
2x TS 4.1.169, R3 1.2.39, found along with <u>unmannerly</u> 7x 'rude.'

<u>-en</u>

representing OE <u>-en</u> :- OTeut <u>-ino-</u> is a suffix added to noun-stems
to form adjs. with the sense 'pertaining to, of the nature of [the noun]'
and, most frequently, 'made of [the noun].' Derivatives in <u>-en</u> alternate
with the simple noun used attributively.

Most of the variants discussed here carry the idea both of material
and of resemblance. <u>Brazen</u> 7x 'made of brass' is found along with <u>brass</u>
1x H5 3.1.11 in the same meaning; and <u>brazen</u> 4x 'resembling brass' is a
synonym of <u>brass</u> 1x TC 1.3.257, the latter being also a syllabic variant
of <u>brassy</u> 1x MV 4.1.31. <u>Golden</u> 44x and <u>gold</u> 3x both mean either 'made of
gold' or 'gold-colored.' And we find <u>silken</u> 1x in the poems as a synonym
of <u>silk</u> 1x AYLI 3.5.46 'silky, resembling silk':

His browny locks did hang in crooked curles,

And every light occasion of the wind

Upon his lippes their <u>silken</u> parcels hurles,   LC 87

and "'Tis not your inkie browes, your blacke <u>silke</u> haire" clearly show
form-variation for the meter. Finally, <u>olden</u> 1x M 3.4.75, "Blood hath
bene shed ere now, i'th'<u>olden</u> time," meaning 'bygone' has as its parallel
<u>old</u> 1x H8 4.1.78, "In the <u>old</u> time of Warre, would shake the prease."
(Other occurrences of <u>old</u> not in the phrase <u>the old time</u> have been excluded to insure parallelism.)

-<u>ern</u>

represents an ancient OTeut suffix and appears only in the four
adjs. denoting geographic location. Shakespeare has them all: <u>eastern</u>
5x - <u>east</u> 2x 2H6 2.1.43, 2.1.47 'situated to the east'; <u>western</u> 10x -
<u>west</u> 1x TG 5.3.9 'situated to the west'; <u>northern</u> 5x - <u>north</u> 4x in the
two meanings 'situated to the north' and (of the wind) 'blowing from the
north'; and <u>southern</u> 3x - <u>south</u> 4x in the same two meanings in reference
to the south.

-<u>ful</u>

was in origin a distinct adj. (OE <u>full</u>); it is commonly used to form
adjs. from nouns. Its etymological sense, 'full of,' had become weakened by Shakespeare's time to 'having, characterized by.' In the following cases, an adj. formally identical with the noun simplex alternates
with the -<u>ful</u> derivative.

<u>Rightful</u> is used 1x 2H6 2.1.205 along with <u>right</u> 5x (2x rhyme) in

the meaning 'just, equitable' (said of <u>things</u>); <u>right</u> has another syllabic

variant, <u>righteous</u> 3x. And the adv. <u>rightfully</u> 1x 2H4 4.5.225 'justly'

alternates with <u>rightly</u> 5x. Similarly, <u>wrongful</u> 2x TG 4.2.102, TA 1.1.293

'unjust' is found along with <u>wrong</u> 2x 3H6 1.1.159, O 1.1.131; and Shake-

speare has the corresponding advs. <u>wrongfully</u> 6x - <u>wrongly</u> 1x M 1.5.23.

In the word <u>cheerfully</u> 6x and its variant <u>cheerly</u> 5x (interjectional

uses omitted) 'joyously,' form-association probably accounts for synonym-

ity. <u>Cheerly</u> first entered the language as an adj. in -<u>ly</u>, and then (ap-

parently because of the -<u>ly</u> suffix) was used as an adv. too. The hybrid

*<u>crimeful</u> 1x H 4.7.7, "So <u>crimefull</u>, and so Capitall in Nature" (Ff only;

Qq have <u>criminall</u>, which would also be acceptable in the caesura), seems

to have been formed by Shakespeare as a synonym for <u>criminal</u> 4x 'involving

crime.' Here, syllabic variation results from the fact that the simplexes

differ in syllabic value. Finally, <u>ingrateful</u> 10x and <u>ungrateful</u> 6x (f.

<u>grateful</u>, which was itself an unusual formation on an adjectival simplex

<u>grate</u>) alternate with the adj. <u>ingrate</u> 5x 'unthankful.'

-iful vs. -eous

In commenting on -<u>ful</u>, OED says that its meaning differs little from

that of L -<u>osus</u>, which gave ModE -<u>ous</u>. The suffixes -<u>ful</u> and -<u>ous</u> are

often added to the same simplex. When this simplex ends in -<u>y</u>, -<u>ful</u> as-

sumes the form -<u>iful</u> (disyllabic) and -<u>ous</u> the form -<u>eous</u> (which can be

monosyllabic); thus synonymous syllabic variants are made possible.

Shakespeare has <u>bountiful</u> 2x T 1.2.178, 1H4 3.1.168 as well as di-

syllabic <u>bounteous</u> 16x 'liberal,' and <u>dutiful</u> 2x H5 2.2.127, TC 5.3.72

as a metrical variant of *<u>duteous</u> 9x 'obedient.' The form <u>plentiful</u> 1x

Cy 5.3.9 'abundant' alternates not only with <u>plenteous</u> 7x but also with the simplex <u>plenty</u> 1x T 4.1.110 (used adjectivally, in a rhyming trimeter line), "Earths increase, foyzon <u>plentie</u>."[6] The advs. <u>plentifully</u> 1x LLL 5.2.2 and <u>plenteously</u> 1x 2H4 4.5.40 also alternate metrically.

-<u>ish</u>,

found in Old English in the form -<u>isc</u>, forms adjs. on nouns or other adjs. with the sense 'of the nature of, having the qualities of [the root word].' As a living suffix, it is used chiefly with deprecatory meaning, but we do not find these strong overtones in Shakespeare's <u>childishness</u> 3x, which is for all practical purposes a synonym of *<u>childness</u> 1x WT 1.2.170 'quality or conduct natural to a child.' Compare "Speake thou Boy, / Perhaps thy <u>childishnesse</u> will move him more" (C 5.3.157) and "And with his varying <u>child-nesse</u>, cures in me / Thoughts, that would thick my blood" (WT 1.2.170).

In two further word-pairs, synonymity is dependent on the fact that the noun simplex of the -<u>ish</u> derivative had a related adj. of the same form. Thus <u>dankish</u> 1x CE 5.1.247, "And in a darke and <u>dankish</u> vault at home," in the sense 'wet, damp' (OED specifically cites the line for this meaning), is a metrical variant of <u>dank</u> 3x. And <u>foolish</u> 31x alternates with <u>fool</u> 2x MV 1.1.102, 2.9.26 (the noun used attributively) in the two meanings 'trifling' and 'unwise.' The occurrences of <u>foolish</u> not preceding a noun are omitted because <u>fool</u> is not used in this way.

-<u>ive</u>

represents, through Fr -<u>ive</u>, L -<u>ivus</u>, which was added to the past ppl. stem of verbs to form adjs. with the sense 'having the nature of [the

action of the verb].' But sometimes the simple ppl. stem was adopted in
English as an adj. along with the -ive word, so that synonymous double
forms were created.

Shakespeare uses attentive 5x 'full of attention' as a variant of
attent 2x H 1.2.193, P 3.Gower.11 (rhyme). He also has conjunctive 1x
H 4.7.14 and conjunct 2x L 2.2.125 (only in Qq; Ff compact), 5.1.12 (om.
F), both meaning 'combined'; and compare also the synonymous past ppl.
adjs. conjoined 2x 1H6 5.2.12, H 3.4.126 and joined 15x (once disyllabic,
but still a syllabic variant of conjunctive). And definitive 1x
MM 5.1.432 'determined' ("Never crave him, we are definitive") is a synonym of definite 1x Cy 1.6.43.

OED makes a distinction between -ive and -ant forms generally by
saying that -ive implies a permanent or habitual quality, but there is no
such difference in meaning between trisyllabic operative 1x L 4.4.14 and
disyllabic *operant 2x TmA 4.3.25, H 3.2.184. Both are used in the sense
'exerting force, active.'

-like,

in origin a shortened form of OE ȝelíc, is appended to nouns and
adjs. When used to form adjs., it carries the sense 'characteristic of,
resembling' [the root word]. In a few cases in the plays, an adjectival
-like form alternates metrically with a noun used attributively. For instance, Shakespeare has Christian-like 2x H5 5.2.381, R3 1.3.316 along
with Christian 6x 'befitting a Christian.' Similarly, we find *rebel-like
1x L 4.3.16 (om. F) along with rebel 2x 2H4 4.5.172, JC 3.1.40 'insub-
ordinate'; the latter is also a syllabic variant of the pr.p. rebelling
1x Cy 5.4.96 and rebellious 7x (only occurrences preceding a noun are

counted).

When used to form advs., -like means 'in the manner of.' The
nonce-word *villain-like 2x L 5.3.98, Cy 5.5.218 is used along with villainously 1x MM 5.1.149 to mean 'in the manner of a villain, wickedly.'

-ous

is a suffix found in words derived from, or formed on the analogy
of, L words in -osus. Affixed to nouns to form adjs., -osus had the
sense 'abounding in' [the quality specified by the noun]. There are two
cases in Shakespeare in which an -ous derivative alternates with the noun
simplex used attributively. One is tyrannous vs. tyrant, which is not
statistically significant because tyrannous is frequently disyllabic; the
other is victorious 12x 'having conquered' as a synonym of victor 1x
L 5.3.132, "Despise thy victor-Sword, and fire new Fortune" (Qq do not
hyphenate victor sword). In famoused in the poems, "The painefull
warrier famosèd for worth" (S 25.9), along with famed 9x 'made famous,'
a verb has been formed both on the -ous derivative and on its root noun.

Metrical variation is often also possible when a word ending in -ous
has a synonym bearing a different adjectival suffix. For example, expeditious 1x T 5.1.315 'speedy' ("And saile, so expeditious, that shall
catch / Your Royall fleete farre off") is a metrical variant of trisyllabic expedient 6x, a basically present ppl. form (e.g. J 4.2.268,
" . . . to my Closset bring / The angry Lords, with all expedient hast").
Similarly, disyllabic odorous 1x MND 2.1.110 'fragrant' alternates with
tetrasyllabic odoriferous 1x J 3.4.26, "Thou odoriferous stench: sound
rottennesse" (oxymoron); -iferous is derived from L -fer 'producing' (f.
ferre 'to bear') + -ous.

-<u>some</u>

represents OE -<u>sum</u>, and is added to nouns, adjs., and verbs to form adjs. meaning 'having the quality of [the root word].' Shakespeare has <u>darksome</u> in the poems with the sense 'characterized by darkness' ("O had they in that <u>darkesome</u> prison died," RL 379) along with <u>dark</u> 37x (1x rhyme). And he uses <u>wearisome</u> 3x 'causing weariness' as a synonym for <u>weary</u> 17x; note the following exchange in R3 3.1.3-5,

Richard. The <u>wearie</u> way hath made you Melancholly.

Prince. No Unkle, but our crosses on the way,

    Have made it tedious, <u>wearisome</u>, and heavie,

where metrical alternation can clearly be seen.

-<u>y</u>

in the variants discussed below represents the OE adjectival suffix -<u>iʒ</u>, and was originally appended to nouns only. Like -<u>en</u> (see p. 125 f.), it could denote either resemblance ('having the qualities of') or material ('full of, made of'). Thus the -<u>y</u> form could in some cases be a synonym of the root noun used attributively.

For example, <u>flinty</u> 5x is found along with <u>flint</u> 1x R2 5.1.3 'consisting of flint'; the lack of parallelism in O 1.3.231, "Hath made the <u>flinty</u> and Steele Coach of Warre," was probably metrically-inspired. In the two senses 'made of steel' and 'resembling steel,' we find <u>steely</u> 2x 3H6 2.3.16, AW 1.1.114 and <u>steel</u> 3x (1x poems); the latter has another syllabic variant, disyllabic <u>steeled</u> 3x, e.g. in 1H6 1.1.85 ("Give me my <u>steelèd</u> Coat, Ile fight for France").

Also from a noun-stem is <u>stony</u> 4x 'made of stone' as in "For <u>stony</u> limits cannot hold Love out" (RJ 2.2.67, referring to a stone wall); its metrical variant, <u>stone</u>, occurs 1x TS Ind.2.90 (printed as part of a compound in F). The use of <u>stone</u> in the proverbial <u>hunger broke stone walls</u> is omitted. In the case of <u>worthy</u> 18x and <u>worth</u> 3x meaning 'deserving,' synonymity is possible because the root noun <u>worth</u> has an adj. of the same form. Examples are "It is a cause <u>worthy</u> my Spleene and Furie" (TmA 3.5.113) and "Me (wretch) more <u>worth</u> your Vengeance" (Cy 5.1.11).

A second group of <u>-y</u> variants is based not on a noun but on an adj. Most of these words arose in the sixteenth and seventeenth centuries. Gordon's comments on the sense carried by the suffix have been discussed in Chapter I; OED suggests that at times this <u>-y</u> expresses the notion 'somewhat, tending to be,' but I can find no support for this in the variants listed below.

The nonce-word *<u>brisky</u> occurs 1x MND 3.1.97 along with <u>brisk</u> 2x TN 2.4.6, 2H4 5.3.48 (F prints as prose) 'nimble, lively, keen'; and <u>browny</u> is used in the poems (LC 85, quoted above on p. 126) along with <u>brown</u> 4x. <u>Haughty</u> 10x and <u>haught</u> 4x both mean 'proud, arrogant'; in 2H6 1.3.71, "Beside the <u>haughtie</u> Protector, have we Beauford," <u>haughtie</u> creates a trisyllabic foot but is corrected to <u>haught</u> by F2-4.

Shakespeare also has <u>paly</u> 3x as well as <u>pale</u> over 150x (predicate uses are omitted), and <u>pale</u> is in addition a syllabic variant of <u>pallid</u> in the poems; all three variants mean 'lacking depth of color.' Two examples are "To <u>paly</u> ashes, the eyes windowes fall" (RJ 4.1.100; this is the Q5 reading--F has <u>many ashes</u>) and "<u>Pale</u> Ashes of the House of Lancaster" (R3 1.2.6). And there is *<u>plumpy</u> 1x AC 2.7.121 along with <u>plump</u> in the poems, both in the sense 'of full and rounded form.'

In one line, TmA 1.1.75, "Bowing his head against the steepy Mount,"
Shakespeare uses steepy to mean 'precipitous'; its metrical variant is
steep 5x, as in H8 1.1.131, "What 'tis you go about: to climbe steepe
hilles." And swarthy 1x TG 2.6.26 'dark of complexion' is used as well
as swart 2x J 3.1.46, 1H6 1.2.84 and its variant swarth 1x TA 2.3.72
(only in Ff; Qq have the metrically inexact forms swarty and swartie).

In reference to the pair *vasty and vast, it has already been noted
on p. 116 that the F unmetrical vaste in MV 2.7.41 is a misprint for
vastie. *Vasty occurs 5x and vast 12x in the sense 'immense'; examples
include "I can call Spirits from the vastie Deepe" (1H4 3.1.52) and "No
Vast obscurity, or Misty vale" (TA 5.2.36). *Vasty, incidentally, is a
form in which -y could not possibly mean 'somewhat, tending to be'; a
word cannot mean 'somewhat vast.'

Negation and Privation

be-

was in Old English and Middle English sometimes used to form verbs
with a privative sense. Identical in origin with the intensive and direc-
tional be- discussed in Chapter III, it added the meaning 'off, away.'
Very few words of this class survive in Modern English. One is bereave,
which Shakespeare uses 4x along with the simple reave 2x AW 5.3.86,
2H6 5.1.187 'to deprive' [of something]; synonymity is possible because
reave itself expresses privation. In the p.p. we find bereft 15x - reft
6x (1x poems) in the two meanings 'deprived' [of something] and 'taken
away' (said of the object taken). Compare, in the first sense, "Bereft
of ships and men, cast on this shore" (P 2.3.89) and "Was by the rough

seas <u>reft</u> of ships and men" (P 2.3.84).

-<u>less</u>

represents OE -<u>léas</u>, which was attached to nouns with the meaning 'devoid of, free from.' Shakespeare has a striking array of -<u>less</u> adjs.; many of them alternate metrically with adjs. which have the negative prefix <u>un</u>- (or <u>in</u>-) and a syllabic adjectival suffix. I have grouped these variants according to the suffix found in the <u>un</u>- or <u>in</u>- word.

-<u>able</u>

Shakespeare uses <u>comfortless</u> 3x as well as *<u>uncomfortable</u> 1x RJ 4.5.60, "<u>Uncomfortable</u> time, why cam'st thou now," to mean 'involving discomfort'; and he has *<u>profitless</u> 1x O 1.3.30,[7] "To wake, and wage a danger <u>profitless</u>," as well as <u>unprofitable</u> 5x to mean 'void of gain.' <u>Reasonless</u> 2x 1H6 5.4.137 ("This proffer is absurd, and <u>reasonlesse</u>"), TG 2.4.198 ("That makes me <u>reasonlesse</u>, to reason thus") is used as a metrical variant of <u>unreasonable</u> 2x RJ 3.3.111, MV 5.1.203 in the two senses 'not based on reason' and 'not acting in accordance with reason.'

-<u>ed</u>

In the meaning 'not limited, uncontrolled,' we find <u>boundless</u> 6x and <u>unbounded</u> 1x H8 4.2.34 ("He was a man / Of an <u>unbounded</u> stomacke, ever ranking"). And <u>doubtless</u> 2x 1H4 3.2.20, J 4.1.130 ("And, pretty childe, sleepe <u>doubtlesse</u>, and secure") is a metrical variant of <u>undoubted</u> 2x 1H6 3.3.41, 3H6 5.7.6, "Three Dukes of Somerset, threefold Renowne, / For hardy and <u>undoubted</u> Champions." The meaning of <u>undoubted</u> here is, I feel, 'free from doubt or fear,' though OED defines it rather as 'not called in question.'[8]

Friendless 1x H8 3.1.80 'unprovided with friends' occurs along with
unfriended 2x TN 3.3.10, L 1.1.206; and houseless 2x L 3.4.26, 3.4.30
'lacking a house' along with trisyllabic unhoused 2x TmA 4.3.229,
O 1.2.26. Similarly, shapeless 1x J 5.7.27 'lacking a definite shape'
has a trisyllabic variant in unshaped 1x H 4.5.8. And in the meaning
'pure, unblemished,' spotless 6x occurs along with unspotted 4x.[9] Finally, stringless 1x R2 2.1.149 'having no strings' ("His tongue is now a
stringlesse instrument") is a metrical variant of trisyllabic *unstringed
1x R2 1.3.162 ("And now my tongues use is to me no more, / Then an un-
stringèd Vyall, or a Harpe").

-en

In the meaning 'unshapely, deformed,' we find shapeless 2x
LLL 5.2.303, CE 4.2.20, "Ill-fac'd, worse bodied, shapelesse every where,"
as a synonym of unshapen 1x R3 1.2.251 (only in Qq; Ff mishapen), "On me,
that halts, and am unshapen thus."[10] These two variants are synonyms
also of the weak form mis-shaped 1x 3H6 3.2.170, "Untill my mis-shap'd
Trunke, that beares this Head," and mis-shapen 5x.

-ful

Cheerless occurs 1x L 5.3.290 and uncheerful in the poems in the
sense 'devoid of cheer'; and Shakespeare uses heedless 2x TS 4.1.169,
1H6 4.2.44 as a synonym for both unheedful 2x TG 2.6.11, 1H6 4.4.7 and
unheedy 1x MND 1.1.237 'careless, rash.' And helpless 2x CE 2.1.39,
R3 1.2.13 ("I powre the helplesse Balme of my poore eyes"), meaning 'affording no help,' alternates metrically with *unhelpful 1x 2H6 3.1.218.

Lawless 1x R3 1.4.224 is a synonym of <u>unlawful</u> 3x 'prohibited by law, illegal'; occurrences of <u>unlawful</u> meaning specifically 'illegitimate' (of offspring) or 'contrary to moral standards' (of illicit love) have been omitted. Shakespeare also has <u>merciless</u> 6x 'pitiless, cruel' along with <u>unmerciful</u> 1x L 3.7.33, a hypermetrical line if the spelling is taken as a guide to pronunciation:

<u>Unmercifull</u> Lady, as you are, I'me none.

But <u>unmerciful</u>, like <u>benefit</u> discussed above on p. 54, could have lost its medial unstressed vowel before <u>f</u>; see Kökeritz, <u>Shakespeare's Pronunciation</u>, p. 285.

<u>Mindless</u> 1x TmA 4.3.93 'negligent, careless' ("How cursèd Athens, <u>mindelesse</u> of thy worth") is a metrical variant of <u>unmindful</u> 1x R3 4.4.444. And <u>skilless</u> 4x occurs along with <u>unskilful</u> 2x 3H6 5.4.19, O 1.3.27 meaning 'ignorant or inexpert.' Finally, <u>thankless</u> 3x 'ungrateful' (e.g. in L 1.4.311, "To have a <u>thanklesse</u> Childe") alternates metrically with <u>unthankful</u> 1x 1H4 1.3.136.

-ly

In J 3.1.45, <u>sightless</u> is used to mean 'offensive to the eye' ("Full of unpleasing blots, and <u>sightlesse</u> staines"); its synonym is <u>unsightly</u> 1x L 2.4.159. And <u>timeless</u> 8x, as in "Must I behold thy <u>timelesse</u> cruell death" (1H6 5.4.5), is found along with <u>untimely</u> 9x in the sense 'ill-timed, especially, occurring before the proper time.'

-ious

There is only one example: <u>graceless</u> 5x 'impious' and its synonym

ungracious 3x, e.g. in R2 2.3.89, " . . . that word Grace, / In an ungracious mouth, is but prophane."

-Y

Hapless occurs 7x along with unhappy 27x meaning 'unfortunate,' and
in the same meaning we find luckless 2x 3H6 2.6.18, 5.6.45 along with un-
lucky 5x. Thriftless 2x R2 5.3.69, M 2.4.28 ("Thriftlesse Ambition, that
will raven up / Thine owne lives meanes") has the sense 'extravagant'; it
is a metrical variant of unthrifty 2x MV 1.3.177, R2 5.3.1. The latter
is also a syllabic variant of unthrift 1x MV 5.1.16, the noun used attributively.

In addition, *worthless 14x is found as well as unworthy 10x in the
two meanings 'lacking merit' and 'undeserving' [of something]; an example
of *worthless in the second sense is in JC 5.1.61, "A peevish School-boy,
worthles of such Honor." One relevant line, 2H6 1.3.108,

If Somerset be unworthy of the Place,

is hypermetrical when read as printed. But the vowel of be may well have
been lost before the following vowel: Kökeritz notes that a Renaissance
orthoepist, John Hart, has tu b'aspi·rd, and that Ben Jonson has
b'un-alterd (where, however, b' stands for by).[11]

When the noun to which the suffix -less was attached was a noun of
action with a related verb, some of the adjs. so formed had the sense 'not
to be ——— ed,' 'un- ——— able.' Several of Shakespeare's -less words
alternate with derivatives in -able and -ed which carry this sense.

*Countless 1x P 1.1.73 'innumerable' is a variant of uncounted 1x
2H4 Ind.18 ("That the blunt Monster, with uncounted heads"); and cureless

2x MV 4.1.142 (only in Qq; Ff _endlesse_), 3H6 2.6.23 alternates metrically
with _uncurable_ 2x 2H6 3.1.286 (F3-4 _incurable_), 5.2.86 and _incurable_ 2x
J 5.1.16, 2H6 3.1.286 (F3-4 only), all meaning 'irremediable.'

Similarly, _matchless_ 2x LLL 2.1.7, TC 4.5.97 occurs along with _un-matchable_ 2x J 4.3.52, AC 2.3.20; _unmatchable_ is also a syllabic variant
of _unmatched_ 4x, and all three variants mean 'not to be matched, having
no equal.' In the sense 'immeasurable,' _measureless_ 2x M 2.1.17,
C 5.6.103 ("_Measurelesse_ Lyar, thou hast made my heart / Too great for
what contains it") and _unmeasurable_ 1x TmA 4.3.178 both occur. Finally,
numberless is used 2x H8 2.1.84, TmA 4.3.263 to mean 'incapable of being
numbered.' Both _numberless_ and _unnumbered_ 2x L 4.6.21, JC 3.1.63 ("The
Skies are painted with _unnumbred_ sparkes") are syllabic variants of _in-numerable_ 1x H8 3.2.326.[12]

On the model of such -_less_ adjs., the suffix -_less_ was appended to
many verbs even when there was no corresponding noun of action. Thus we
find in Shakespeare *_dauntless_ 4x - _undaunted_ 4x, which are for all practical purposes synonymous in the meaning 'fearless' (when, for example,
they modify _spirit_). And Shakespeare has *_shunless_ 1x C 2.2.116 'inevit-
able' ("With _shunlesse_ destinie . . . ") along with *_unshunnable_ 1x
O 3.3.275 ("'Tis destiny _unshunnable_, like death"), a clear case of alternation for the meter.

Finally, there is one variant in which -_less_ is used adverbially:
doubtless 6x 'without doubt,' which has as its synonym _undoubtedly_ 1x
H8 4.2.49.

_un-,_

representing the OE negative prefix _un-_, is used redundantly in _un-_

loose 5x, which Shakespeare has as a variant of loose 2x CE 5.1.339,
H 2.2.162 in the two meanings 'to untie' and 'to set at liberty.' In
MM 1.3.32,

> To unloose this tyde-up Justice, when you pleas'd,

the vowel of to was undoubtedly meant to be elided before the following
vowel, as represented orthographically in L 2.2.81, t'unloose. Here, as
with bereave and reave discussed on p. 133, the simplex itself carries a
privative sense.

CHAPTER VI

NONDERIVATIONAL VARIANTS

Etymological Variants

As I have stated in Chapter II, etymological variants are unlike
true derivational variants in that the syllabic difference between synonymous words is not due to recognizable prefixes or suffixes, but to
so-called "etymological elements" which may have originally been affixes
but are not now living formatives. Such variants usually arise as a result of modification of a form when it passes from one language into
another. Elsewhere in this study, I have occasionally discussed words
which contain hidden etymological variants (e.g. simpleness and simplicity); here I will list all of the remaining cases, beginning with those
involving non-Romanic words.

In English, ancient double forms gave the verbal variants listen
11x and list 21x in the two meanings 'to give ear to' and (intr.) 'to
give ear.' In the F version of MA 3.1.12, "To listen our purpose, this
is thy office," listen creates a trisyllabic foot where list would be exact; but Q has propose 'conversation' instead of purpose, which regularizes the meter and is acceptable for the sense. In addition, F2-4 read "To
listen to our purpose, this is thy office," which is regular with a per-

missible extra syllable before the caesura.[1] A parallel pair of verbs is
threaten 17x along with threat 13x 'to menace' (trans. or intr.).

When words of L, Fr, Sp, or It origin were introduced into English,
they were frequently anglicized by shortening, just as they usually are
today. But sometimes the longer form also remained. Thus in Shakespeare
the L form balsamum is found 1x CE 4.1.89 along with the shorter balsam
1x TmA 3.5.110 'a soothing medicinal preparation.' And lavolta 1x
H5 3.5.33 (It la volta), a dance of It origin, is used along with the
anglicized form lavolt 1x TC 4.4.88.

There are three pairs of metrical variants involving alternation of
a form which came through Spanish or Italian with one which came through
French. First, we find battalia 2x R3 5.3.11 (only in Ff; Qq battalion,
in various spellings), H 4.5.79 (only in F1-2; Qq battalians, F3-4
battels, making the line headless) meaning 'a large body of armed men.'
The word was taken up in the late sixteenth century from It battaglia or
perhaps Sp batalla. Thus an etymological variant of the pre-existing
battle (a. OF bataille :- vulgar L battalia) was introduced into English;
battle occurs 20x in this sense, as in H5 4.Prol.9, "Each Battaile sees
the others umber'd face."

A second example is *figo 2x H5 3.6.60, 4.1.60 'a contemptuous ges-
ture' (adopted from OSp figo); it alternates metrically with fig 1x
H5 3.6.61 (ad. Fr figue). And, finally, motto, adopted from Italian,
occurs 3x along with mot, adopted from French, in the poems. Both mean
'a phrase placed on a heraldic crest (lit. or fig.).'

The remaining etymological variants show variation between a form
which corresponds fairly closely to the original Latin, and one which
shows evidence of having been altered when transmitted through French.

For example, L words with initial <u>sp</u>, <u>st</u>, and <u>sc</u> which were adopted in French before the fifteenth century usually assumed a euphonic initial <u>e</u> in French. When these words came into English, they were sometimes assimilated to the L type without <u>e</u>; but often the Fr form persisted as well.

Shakespeare has the double forms <u>especial</u> 2x 1H6 4.1.55, H 4.3.42 (a. OF <u>especial</u>, ad. L <u>specialis</u>) – <u>special</u> 27x 'particular,' and the corresponding advs. <u>especially</u> 4x – <u>specially</u> 1x TS 1.1.20 'particularly.' <u>Espy</u> 5x 'to perceive' is a. OF <u>espier</u>, ultimately representing Common Romanic *<u>spiare</u>; <u>espy</u> alternates metrically with <u>spy</u> 13x. In the same meaning, we have the p.ts. <u>espied</u> 1x TA 2.3.194 and <u>spied</u> 2x LLL 4.3.103, TS 4.2.60, and the p.ps. <u>espied</u> 1x TA 2.3.48 and <u>spied</u> 1x O 1.1.77. Related nouns are <u>espial</u> 3x and <u>spy</u> 9x 'one who observes others secretly.' In 1H6 1.4.8, "The Princes <u>espyals</u> have informèd me," <u>Princes</u> must have been read as a haplologized genitive; it would then have been pronounced like <u>Prince</u>.[2] Notice that <u>spies</u> would not improve the meter of this line.

Also alternating in Shakespeare are <u>esquire</u> 4x 'a man next in rank below a knight' (occurrences as an appositive title are omitted) and <u>squire</u> 6x; <u>esquire</u> is a. OF <u>esquier</u>, ultimately representing L <u>scutarius</u>. Also there is <u>establish</u> 5x (a. OF <u>establiss-</u>, lengthened stem of <u>establir</u> :– L <u>stabilire</u>) along with <u>stablish</u> 1x 1H6 5.1.10 'to settle, fix.' And finally, <u>estate</u> (a. OF <u>estat</u>, ad. L <u>status</u>) occurs 41x in the three meanings 'condition,' 'property,' and 'a body politic'; its variant <u>state</u> occurs over 200x. Examples in the second meaning are "How much I have disabled mine <u>estate</u>" (MV 1.1.123) and "And that my <u>state</u> being gall'd with my expence, / I seeke to heale it onely by his wealth" (MW 3.4.5). And in the third meaning we find, for example, "By how much the <u>estate</u> is

greene, and yet ungovern'd" (R3 2.2.127, an alexandrine) and "Papers of
State he sent me, to peruse" (H8 3.2.121).

In the preceding word-pairs, the shorter form is the one closer to
the original L root. This is true also of mount 4x 'a very large hill'
which occurs along with mountain 29x, both of which are ultimately derived from L mons, montem. Synonymous variants arose because the popular
L adj. *montaneus 'pertaining to mountains' happened to develop a substantival sense, giving OF montaigne, ModE mountain. (Occurrences of
mount in proper names and fig. occurrences of mountain have been omitted.)

Far more commonly, it is the longer word which is closer to the L
original. This is so, for example, in debitor 1x O 1.1.31 (a Fr literary
borrowing from Latin) as opposed to debtor 9x (2x rhyme), which represents
a form that came down from L debitor through colloquial French. It is
also true of the interesting pl. variants pyramides 1x AC 5.2.61 (tetrasyllabic) and pyramids 1x M 4.1.57 'structures of pyramidal form.' The
original forms from Latin (and Greek) were pyramis in the sg. and pyramides in the pl., but then a new sg. pyramid was inferred from the pl.
(probably after Fr pyramide), and finally a regular pl. pyramids was
formed on this new sg.[3]

In two further word-pairs, the L -ium suffix has come down either as
-y (through AF -ie) or as -e (through continental French). Again, the
longer forms are those closer to the L original. In the meaning 'divina-
tion,' we find augury 1x TG 4.4.73 and augure 1x M 3.4.124, both ultimately
from L augurium. Similarly, as representatives of L imperium, Shakespeare
has empery 6x along with empire 16x in the two senses 'supreme power' and
'a region subject to an emperor or powerful ruler.'

Name-Variants

I include here with these etymological variants a group of proper names of classical, It, or Sp origin which sometimes lost their final syllable when they were adopted in French. Thus a long and a short form were conveniently available for Shakespeare's use as syllabic variants. Though it has been asserted that "proper names are often extra-metrical in Elizabethan drama,"[4] little support for this view is to be found in Shakespeare's plays.

Shakespeare has Adon in the poems (the Fr form, though also in Latin and Greek) along with Adonis 2x TS Ind.2.52, 1H6 1.6.6 (the dominant L form, from Greek). He also has Afric 2x C 1.8.3, Cy 1.1.167 (Fr Afrique) - Africa 1x 2H4 5.3.104 (L); Clothair 1x H5 1.2.67, stressed on the first syllable - Clotharius 1x H8 1.3.10, the Fr king; and Cressid 34x - Cressida 4x, the Trojan girl loved by Troilus.

Desdemon (which would be the Fr form)[5] occurs 6x in F, replacing the full form Desdemona of the Qq. Though Desdemon is metrically preferable, Desdemona would be possible in all cases, even in O 3.1.56, "With Desdemon alone. // Pray you come in" (Qq Desdemona) if we assume an unmarked cae- sura before alone. Desdemona occurs a total of 31x.[6] Shakespeare also has Dian 23x (Fr Diane) - Diana 16x (L), referring either to the goddess or to the character in AW. And trisyllabic Diomed 30x and Diomede 1x 3H6 4.2.19 alternate with tetrasyllabic Diomedes 2x TC 3.3.30, 4.2.67 (L, from Greek), the Greek soldier in the Trojan War. In TC 4.2.67, "We must give up to Diomeds hand," Q and F2-4 have Diomedes, thus giving the line five iambic feet. Similarly, in TC 5.2.137, "This she? no, this is Diomids Cressida," F4 has Diomede's Cressid, undoubtedly an error for Diomedes' Cressid, which would regularize the meter.[7]

We also find Europe 6x (Fr) along with Europa 1x MA 5.4.45 (L), referring to the geographical area. And Helen 6x (Fr Hélène) is used as
well as Helena 22x (L), the character in MND. In MND 2.2.113, Q2 and Ff
have "Not Hermia, but Helena now I love," but Q omits now so that the
line scans. And F misprints MND 2.2.104, "Transparent Helena, nature her
shewes art," in which Qq omit her and F2-4 substitute here for her (which
would also be possible with an extra syllable before the caesura). As
the name of the wise counselor in P, Shakespeare uses Helicane 5x (in
Book 8 of the Confessio Amantis, Shakespeare's source, Gower has the form
Hellican); its variant is Helicanus 13x (L Hellicanus).

Trisyllabic Isabel 22x[8] (Fr Isabelle) alternates metrically with
tetrasyllabic Isabella 4x as the name of the heroine in MM. Also in MM
we find disyllabic Juliet 4x along with trisyllabic Julietta 1x
MM 1.2.150.[9] Disyllabic or trisyllabic Katharine is used 19x to refer to
the heroine of TS, as a variant of tetrasyllabic Katharina 8x (L Katharina, Katerina). And in the plays, we find also Lucrece 4x - Lucretia 1x
AYLI 3.2.156 (L), Collatine's wife; and Mede 1x AC 3.6.75 - Media 2x
AC 3.1.7, 3.6.14 (L, from Greek), the country in Asia.

To refer to the river in Egypt, Shakespeare uses either Nile 6x (Fr
Nil) or Nilus 5x (L); and as a proper name, he has Pandar 5x (the AF form
was Pandare) along with Pandarus 6x (L), as in TC 1.1.97-98: "But Pandarus: O Gods! How do you plague me? / I cannot come to Cressid but by Pandar." Similarly, Philomel 6x (Fr Philomèle) is present along with Philo-
mela 3x (1x poems; the L form, from Greek), referring to the daughter of
Pandion or used as a poetic name for the nightingale. And Priam 27x alternates metrically with Priamus 2x TC 2.2.207, 5.3.54 (L), the king of
Troy. Prosper occurs 2x T 2.2.2, 3.3.99 (the Fr form would be Prospère)

as well as Prospero 10x.

The heroine of AYLI is called Rosalind 24x (10x rhyme) and also Rosalinda (Sp) in one case, AYLI 3.2.145. And in TA, we find both Saturnine 17x (Fr Saturnin) and Saturninus 5x (L), e.g. in TA 1.1.232-233: " . . . we Create / Lord Saturninus Romes Great Emperour. / And say, Long live our Emperour Saturnine." Tyre 21x (5x rhyme), the city in Phoenicia, is a metrical variant of Tyrus 5x (L). Finally, in TG the name Valentine is found 49x (Fr Valentin) along with Valentinus 1x TG 1.3.67 (only in F; F2-4 Valentino; L). In TG 2.4.196 ("It is mine, or Valentines praise?"), perhaps the genitive ending was to be syllabic as in Queenes discussed above, p. 105. Then, if It is were emended to Is it in accordance with the practice of most modern editors, the line would be satisfactory both in sense and in meter, though of course headless. But the line is really too corrupt for Valentines to be regarded as an "irregular" use; Cambridge Ed. remarks (p. 80) that "the text has been tampered with at this point, in order to shorten the soliloquy."

Though they are not etymological variants, the proper nouns Rape 4x and Rapine 4x, alternating as the assumed name of Chiron in TA, may perhaps be mentioned here. Rapine is not ordinarily a synonym of rape, except possibly as meaning 'the act of taking away something by force,' but evidently the two words were supposed to be synonymous in this particular use.

Morphological Variants

As noted in Chapter II, morphological variants are traceable to a conjugational sign of a verb (usually the past ppl. stem or an infinitive ending) or to an oblique case-ending of a noun.

Verbs and verbal derivatives

In several words, the L ppl. stem -at- of first conjugation verbs gave rise to a morphological variant. Among these are illuminate 1x JC 1.3.110 from the past ppl. stem, meaning 'to light up (lit. or fig.)'; its variant is *illume 1x H 1.1.37, an apocopated form of illumine, which is from the infinitive stem. (Illumine occurs only in the p.p. and -eth forms in Shakespeare.) Similarly, we find invocate 2x 1H6 1.1.52, R3 1.2.8 from the ppl. stem and invoke 1x H5 1.2.104 from the infinitive, both in the sense 'to call on in prayer.' And ruinate 2x 3H6 5.1.83, TA 5.3.204 (rhyme) from the ppl. stem is used along with ruin 2x C 3.2.69, AC 5.2.51 from the infinitive; both mean 'to destroy, overthrow.' Compare also, in the p.p., ruinate 1x CE 3.2.4 (perhaps an error for ruinous) along with ruined 2x H8 3.2.382, R2 3.3.34 'fallen into ruin.'[10]

In the class of adjs. derived from p.ps., we find calumniating 1x TC 3.3.174 'slanderous' as well as trisyllabic calumnious 2x H8 5.1.112, H 1.3.38 (originally formed on the L noun). Similarly, the L ppl. stem gave the English ppl. adj. captivate 2x 1H6 2.3.42, 5.3.107, while the infinitive captivare gave captived 1x H5 2.4.55 and the related adj. captivus gave captive 5x; all three variants mean 'made captive.' In the nonce-word *compulsative 1x H 1.1.103 (Ff only; Qq have *compulsatory, which would also be metrically acceptable because in the caesura) and its synonym *compulsive 2x H 3.4.86, O 3.3.454 'compelling, acting by force,' both variants are from ppl. stems. But *compulsative is ultimately from L compulsare, frequentative of compellere, the verb from which *compulsive is derived.

The L agent-noun conspiratorem, formed on the ppl. stem of conspirare, gave ModE conspirator, which is found 8x along with conspirer 1x

M 4.1.91, ultimately from the L infinitive. Servitor 5x is of the same type, though its suffix shows the -i- vowel of agent-nouns formed on second and fourth conjugation verbs. It alternates metrically with servant 125x, ultimately from the pr.p. Examples are " . . . fearfull commenting / Is leaden servitor to dull delay" (R3 4.3.52) and "Our will became the servant to defect" (M 2.1.18).

The word party (through Fr partie) represents a substantival use of the L feminine p.p. partita of partire, which in turn was derived from pars, partem. But since partem also has an English representative, part, synonymous metrical variants became possible. Party occurs 28x and part 49x in the two senses 'side, cause' and 'faction'; note the metrical alternation in J 2.1.359-361:

Bastard.   Then let confusion of one part confirm

The others peace: till then, blowes, blood, and death.

John.   Whose party do the Townesmen yet admit?

The past ppl. endings of other languages besides Latin also gave rise to morphological variants. Shakespeare has *ambuscado 1x RJ 1.4.84 (F prints as prose), -ado being the Sp masculine ppl. ending substituted for the etymologically correct -ada. Its metrical variant is ambush 2x 3H6 4.6.83, R2 1.1.137 (ultimately from the Sp infinitive stem embusc-); the meaning of both is 'a military disposition of concealed troops,' and occurrences of ambush denoting the troops themselves are omitted.

Similarly, the word parley 13x 'conversation, conference' may represent OF parlée, a feminine noun from the p.p. of the verb parler; the shorter English word parle 9x is ultimately from the infinitive. And in the word valley, the suffix also represents an original Fr ending -ée.

Valley is used 5x along with vale 7x meaning 'a low tract of land between hills'; the fig. occurrences of both have been excluded.

In two further cases, the ppl. sign is a prefix rather than a suffix: the y- representing OE ȝe-. First we have yclad 1x 2H6 1.1.33 'clothed,' used by King Henry VI in a nonarchaic context, which alternates metrically with clad 4x. In ycleped 1x LLL 5.2.602 'called, named,' the intention may have been seriocomic, for the word is used by the pedant Holofernes. But again, the context is not archaic; and OED comments that the y- form was quite common in this sense in the sixteenth century. Its synonym, cleped, occurs 1x M 3.1.94.

Finally, there is one variant which shows an infinitive ending rather than a past ppl. sign. This is remainder 8x (originally OF remaindre 'to remain,' but in AF used substantivally as a law term). Remainder alternates metrically with remain 3x (a. OF remain, vbl. sb. f. remaindre) in the sense 'that which is left; those who are left.' Provender 4x 'dry food for beasts' bears a superficial resemblance to remainder, but it was not an infinitive in Old French. The OF source-word provendre was, rather, a phonetic variant of the simple provende, which gave ModE provand, used 1x C 2.1.267 as a synonym of provender.

Nouns

The oblique cases of L clima were formed on the stem climat-, so that we have the double forms clime 8x (1x rhyme) and climate 8x in the two meanings 'the condition of a place with respect to atmospheric phenomena' and 'a region.' In the second sense, there is a third variant, *climature 1x H 1.1.125 (om. F).

The word mead (representing OE mǽd, nominative sg.) occurs 7x as a

metrical variant of meadow (OE mǽdwe, oblique case of mǽd), which occurs 2x LLL 5.2.907, TA 3.1.125 'a piece of grassland.' In the same way,
shade 24x (2x poems; 2x rhyme) represents the OE nominative sg. sceadu
and the dative sceade, whereas shadow 38x represents the OE sceadwe of
the other oblique cases. The two words are used in the four meanings
'darkness,' 'a spectral form,' 'an image cast by a body intercepting
light,' and 'an unreal image produced by the imagination,' e.g. in
S 43.5-8,

> Then thou, whose shadow shadows doth make bright,
>
> How would thy shadow's form form happie show
>
> To the clear day with thy much clearer light,
>
> When to unseeing eyes thy shade shines soe,

a complex piece of word-play describing a dream-vision of an absent friend.

Analogical Variants

Shakespeare makes good metrical use of many words formed analogically
after derivational, etymological, and morphological variants. A few of
these have been discussed previously and the rest will be treated here.
It is important to recognize, however, that "analogical," taken in its
widest sense, could apply to almost every variant included in this study,
for the process of analogy is as basic to word-formation as it is to
creative thinking in general.

Derivational analogy

On the model of a- from various older sources (OE a-, ȝe-, of-, on-;

L ab-, ad-, ex-, etc.), an excrescent a- was added to many words in the sixteenth century. Because forms with the older a- frequently had synonymous simplexes (e.g. arise and rise), Renaissance writers apparently felt that they could add an a- prefix to words of their own choice to produce (according to OED) a "vaguely intensive, rhetorical, euphonic" effect without altering the lexical meaning of the simplex. In Shakespeare we have the nonce-word *abrook 1x 2H6 2.4.10 along with brook 26x 'to endure'; *arouse 1x 2H6 4.1.3 along with rouse 13x 'to awaken from slumber or repose'; and the predicate adj. aweary 5x along with weary 22x (predicate occurrences only were counted), both meaning 'tired.'

In the verb affright, the f has been doubled after the analogy of forms like affirm derived from L ad-. Affright is used 13x as a synonym of fright 28x 'to frighten.' The modern reader will find an extra syllable in LLL 4.3.275,

No Divell will fright thee then so much as shee,

but see Gabriel Harvey's comments on divel quoted above, p. 41; his spelling indicates that it was pronounced with v and nonsyllabic l. So also the old editions of Shakespeare have div'll in TN 2.3.159.[11] In R2 2.4.9,

And Meteors fright the fixèd Starres of Heaven,

a disyllabic pronunciation of meteors must be assumed if the meter is to be regular. According to Kökeritz, this was achieved either by consonantization or by suppression of the medial e: in support of the latter hypothesis, he cites on p. 290 of Shakespeare's Pronunciation the Renaissance phonetic spellings meator (MW 2.2.293, Q) and meatu(a)re (recorded in OED). Shakespeare also has the corresponding p.ts. affrighted 1x

R3 1.4.64 - <u>frighted</u> 1x AC 3.13.6 and the p.ps. <u>affrighted</u> 5x - <u>frighted</u>
13x 'frightened.'

The verbs <u>defiled</u> and <u>surcease</u> represent a special type of derivational analogy. They were altered from their original spellings by association with their supposed simplexes <u>filed</u> and <u>cease</u>, respectively,
though they were totally unrelated to these verbs in origin. We find
<u>defiled</u> 6x - <u>filed</u> 1x M 3.1.65, "For Banquo's Issue have I <u>fil'd</u> my
Minde," meaning 'sullied.' And <u>surcease</u> 2x C 3.2.121, RJ 4.1.97 occurs
along with <u>cease</u> 26x in the two intr. meanings 'to stop' and 'to come to
an end.' This last pair also has related nouns: <u>surcease</u> 1x M 1.7.4 and
<u>cease</u> 1x H 3.3.15 'cessation.'

And there are other nouns formed by derivational analogy. For ex-
ample, since the noun <u>even</u> had a synonym <u>evening</u>, ultimately derived from
the OE verb <u>ǽfnian</u> 'to grow towards evening,' so also <u>morning</u> arose as a
synonym of <u>morn</u>, even though there was no intermediary verb in this case.
<u>Morning</u> is found 68x meaning 'the early part of the day; dawn' (often
personified) as a synonym of <u>morn</u> 34x (1x poems, 1x rhyme). The occurrences of <u>good</u> <u>morning</u> are omitted, as <u>morn</u> is not used in this phrase.
One relevant line, Cy 3.3.4, is hypermetrical as printed: "To a <u>mornings</u>
holy office. The Gates of Monarches." But <u>a</u> may well be an erroneous
interpolation before <u>mornings</u> (which may have been intended as a personi-
fication). Walker points out that this error is frequent in F, and includes among his examples the following: "Ther's <u>a</u> language in her eye,
her cheeke, her lip" (TC 4.5.55; Q and F2-4 omit <u>a</u>, thus regularizing the
meter); and "Fy, what <u>a</u> man of good temper would endure this tempest of
exclamation?" (2H4 2.1.87; prose; Q <u>what</u> <u>man</u>).[12] Unfortunately, we have
no quarto of Cy for comparison with the F reading given above.

Behaviour 21x was an analogical formation after havour, haviour,
originally meaning 'possession' and spelled aver. Since havour and
haviour were commonly regarded as nouns related to English have (hence
the addition of initial h), behaviour was formed as a supposedly parallel
derivative of behave, which etymologically = be- + have. And after this
took place, haviour may have been regarded as a short form of behaviour;
in any case, it then took on the primary sense of behaviour--'external
deportment.' Haviour occurs 6x in this meaning, 1x only in Q and F2-4,
in a line in which F and the other Qq have behaviour erroneously: "And
therefore thou maist thinke my behaviour light" (RJ 2.2.99).

On the analogy of the adj. revengeful 7x 'vindictive, inflicting
vengeance' from the noun revenge (which has a verb of the same form),
vengeful was formed from the verb venge. Shakespeare uses it 2x in
2H6 3.2.198, TA 5.2.51 as a synonym of revengeful; and it has two other
syllabic variants--the nonce-word *revengive 1x L 2.1.47 (Qq only; Ff
revenging) and the present ppl. adj. revenging 2x 2H6 4.1.97, L 2.1.47,
"But that I told him the revenging Gods, / 'Gainst Paricides did all the
thunder bend."

Etymological analogy

On the model of ancient verbal variants such as listen and list,
many verbs in -en arose in late Middle English and early Modern English,
some being an extension of an existing simple verb. Of this type is
hasten 7x (1x poems), which occurs along with haste 22x in the two meanings 'to urge on' and (intr.) 'to make haste.' Happen 5x may be a similar
case, though perhaps it was derived from the noun hap instead. It is
found as a metrical variant of hap 9x 'to come to pass,' an intr. sense.

Lengthen is definitely from the noun, and is used 5x as a synonym of length in the poems 'to make longer.' Note that in all of these verbs the -en was added to a verb or noun, whereas (according to OED) the -en derivatives discussed in Chapter III had adjectival roots.

Shakespeare may have formed the word *fount 'a spring or source' by adapting it from Fr font or L fontem on the analogy of mount, an etymological variant of mountain. In any case, *fount 3x alternates metrically with the earlier fountain 13x.

We have several variants formed on the analogy of nouns in -y. Thus entreaty 18x 'a petition, request' was formed from the verb entreat on the model of treaty 3x (e.g. "To the young man send humble Treaties, dodge," AC 3.11.62), an originally past ppl. form like party discussed above, p. 148. And since the verb entreat was also used as a noun, entreaty has a second syllabic variant: entreat 3x.

On the analogy of -y derivatives ultimately representing L nouns in -ium, many of which were formed on verbs ending in an r-sound (e.g. augury and empery above), inquiry was formed from the verb inquire. Stressed on the second syllable, inquiry occurs 2x MM 5.1.5, H 2.1.4 (Ff only; Qq inquire, also metrically possible because in the fifth foot). Its metrical variants are the two related nouns inquire 2x P 3.Gower.22 (rhyme), H 2.1.4 (Qq only) and inquisition 2x T 1.2.35, AYLI 2.2.20, which was formed on the L past ppl. stem; the meaning of all three words is 'a seeking for information.'

The noun mutiny was formed from mutine + -y, possibly after felony, in which the suffix represents L -ia. The two substantival forms mutiny and mutine are not synonymous in Shakespeare, but they gave rise to related verbs which are synonyms in the intr. sense 'to rebel': mutiny 2x

JC 3.2.234, 3.2.235 and <u>mutine</u> 1x H 3.4.83, "If thou canst <u>mutine</u> in a Matrons bones."

Morphological analogy

<u>Breech</u> 1x 3H6 5.5.24 'trousers' found along with <u>breeches</u> 5x is an interesting case showing analogical extension of the old umlaut pl. <u>breech</u> (OE <u>bréc</u>) after plurals in -<u>s</u> in early Modern English. And the word <u>accomplice</u> 1x 1H6 5.2.9 'confederate' from the earlier <u>complice</u> 5x may have arisen after the analogy of the phonetically similar <u>accomplish</u>, or perhaps the indefinite article in the phrase <u>a</u> <u>complice</u> was taken as a prefix instead.

The usual ending employed in forming the comparative degree of advs. and adjs. is -<u>er</u>, representing OE -<u>or</u>. But in Old English, some comparatives did not have this ending: these include the adj. <u>lǽssa</u> and adv. <u>lǽs</u> 'less,' the adv. <u>néar</u> 'nearer,' and the adj. <u>wyrsa</u> and adv. <u>wyrs</u> 'worse.' In early Modern English, however, -<u>er</u> was frequently added even to these forms which were already comparative, so that the double comparatives <u>lesser</u> (which has survived in the adj.), <u>nearer</u> (which has survived), and <u>worser</u> arose.

In the plays, we find both <u>less</u> 127x (5x rhyme) and <u>lesser</u> 19x used as adjs. meaning 'smaller.' In RJ 4.4.10, "All night for <u>lesse</u> cause, and nere beene sicke," F has <u>less</u> unmetrically, but Q2 has <u>lesser</u> and F2-4 have <u>a less</u>. As an adv., <u>less</u> also occurs 41x along with *<u>lesser</u> 7x 'in a smaller or lower degree.' And similarly, <u>near</u> is used 3x as an adv. (e.g. in M 2.3.146, "The <u>neere</u> in blood, the neerer bloody") meaning 'closer'; and <u>nearer</u> is used 4x (e.g. in R3 2.1.92, "<u>Neerer</u> in bloody thoughts, and not in blood"). <u>Worse</u> is found 90x (2x rhyme) as an adj.

along with <u>worser</u> 10x, and as advs. Shakespeare has <u>worse</u> 21x (1x rhyme)
and <u>worser</u> 3x 'more badly.'

A related, though not exactly parallel, case is that of <u>oft</u> as an
adv. along with <u>often</u>, for the latter arose through an analogical extension of <u>oft</u> to <u>ofte</u> in early Middle English, in imitation of other advs.
in -<u>e</u>, and a subsequent extension still further to <u>often</u>. Thus we find
in the plays the double forms <u>oft</u> 37x 'frequently' and <u>often</u> 34x (both
figures incomplete). And, in the same meaning, Shakespeare also has <u>oft-
times</u> 1x Cy 1.6.62 (F prints as two words) and <u>oftentimes</u> 7x. <u>Often</u> is
used irregularly in H8 4.1.29,

She was <u>often</u> cyted by them, but appear'd not,

where probably it is an error for <u>oft</u>.

The demonstrative adv. <u>yon</u> 'over there' was extended (through its
variant <u>yond</u>) to <u>yonder</u> in Middle English, probably after advs. like
<u>hither</u> or comparative advs. and adjs. like <u>further</u>. The first meaning
listed by OED for <u>yonder</u> as an adv.--'more distant' (more <u>yon</u>)--actually
shows a comparative sense. <u>Yon</u> occurs 1x R2 3.3.91 (Qq only; Ff <u>yond</u>)
along with <u>yond</u> 7x and <u>yonder</u> 23x. And in the related adjs., we find
<u>yon</u> 26x - <u>yond</u> 29x - <u>yonder</u> 20x, all meaning 'that, those.'

Back-Formation

Back-formation is a special type of morphological analogy. The
variants previously discussed involve analogical <u>extension</u> of a word
(e.g. <u>worse</u> extended to <u>worser</u>); back-formation usually involves analogical <u>reduction</u>.

For example, the variation between the advs. <u>seld</u> 1x TC 4.5.150 and

seldom 18x 'not often' illustrates the worse - worser process in reverse.
Seld was formed in late Old English as an inferred positive to seldor and
seldost, though there was already a positive form seldan (itself later
analogically altered to seldom). If spelling is taken as a guide to pronunciation, AW 2.1.100 shows trisyllabic substitution in the second foot
resulting from the use of seldom:

His Majesty seldome feares, I am Cresseds Uncle.

But it is possible that majesty was meant to be disyllabic here; for parallels see the discussion of magical above, p. 121. An alternate explanation is that seldom is simply an error for an intended seld, but
there is no quarto for comparison.

By far the most common origin of back-formation was the misappre-
hension of certain endings as inflectional when in fact they were part of
the simplex itself. Then these forms with pseudo-inflectional endings
were reduced after the analogy of other words which really did show inflectional terminations. In this group belongs beck 1x J 3.3.13 'to make
a mute signal to,' shortened from beckon 1x H 1.4.58. One of the ME
forms of beckon was bekenen, and after the -en infinitive endings were
lost in late Middle English, the remaining -en of the stem beken- was apparently sometimes taken as also representing an infinitive ending.
Therefore, a further reduction took place and an assumed stem bek- gave
the verb beck.

A somewhat similar case is the reduced form ope, from open. The
-en ending of the adj. open was sometimes regarded as the ending of a
strong p.p. (though in fact there was originally no verb ope), and con-
sequently was dropped along with the endings of true strong p.ps. such as

bounden. Thus Shakespeare has two forms of the adj.: <u>ope</u> 7x 'not closed, not shut' and <u>open</u> 14x (occurrences preceding a noun omitted because of lack of parallelism). These two forms passed also into related verbs; in Shakespeare, we find not only the original <u>open</u> 42x but also <u>ope</u> 23x meaning either 'to unclose, spread apart' or (intr.) 'to become unclosed or spread apart.' One relevant line, 3H6 1.3.23, is typographically hypermetrical:

Then let my Fathers blood <u>open</u> it againe.

Here, however, <u>it</u> was probably meant to be reduced to '<u>t</u> and added enclitically to <u>open</u>. Such contractions are often represented orthographically in the old editions; Kökeritz mentions, for example, <u>on't</u> T 1.2.87, <u>sworn't</u> H 1.5.112 (<u>Shakespeare's Pronunciation</u>, p. 273).

There are also two cases in which an ending that was in fact inflectional was apparently not recognized as such and was taken to be part of the simplex, so that a new extended form arose. For instance, Kökeritz feels that Shakespeare's <u>county</u> as the title of nobility was a back-formation from disyllabic <u>count's</u> or <u>counts</u>, as in TN 1.5.320, "The <u>Countes</u> man: he left this Ring behinde him." The syllabic genitive (or pl. form) was not recognized as such, and a -<u>y</u> ending, pronounced $[ɪ]$, was appended to the simplex.[13] Shakespeare has <u>county</u> 13x along with <u>count</u> 20x (both figures are too small because of incomplete listings). Compare, for example, " . . . a ring the <u>Countie</u> weares" (AW 3.7.22) and " . . . the <u>Count</u> he is my husband" (AW 3.7.8). Finally, a similar type of back-formation can be seen in the development of the form <u>hoisted</u>. Shakespeare uses the original p.p. <u>hoised</u> 1x H 3.4.207 'raised aloft' (om. F; sp. <u>hoist</u> in the other old editions), which was from the verb

hoise, according to OED. But since the p.p. in the hoist spelling could
have been short for hoisted, a new verb-stem with -t seems to have been
analogically inferred (hoist). Thus Shakespeare also had available an
extended ppl. form hoisted, which he uses 1x CE 5.1.21.

Clipped Forms

Aphesis

As mentioned in Chapter II, many of the forms here classified as
aphetic could equally well be regarded as representing the simplex of a
derivational variant; for example, the verb bide could be either an
aphetic form of abide or the modern representative of OE bídan. With
this qualification, I list below those variants in Shakespeare's verse
which are aphetic, classified according to part of speech. Since, by the
very definition of "aphetic" (and of "clipped forms" in general), synonymity is assumed, I give a minimum of supporting examples.

Verbs

We find the aphetic form bate 8x alternating metrically with abate
14x in the four senses 'to blunt,' 'to weaken,' 'to deduct,' and (intr.)
'to decrease.' Pistol uses both variants in the second meaning in
H5 3.2.24-26, which F prints as prose: "Abate thy Rage, abate thy manly
Rage; / Abate thy Rage, great Duke. / Good Bawcock bate thy Rage." In
the first sense, bate has another syllabic variant, rebate 1x MM 1.4.60,
"But doth rebate, and blunt his naturall edge." In the p.p., Shakespeare
uses bated 4x along with abated 2x 2H4 1.1.117, C 3.3.132 meaning either
'weakened, blunted' or 'beaten down, humbled.'

Bide 17x has three senses in which it is a synonym of abide 26x: 'to
endure,' 'to meet in combat,' and (intr.) 'to stay, dwell.' And the p.p.
debted 1x CE 4.1.31 'owing something' is an aphetic form of indebted 2x
MV 4.1.413, 2H6 1.4.47. If the 2H6 line is pronounced as printed, indebted creates a trisyllabic foot:

Are deepely indebted for this peece of paines.

But here, the [I] vowel of the adverbial ending -ly could have been fused
with the following i of indebted, either by absorption or by consonantization to [j]; see Kökeritz, Shakespeare's Pronunciation, p. 291.

Shakespeare also has gage in the poems 'to pawn, pledge' along with
engage 5x. And gin 5x in the two meanings 'to start' and (intr.) 'to
start' [to do something] is a metrical variant of begin 69x. In the intr.
sense, we find the p.ts. gan 1x Cy 5.3.37 and began 6x. Similarly, greed
occurs 5x as a synonym of agreed 10x in the two meanings 'arranged by
common consent' and (intr.) 'come to one opinion'; and in the pr.p.
Shakespeare has greeing in the poems as well as agreeing 3x 'being in con-
cord.'

The aphetic form mend 36x and amend 7x both mean either 'to make better' or (intr.) 'to become better,' and in the p.ps. we find mended 6x
and amended 4x 'made better.' In the sense 'smeared with any unctuous
matter,' the p.p. nointed 1x MND 3.2.351 occurs as well as anointed 19x;
this particular aphetic form arose because anointed was interpreted as a
+ nointed, though etymologically it was an + ointed (ultimately representing L inunctum). Palled 1x AC 2.7.88, "For this, Ile never follow
thy paul'd Fortunes more" (F prints as two short lines, dividing after
follow), means 'impaired'; its variant, appalled, occurs 1x 1H6 1.2.48,

"Me thinks your looks are sad, your chear appal'd." And ply 4x 'to de-
vote one's energy to' occurs along with apply 1x TS 1.1.19.

Shakespeare also uses point 1x TS 3.2.15 meaning 'to fix' [a time,
meeting, etc.]; its metrical variant is appoint 3x. And in the p.ps. he
has both pointed 2x TS 3.1.19, 3.2.1 and appointed 4x. Similarly, rested
1x CE 4.4.3, "Ile give thee ere I leave thee so much money / To warrant
thee as I am rested for," is used as a short form of arrested 3x 'apprehended by legal authority.' And the word side in S 46.9, "To side this
title is impannellèd / A quest of thoughts, all tennants to the heart,"
is regarded by most editors as an aphetic form of decide (hence = a nonce-
word *cide), though OED defines it rather as a nonce-use of the verb side
meaning 'to assign to one of two sides or parties.' Note that decide,
which occurs 3x in the sense 'to settle,' was sometimes spelled deside or
dissyde in the fifteenth and sixteenth centuries, according to OED.

The aphetic form spend 43x alternates metrically with expend 4x 'to
pay away, lay out,' and Shakespeare uses stain 9x meaning 'to blemish,
defile' (occurrences in lit. sense are omitted) along with the full form
distain 3x. Interesting parallel forms are the compounds *tear-stained
1x 2H6 2.4.16 and *tear-distained (a nonce-word) in the poems, both in
the sense 'tinged or discolored by tears.' And stalled 1x R3 1.3.206,
"Deck'd in thy Rights, as thou art stall'd in mine," is an aphetic variant of installed 5x 'placed, instated.'

Shakespeare also has stonished in the poems for astonished 2x
1H6 1.2.93, 5.5.2 'stunned mentally.' Stroyed 1x AC 3.11.54, "Stroy'd in
dishonor. // Oh my Lord, my Lord," is an aphetic form of destroyed 5x,
and shows how a prefix with privative force (L de-) has been removed but
the sense of the full form retained, even though the original simplex (L

struere 'to pile up') expressed constructive action. We also find void
1x H5 4.7.62 'to depart from' as a synonym of avoid 1x H8 5.1.86, "Avoyd
the Gallery. / Ha? I have said. Be gone." And in a slightly different
sense, 'shunned,' we find the p.ps. voided 1x C 4.5.88 ("I would have
voided thee . . . ") and avoided 8x. Vow 4x 'to assert' is an aphetic
variant of avow 2x H8 4.2.142, TC 1.3.271.

Finally, Shakespeare has witch 4x along with the full form bewitch
2x 2H6 1.1.157, 3H6 3.3.112 'to enchant.' The related p.ps. are witched
1x 2H6 3.2.119 and bewitched 6x; one relevant line, MND 1.1.27 ("This
man hath bewitch'd the bosome of my childe"), is hypermetrical as printed
in F. F2-4, however, regularize the meter by omitting man, making this a
demonstrative pronoun rather than an adj.[14] Such an alteration would be
satisfactory for the sense, for the meaning of this would be clarified by
the antithetical "This man hath my consent to marrie her" occurring two
lines above in the play.[15]

Verbs with Related Nouns

There are several verbs whose related nouns are also statistically
significant. These include plot 8x 'to contrive, plan,' whose variant is
complot 1x R2 1.3.189, "To plot, contrive, or complot any ill." Shakespeare also has the p.ps. plotted 6x and complotted 1x R2 1.1.96. The
related nouns, plot 31x and complot 6x, mean 'a scheme, plan'; plot probably represents an aphetic shortening of complot when the latter was
still stressed on the final syllable as in French. In R3 3.4.62,

That doe conspire my death with divellish Plots,

divellish was undoubtedly meant to be read as a disyllable; see above, p.

151, for a discussion of monosyllabic _divel_.

Scape 28x, an aphetic variant of _escape_ 5x, is used in the two meanings 'to be saved from, avoid' and (intr.) 'to get out of danger.' And
in the p.t. we find scaped 2x JC 4.3.150, P 1.3.29 along with escaped 3x
'avoided.' The related p.ps. are scaped 4x - escaped 3x 'gotten out of
danger' (intr.); and the related nouns are scape 3x (1x poems) - escape
10x meaning either 'a getting out of danger' or 'a serious transgression'
(escape in the latter meaning occurs only in Shakespeare, according to
OED). Note the juxtaposition of variants in 3H6 2.1.6-7, "Or had he
scap't, me thinkes we should have heard / The happy tidings of his good
escape."

Similarly, the verb sport 3x occurs along with disport 2x 3H6 4.5.8,
TmA 1.2.141, both meaning 'to divert' [oneself], a reflexive sense. The
related nouns are sport 22x and disport 1x O 1.3.272, "That my Disports
corrupt, and taint my businesse," in the sense 'a pastime, diversion.'
And the verbs story in the poems and history 1x 2H4 4.1.203 'to relate,
recount' ("And keepe no Tell-tale to his Memorie, / That may repeat, and
Historie his losse") also have related nouns. Story 60x alternates metrically with history 14x[16] meaning either 'the formal record of past events'
or 'any relation of incidents, narrative.' A comment of the Chorus in the
history play Henry V, "Vouchsafe to those that have not read the Story, /
That I may prompt them" (H5 5.Prol.1), shows that story does not necessarily refer to imaginary events.

The complex group of variants related to taint and attaint are discussed here because an aphetic shortening was at the base of all of the
confusion. The nonaphetic verb taint was derived from OF teint, p.p. of
teindre :- L tingere 'to dye, tinge, stain.' And the verb attaint was

derived from OF _ateint_, p.p. of _ateindre_ 'to attain' :- L _attingere_, f. _ad-_ + _tangere_ 'to touch.' But because _attaint_ had an aphetic form _taint_, two words of distinct origin and of originally distinct meaning ran together under one spelling: _taint_. The next step was an interaction between the composite verb _taint_ and _attaint_, so that the latter also attracted much of the meaning of the original _taint_, e.g. 'to infect, sully.'

Taint 5x 'to infect, impair' is used as a synonym of _attaint_, which occurs in the poems, "When time with age shall them _attaint_" (PP 344). The p.ps. first remained as _taint_ and _attaint_ (after the Fr forms), so that we have _taint_ 1x 1H6 5.3.183 (" . . . a pure unspotted heart, / Never yet _taint_ with love, I send the King") and _attaint_ 1x 1H6 5.5.81 ("My tender youth was never yet _attaint_ / With any passion of inflaming Love"; F has _Jove_ instead of the F2-4 reading _Love_). The meaning of both is 'touched' [_with_ some emotion]. Soon the p.ps. attracted a weak form, so that we find _tainted_ 9x - _attainted_ 3x 'touched by dishonor, condemned.' And compare also the negative ppl. adjs. _untainted_ in the poems and *_unattainted_ 1x RJ 1.2.90 'unimpaired.'

In Old French, nouns developed from a substantival use of the p.ps. _teint_ and _ateint_, and the English representatives of these nouns also ran together in meaning. Therefore Shakespeare can use _taint_ 5x and _attaint_ 1x CE 3.2.16 (rhyme; F has the misprint _attaine_) as synonyms meaning 'stain or touch of dishonor.' For _taint_ and _attaint_ as nouns alternating with _tainture_, see p. 100 above.

Another verb with a statistically significant related noun is _tend_, which occurs 20x along with _attend_ 60x in the two trans. senses 'to wait on, guard, accompany' and 'to expect,' and the two intr. senses 'to be ready for service' and 'to wait.' In one typographically irregular line,

TA 2.2.8,

> To attend the Emperours person carefully,

the vowel of to must be elided before the following vowel (and Emperours must be syncopated to a disyllable). The p.ps. tended 2x AW 2.1.210, TN 5.1.102 and attended 1x P 4.4.11 also occur meaning 'waited' [on or upon someone], an intr. sense.

The related nouns of action are tendance 3x - attendance 3x (occurrences in the phrase dance attendance are omitted) 'ministration.' And attendance is also a syllabic variant of the vbl. sb. *tending, which is used 1x M 1.5.38. In addition, tendance is once a collective sg. meaning 'train or retinue' (TmA 1.1.80, "Follow his strides, his Lobbies fill with tendance"), and in this use it corresponds in sense to the related pl. noun attendants except in certain constructions (e.g. when there is a pl. verb). With all such cases omitted, attendants is found 3x as a metrical variant of tendance.

Venture 18x is used along with adventure 8x in the two senses 'to hazard, risk, dare' and (intr.) 'to dare.' And in the second meaning, Shakespeare also has the p.ps. ventured 4x, e.g. in L 3.4.157, "Yet have I ventured to come seeke you out," and adventured 1x Cy 1.6.172, "Be not angrie / (Most mighty Princesse) that I have adventur'd / To try your taking of a false report." In the pr.p., Shakespeare uses disyllabic venturing in the poems to mean 'hazarding, risking, daring': "So that in ventring ill, we leave to be / The things we are." Its metrical variant is adventuring 1x MV 1.1.143, "To finde the other forth, and by adventuring both," which also must be syncopated and is so spelled in Q: adventring. The related nouns are venture 3x and adventure 13x 'a risk, risking; hazardous enterprise'; the aphetic venture is probably partly due to the

initial a of aventure (the original form from French) having been taken

as the indefinite article. There are two relevant lines that are irregu-

lar if the spelling is taken as a guide to the meter. These are M 1.3.91,

Thy personall Venture in the Rebels fight,

where the o of personall must be elided (cf. card'nall in 2H6 3.3.27,

cited by Kökeritz on p. 371 of Shakespeare's Pronunciation); and 3H6 4.2.18,

Our Scouts have found the adventure very easie,

where the vowel of the must be elided before adventure, as represented

orthographically in WT 5.1.156.

Nouns

The aphetic form fence 1x 3H6 4.1.44 'that which serves as a bulwark'

("Let us be back'd with God, and with the Seas, / Which he hath giv'n for

fence impregnable") alternates metrically with defence 6x.[17] And larum

3x 'a loud sound to warn of danger, or to arouse' occurs along with the

full form alarum 9x, a variant of alarm (which occurs only in the fifth

foot). Alarum seems to be used irregularly in C 2.2.80, if alarm is con-

sidered a possibility:

When the Alarum were strucke, then idly sit.

But as Kökeritz notes, it may be merely an error for an intended alarm.[18]

Such an error actually occurred in the transmission of H 2.2.532 ("A

blanket in th'Alarum of feare caught up"), in which alarum is used in a

different sense, 'a state of apprehension'; in this line, the Qq reading is alarme. Compare also the compounds larum-bell 1x 2H4 3.1.17 and *alar-um-bell (not hyphenated in F) 2x M 2.3.79, 5.5.51.

Shakespeare has noyance 1x H 3.3.13 'harm, suffering, discomfort' ("To keepe it selfe from noyance . . . ") as an aphetic form of annoyance 5x. And in the sense 'clothing,' both parel 1x L 4.1.51 and apparel 12x are used. Shakespeare twice has pothecary (RJ 5.3.289, P 3.2.9) along with apothecary 4x 'one who prepares and sells drugs'; one line, 2H6 3.3.17, "Give me some drinke, and bid the Apothecarie," is irregular as printed in F. But Q has Pothicary (in a slightly different line); and, in any case, the could easily have been apocopated before the following vowel.

*Rouse 1x H 1.2.127 'a full draught of liquor' came to be used as an aphetic form of carouse because the phrase to drink carouse was mistakenly interpreted as to drink a rouse. Carouse, which occurs 2x TS 1.2.277, AC 4.8.34, was originally an adv. representing German gar aus 'completely,' and itself came to be used as a noun by being taken for a direct object in the phrase to drink carouse.

In the sense 'a person or action that induces imitation,' Shakespeare once uses sample, "A sample to the yongest . . . " (Cy 1.1.48). The full form example occurs 12x, twice creating trisyllabic feet if the line is pronounced as printed. In H8 1.3.62,

They are set heere for examples. // True, they are so,

the first they are must be read as they're or th'are to regularize the meter; orthographic representation of such a contraction is to be found in the very next act (" . . . th'are breath I not beleeve in," H8 2.2.54). See also the discussion of we are in WT 1.2.394, p. 98 above. The other trisyllabic foot, in AC 3.10.28,

Oh his ha's given example for our flight,

can easily be eliminated by a monosyllabic pronunciation of given, orthographically represented (giv'n) in 3H6 4.1.44, quoted above on p. 166.[19]

Scuse is used 2x MV 4.1.444, O 4.1.80 as an aphetic form of excuse
19x meaning 'a plea offered in extenuation.' In 1H4 5.2.17,

It hath the excuse of youth, and heate of blood,

and in RJ 2.5.33,

The excuse that thou dost make in this delay,

the vowel of the must be elided before excuse if the line is to be metrically exact. This elision is orthographically indicated (th'excuse) in
H5 5.Prol.3.

Similarly, spite 17x is aphetic for despite 11x 'malice.' There are
two relevant lines which contain trisyllabic feet if read as printed:
1H6 4.1.185,

More rancorous spight, more furious raging broyles,

and TmA 1.2.144,

With poysonous Spight and Envy.

Both can be regularized, however, by elision of an unstressed medial
vowel: ranc'rous, poys'nous.[20] And (in) spite of is also found 20x along
with (in) despite of 14x 'notwithstanding'; further, the related adjs.
spiteful 2x 2H6 1.3.158, M 3.5.12 and despiteful 7x 'malicious' also occur.

Shakespeare uses surance 1x TA 5.2.46, "Now give some surance that thou art Revenge," as an aphetic synonym of assurance 10x 'surety.' And test 2x TC 5.2.122, O 1.3.107 'evidence' may be an aphetic form of *attest 1x TC 5.2.122 (only in Q). The TC line as it stands in F is "That doth invert that test of eyes and eares"; Q has th'attest instead of that test. Both variants alternate metrically with a third form, testimony 7x. A final noun is tire, used in the poems to mean 'apparel': "And you in Grecian tires are painted new," S 53.8. Its synonym, attire, occurs 11x.[21]

Adjectives and Adverbs

In the adjectival class, like 4x alternates metrically with alike 5x 'mutually similar or identical.' Only the occurrences of like in the predicate have been included in the reckoning. Examples are " . . . they say we are / Almost as like as Egges; Women say so" (WT 1.2.130) and "Creatures may be alike: were't he, I am sure / He would have spoke to us" (Cy 5.5.125). And these variants have corresponding advs.: like is used 7x and alike 2x RJ 2.Prol.6, WT 1.2.310 in the two senses 'equally' (qualifying an adj.) and, in the phrase a)like as, 'in the same way as.' Compare, in the first sense, "Like warlike as the Wolfe, for what we eate" (Cy 3.3.41) and "Alike bewitchèd by the charme of lookes" (RJ 2.Prol.6).

Prepositions, Conjunctions, Interjections

Unfortunately, full statistics cannot be given for these words, but on the basis of the listings in Schmidt's Shakespeare-Lexicon and the Concordance combined, the following figures were obtained. The aphetic prep. _bout_ occurs 4x along with _about_ 34x meaning 'surrounding, around,' 'approximately,' and 'to and fro in.' In Puck's speech in MND 3.1.109,

> Ile follow you, Ile leade you _about_ a Round,

hypermetrical as printed, the meaning of _Round_ has puzzled commentators. Var. Ed. offers as an emendation "Ile follow you--Ile leade you--about-- around"; if this were accepted, the first syllable of _about_ would be a permissible extra syllable in the caesura. Two other possibilities are that _about_ was an intentionally irregular use for purposes of character- ization, or that the vowel of _you_ was meant to be elided before _about_.[22]

In the senses 'higher than' and 'more than,' the prep. _bove_ is used 4x along with _above_ 33x. And _cross_ 1x 2H6 4.1.114, "I charge thee waft me safely _crosse_ the Channell," meaning 'over,' is a metrical variant of *_across_ 1x WT 4.4.15, "When my good Falcon, made her flight _a-crosse_ / Thy Fathers ground." Similarly, the preps. _mong_ 4x and _mongst_ 22x are aphetic variants of _among_ 16x and _amongst_ 22x, respectively, 'surrounded by, associated with.' In TmA 3.3.21, F has "To th'rest, and '_mongst_ Lords be thought a Foole"; the word _I_, erroneously omitted here after _Lords_, is inserted by F2-4 (there is no quarto).

Shakespeare also has the prep. _tween_ 14x along with _between_ 44x, and _twixt_ 47x along with _betwixt_ 34x; metrical alternation can be seen clear- ly in R2 5.1.71-74,

> . . . ye violate
>
> A two-fold Marriage; '_twixt_ my Crowne, and me,
>
> And then _betwixt_ me, and my marryed Wife.
>
> Let me un-kisse the Oath '_twixt_ thee, and me.

Finally, gainst occurs 49x as a prep. along with against 59x (in two
cases, LLL 4.3.293 and MM 5.1.244, F has against in a trisyllabic foot,
but F2-4 correct to gainst). The meanings are 'towards' (of place), 'before' (of time), and 'in opposition to.' If the printed form is accepted,
gainst is responsible for the irregularity in Cy 3.1.29,

As easily 'gainst our Rockes. For joy whereof,

for against would create a regular alexandrine; but here, the medial i of
easily was probably meant to be elided. Such an elision is orthographically indicated (easlie) in J 2.1.515 and LLL 5.2.190.[23]

Gainst and against can also be used as conjs. meaning 'before'; in
this sense, they occur 2x (H 1.1.158, TA 5.2.206--the latter only in Ff;
Qq have against, also possible in the caesura) and 4x respectively. And
as interjections, Shakespeare has lack 2x Cy 4.2.374, 5.3.59 as an aphetic
form of alack 35x; and *las 1x O 5.1.111 (only in Qq, in a hypermetrical
caesura; Ff alas) along with alas 27x. The aphetic interjectional forms
are not used solely by "low" characters; both Posthumus and Lucius use
lack in Cymbeline.

Syncope

In Shakespeare's verse, there are many words in which syncopation is
indicated by an apostrophe or can be inferred from the meter, but in this
section I discuss only those variants which acquired the status of independent words and are so listed by OED.

First, Shakespeare has canstick 1x 1H4 3.1.131 (Qq only) as well as
candlestick 2x H5 4.2.45, 1H4 3.1.131 (Ff only; an error for canstick of
the Qq). And he uses *votress 2x MND 2.1.123, 2.1.163 along with votaress

1x (rhyme) P 4.Gower.4 to mean 'a female votary'; both words have another synonym in disyllabic *votarists 1x MM 1.4.5 (an alexandrine), "Upon the Sisterhood, the Votarists of Saint Clare." Notice that *votarist is the only one of the three variants which could have been disyllabic in the pl. form. Finally, we find the adj. wondrous 14x, an alteration of the adj. wonders after marvellous by substitution of -ous for the genitival -s, with subsequent loss of medial e. Its synonym wonderful occurs 9x.

Apocope

Shakespeare took from Arthur Brooke's Tragicall History of Romeus and Juliet the apocopated name-variant Capel 2x RJ 5.1.18, 5.3.127, which he uses along with the full form Capulet 16x (1x rhyme). In RJ 4.1.112,

Where all the kindred of the Capulets lie,

Capulets creates a trisyllabic foot unless we allow the possibility of a syncopated form Cap'let (suggested by Kökeritz in Shakespeare's Pronunciation, p. 282); as pointed out on p. 44 above, loss of a medial vowel before l is frequent in the plays. Kökeritz puts forward still another explanation in "Elizabethan Prosody," pp. 89-90, noting that the line has no exact parallel in Q, where we find instead "And when thou art laid in thy Kindreds Vault": "Since elsewhere Capels appears in a similar context, namely 'in Capels Monument' (5.1.18) and 'in the Capels Monument' (5.3.127), the probability of miswriting or a printer's error in Q2, the basis of F, is very strong." Capulets could thus have been printed erroneously instead of an intended Capels.

Shakespeare also has coz 14x as well as cousin 76x (probably too small a figure; the listings are incomplete). Occurrences of cousin with

proper names, in the pl. form, or not in direct address are omitted. And
we find the nonce-word *intrince 1x L 2.2.81 'involved, entangled' ("Like
Rats oft bite the holy cords a twaine, / Which are t'intrince, t'unloose"), which is probably an abbreviated form of intrinsicate, used 1x
AC 5.2.307 ("With thy sharpe teeth this knot intrinsicate, / Of life at
once untye").[24] Both words appear to combine the senses of intricate--
which also occurs in Shakespeare, but has the slightly different sense
'complicated in meaning'--and intrinsic 'situated within.'

Maid is used 129x (14x rhyme) as a shortened form of maiden 23x
'virgin, girl' (occurrences of maid meaning specifically 'a female servant' have been excluded). The variants alternate metrically in Puck's
tetrameter speech in MND 2.2.73-74: "This is he (my master said) / De-
spisèd the Athenian maide: / And heere the maiden sleeping sound."

One further variant, the p.p. *cowed 1x M 5.8.18, "For it hath Cow'd
my better part of man," may be mentioned as a possibly apocopated form;
the meaning is 'dispirited by fear.' Though OED tentatively classifies
*cow as adopted from Old Norse kúga 'to cow, tyrannize over' (and appar-
ently often associated with the bovine cow), it seems probable that if
Shakespeare introduced the verb, it may simply be a shortening of the
established verb coward. Cowarded is also used 1x in the p.p.: "That
have so cowarded and chac'd your blood," H5 2.2.75.

CHAPTER VII

SUMMARY

Out of 12,814 lines analyzed, only 63, or less than 0.5%, may show irregular use of a variant. (It is necessary to stress may here because irregularity is present only if the spelling is taken as an indication of the meter.) And if we exclude those lines which would become alexandrines with the alternate variant, the figure is further reduced to 48. Thus the amount of even possible irregular usage is negligible.

Moreover, even these 63 lines probably owe their seeming irregularity to textual corruption or inconsistent orthography, for almost all can easily be regularized by a syncopation, elision, or expansion of the type outlined by Kökeritz in Shakespeare's Pronunciation. In the next section, the lines have been tabulated and grouped according to the specific reduction or expansion which would be necessary to produce metrically exact iambic verse.

No lines have been included in this summary in which obvious textual corruption has occurred, as evidenced by Q or later F variant readings. In addition, the following four lines which occur in plays for which we have no quarto have been excluded, because they are clear cases of erroneous interpolation, mislineation, or careless cutting:

To a mornings holy office. The Gates of Monarches   Cy 3.3.4 (152)[1]

174

For in the ingrafted love he beares to Caesar   JC 2.1.184 (70)

but shorten thy life one weeke. And thou, fresh peece   WT 4.4.433 (80)

It is mine, or Valentines praise   TG 2.4.196 (146)

Had all of these lines been included, there still would have been fewer
than 100 cases involving the possibility of haphazard usage not in accord
with metrical requirements.

Possibly irregular usage

Fusion of Two Adjacent Vowels

1. By suppression of the first vowel (apocope)

The_ excuse that thou dost make in this delay   RJ 2.5.33   (168)

The_ Hircanion deserts, and the vaste wildes   MV 2.7.41   (116)

And summ'd the_ accompt of Chance, before you said   2H4 1.1.167(49)

Our Scouts have found the_ adventure very easie   3H6 4.2.18 (166)

It hath the_ excuse of youth, and heate of blood   1H4 5.2.17 (168)

To_ unloose this tyde-up Justice, when you pleas'd   MM 1.3.32   (139)

To_ intrap the wisest. Therefore then thou gaudie gold   MV 3.2.101 (76)

To_ enforce the painèd impotent to smile   LLL 5.2.864(78)

To_ inforce these rights, so forcibly with-held   J 1.1.18   (78)

To_ emblaze the Honor that thy Master got   2H6 4.10.76(69)

To_ attend the Emperours person carefully   TA 2.2.8   (165)

That were to_ enlard his fat already, pride   TC 2.3.205 (75)

If Somerset be_ unworthy of the Place   2H6 1.3.108(137)

Ile follow you, Ile leade you_ about a Round   MND 3.1.109(170)

For that it made m<u>y</u> imprisonment, a pleasure   3H6 4.6.11 (77)

2.   By suppression or consonantization of the first vowel

Such friends (as time) in Pad<u>u</u>a shall beget   TS 1.1.45 (60)

Are deepel<u>y</u> indebted for this peece of paines   2H6 1.4.47 (160)

And Met<u>e</u>ors fright the fixèd Starres of Heaven   R2 2.4.9   (151)

3.   By suppression of the first or second vowel

In whose successe w<u>e</u> <u>a</u>re gentle: I beseech you   WT 1.2.394 (98)

Th<u>ey</u> <u>a</u>re set heere for examples. // True, they are so   H8 1.3.62 (167)

4.   By suppression of the second vowel (synaeresis)

Saw his Hero<u>i</u>call Seed, and smil'd to see him   H5 2.4.59 (121)

And never go<u>i</u>ng a right, being a Watch   LLL 3.1.194(46)

Whose infl<u>ue</u>nce is begot of that loose grace   LLL 5.2.869(60)

Loss of Vowel and Preceding Consonant

There's no hope she <u>wi</u>ll return. I'll swear she's dead   P 4.1.99   (40)

She <u>wo</u>uld mocke me into ayre, O she would laugh me   MA 3.1.75 (64)

A halter pardon him: And hell gnaw <u>hi</u>s bones   O 4.2.136 (61)

And e<u>ve</u>n before this truce, but new before   J 3.1.233 (53)

Loss of Vowel between Consonants (Syncope)

1.   Before <u>f</u>

A ben<u>e</u>fit in this change: but if you seeke   AC 5.2.128 (54)

Unmerc<u>i</u>full Lady, as you are, I'me none   L 3.7.33   (136)

2.   Before l̲

As easil̲y 'gainst our Rockes. For joy whereof   Cy 3.1.29   (171)

That doe conspire my death with divel̲lish Plots   R3 3.4.62   (162)

No Divel̲l will fright thee then so much as shee   LLL 4.3.275(151)

And credul̲ous to false prints. // I thinke it well   MM 2.4.130 (72)

3.   Before n̲

Thy person̲all Venture in the Rebels fight   M 1.3.91   (166)

With poyson̲ous Spight and Envy   TmA 1.2.144(168)

Oh his ha's giv̲en example for our flight   AC 3.10.28 (168)

How more unfortun̲ate then all living women   C 5.3.97   (92)

Let Heav̲en requit it with the Serpents curse   O 4.2.16   (41)

Let heav̲en revenge: for I may never lift   R2 1.2.40   (51)

4.   Before r̲

Shall be the Gener̲als fault, though he performe   C 1.1.271   (66)

Commotions, uprores, with a gener̲all Taint   H8 5.3.28   (100)

The liber̲all opposition of our spirits   LLL 5.2.743(90)

And ventur̲e madly on a desperate Mart   TS 2.1.329 (43)

Of what your rever̲ence shall incite us to   H5 1.2.20   (55)

More rancor̲ous spight, more furious raging broyles   1H6 4.1.185(168)

With twisted mettle amor̲ously empleacht   LC 205   (71)

5.   Before t̲ (enclitic)

Then let my Fathers blood open it̲ againe   3H6 1.3.23 (158)

6.   Possible syncope

That magicall word of Warre we have effected	AC 3.1.31 (121)
And his love Thisby; very tragicall mirth	MND 5.1.57 (122)
His Majesty seldome feares, I am Cresseds Uncle	AW 2.1.100 (157)
When the Alarum were strucke, then idly sit	C 2.2.80 (166)
Where all the kindred of the Capulets lie	RJ 4.1.112 (172)
May make it probable neede. // What more commands hee	AW 2.4.52 (184)

Addition of Vowel

1. Before r

Intelligent of our State. What hath bin seene	L 3.1.25 (92)
For our best Act: if we shall stand still	H8 1.2.85 (95)
And not endure all threats? Sleepe upon't	TmA 3.5.43 (89)
And the desire of the Nobles	C 2.1.255 (101)
Good, good, my Lord, the secrets of nature	TC 4.2.74 (106)

2. In an inflectional ending

And that the Queenes Kindred are made gentle Folkes	R3 1.1.95 (104)
Partly for that her promis'd proportions	MM 5.1.219 (56)

Substitution of Alternate Variant

She was often cyted by them, but appear'd not	H8 4.1.29 (156)
Powres into Captaines wounds? Banishment	TmA 3.5.111 (90)
In you, which I account his beyond all Talents	Cy 1.6.80 (48)

Thus all of these lines can easily be regularized if we simply recognize that Elizabethan pronunciation and orthography in some ways differed from our own, and that printers' errors could and did occur. Even the

three cases listed at the end could very well have resulted from the mis-
takes of a copyist or compositor. (Unfortunately, but perhaps signifi-
cantly, we have no quarto for H8, TmA, and Cy.) It is interesting, also,
that of the eight plays showing the greatest amount of possibly irregular
usage, five (H8, TmA, C, AC, MM) have no quarto, two (2H6, 3H6) exist
only in "bad" quartos, and only one (LLL) has what may be called a "good"
quarto. The implication is that if good quartos existed for all of these
plays, variant readings might provide evidence pointing to corruption in
the F text.

However, the evidence that we do have clearly shows that, at least
in the lines investigated in this study, Shakespeare chose particular
word-forms with metrics in mind. These 12,814 lines make up more than
one-sixth of his total output of 74,817 lines of dramatic verse. And,
since there would have been no motive for his failing to follow the same
metrical principles in the remainder of his verse, it seems certain that
Shakespeare was deliberately and carefully writing iambic verse in his
works as a whole.

Meter and style

In this study, after making every effort to hold stylistic connotations constant, I have found that the metrically preferable variant was
chosen in over 99.5% of the lines. Therefore it is obvious that in these
cases meter was the major determinant of word choice, and probably the
only determinant. Another interesting finding was that none of the variants which would be expected to have the strongest stylistic connotations
--the neologistic variants--were used except in strict accord with the demands of the meter.[2]

But it is impossible to make sweeping pronouncements as to which factor, meter or style,[3] was uppermost in Shakespeare's mind as he wrote, for the role of style cannot be assessed by means of an objective statistical survey. We could, of course, choose variants of identical syllabic value but differing connotations, such as <u>Richard</u> and <u>Dicky</u>, and then examine them in context to see in what per cent of the cases they were used "correctly." But I cannot imagine that anyone would often presume to decide "against" Shakespeare in these matters, since, after all, there would always be the possibility that he had <u>intended</u> an incongruity. And there would surely be many neutral contexts in which either of two variants would have been acceptable.

Thus an investigator with a normal amount of admiration for Shakespeare would be likely to find close to 100% stylistic "correctness" in his verse; but this would not have the same significance as my 99.5% figure, for it would be based primarily on doubtful cases which could have been decided either way. And the fact that, as Evelyn Scholl points out on p. 425, some lines do have extra syllables "which cannot be reduced even by . . . tortuous methods" is also inconclusive, since we cannot know whether or not textual corruption has occurred in these instances. It is necessary, then, to abandon the thought of a thorough, impartial, scientific comparison. We must content ourselves with remarking that both stylistic and metrical suitability appear to have been important to Shakespeare, and that in the works of a man of his genius it is hardly possible to separate the two.

<u>Stylistic implications</u>

Once the importance of meter in Shakespeare's verse has been established, however, it becomes possible to make certain generalizations about the situations in which style is likely to have determined word-choice. Just as our most reliable examples of purely "stylistic" inversion are in lines which would have been rhythmically acceptable in a noninverted form, so also our best examples of purely "stylistic" word choice are in those lines which would have been <u>metrically</u> acceptable whichever variant had been used.

A frequent location of such stylistic variants is at the beginning of the line, where one variant would create a permissible headless line and the other would not. An example in an inverted foot is the single occurrence of <u>Dicky</u>, used in 3H6 1.4.76 to refer to Richard, Duke of Gloucester (later Richard III), who elsewhere in the play is called <u>Dick</u> or <u>Richard</u>. Queen Margaret is here taunting the defeated York with the absence of his son, and the diminutive, ordinarily affectionate, carries the full weight of her contempt:

> And where's that valiant Crook-back Prodigie,
>
> <u>Dickie</u>, your Boy, that with his grumbling voyce
>
> Was wont to cheare his Dad in Mutinies?

Though <u>Dick</u> also may have slightly derogatory overtones in the one line in which it occurs, 3H6 5.5.35 ("Lascivious Edward, and thou perjur'd George, / And thou mis-shapen <u>Dicke</u>, I tell ye all"), the effect is not nearly so marked as that produced by <u>Dicky</u> when applied to a youth old enough to participate in a battle.[4]

Since certain caesural irregularities were also allowed, a variant placed in the caesura might also have a synonym which would have been equally acceptable metrically. Such is the case with <u>prick</u> in AYLI 3.2.118

(at one level = <u>prickle</u> 'the thorn of a rose,' used in VA 574):

> He that sweetest rose will finde,
>
> Must finde Loves <u>pricke</u>, & Rosalinde.

Here <u>prickle</u> would have been possible in the caesura, but <u>prick</u> was chosen to supply a bawdy quibble. This is a case in which stylistic variation, by introducing an ambiguity, shades into an actual lexical distinction between words.

Finally, variants placed at the end of the line frequently could have been replaced by syllabic variants with no metrical change other than addition or loss of a feminine ending. A most interesting case is the lone occurrence of <u>Enobarbe</u> (for <u>Enobarbus</u>) in AC 2.7.129. Caesar, commenting on the effects of wine-drinking, also incidentally explains the presence of this variant:

> . . . Strong <u>Enobarbe</u>
>
> Is weaker then the Wine, and mine owne tongue
>
> Spleet's what it speakes: the wilde disguise hath almost
>
> Antickt us all.

For an example of a more serious physical disability similarly affecting speech, see Mardian's description of Cleopatra's supposed death in AC 4.14.29-34.

In other instances, such as <u>Duff</u>, <u>Dansker</u>, *<u>an-hungry</u>, and *<u>carlot</u> discussed in Chapter I, the style-oriented critic can point out that by a relatively minor change in the line, the more "usual" variant would have been metrically possible:

> Deare <u>Duff</u>, I prythee contradict thy selfe   M 2.3.94

<u>Macduff</u>, I prythee contradict thy selfe

Enquire me first what <u>Danskers</u> are in Paris   H 2.1.7

Enquire me first what <u>Danes</u> <u>there</u> are in Paris

They said they were <u>an</u> <u>hungry</u>, sigh'd forth Proverbes C 1.1.209

They said <u>that</u> they were <u>hungry</u>, sigh'd forth Proverbes

That the old <u>Carlot</u> once was master of   AYLI 3.5.108

That the old <u>Carl</u> <u>before</u> was master of.

A similar case could be made for *<u>repasture</u> 'food' in LLL 4.1.95 as a
stylistic variant pedantically conflating <u>repast</u> and <u>pasture</u>. Armado,
representing himself as a lion, advises Jaquenetta to submit to him:

But if thou strive (poore soule) what art thou then?

Foode for his rage, <u>repasture</u> for his den.

Here, the neologism was apparently used so as to emphasize the pompous,
affected quality of the "sonnet," for <u>pasture</u>, preceded by <u>and</u>, would
have been equally possible both metrically and lexically--it is found
elsewhere in the plays and meant 'animal food' in Shakespeare's time.

Even when no such minor alterations can be made, the critic who feels
a certain word-form as stylistically determined can appeal to the commun-
ity of taste for support. But the fact remains that style studies involving variant forms will be most convincing if, and only if, they make
an allowance for the fact that metrics and not stylistics may have been
the determining factor.

Phonological implications

When we see that Shakespeare was adhering to an iambic prosody, important phonological implications also become clear. As explained previously, up to this point I have excluded phonological material from my discussion as much as possible, in order to avoid circularity of reasoning. However, the fact that Shakespeare _was_ concerned about metrical regularity enables us to form hypotheses about the ways in which words must have been pronounced.

On p. 178, one line is listed that has not been previously mentioned. This is AW 2.4.52,

May make it probable neede. // What more commands hee,

in which _probable_ creates a trisyllabic foot if pronounced as printed. But the very existence of a disyllabic variant *_probal_ 'such as to approve itself to the mind, worthy of acceptance' in O 2.3.344,

When this advise is free I give, and honest,

Proball to thinking, and indeed the course

To win the Moore againe,

a nonce-word according to OED,[5] strongly suggests that _probable_ had a variant pronunciation _probble_. The process involved would have been the special form of syncope called haplology, or the elimination of an unstressed vowel (in this case, _a_) between two identical or phonetically similar consonants. Such a haplologized form would be paralleled by the form _probbly_ (= _probably_) commonly heard in rapid speech today.[6]

In addition, there are parallels elsewhere in the plays themselves. I have discussed on p. 142 one interesting form (_Princes_) which may show

haplology. And many other examples are to be found, some involving haplology at work even between words. Shakespeare has, for instance, "And put
upon him such a deale of Man, / That (= That it) worthied him, got praises
of the King" (L 2.2.128) and "Alacke there lies more perill in thine eye, /
Then (= Than in) twenty of their Swords" (RJ 2.2.72). Another interesting
case is the alternation between the short form ignomy and the full form
ignominy throughout the quartos and folios (though ignomy is almost always
metrically preferable), indicating that the spelling ignominy could have
concealed a trisyllabic variant pronunciation. The lines involved are:

Thy ignomy sleepe with thee in the grave   1H4 5.4.100

    (Q1-3, 8 and F3-4 ignominy)

Ignomie in ransome, and free pardon   MM 2.4.111

    (F2-4 ignominy; no quarto)

Hence broker, lackie, ignomy, and shame   TC 5.10.33

    (F3-4 ignominy; Q ignomyny with omission of and)

I blush to thinke upon this ignominie   TA 4.2.115

    (Qq ignomy)

If ignominy was indeed pronounced ignomy in colloquial usage, by loss of
medial i and subsequent reduction of the consonant group mn to m,[7] this
would furnish a further parallel for probable pronounced as probble.

Lexical implications

Shakespeare's adherence to an iambic prosody has, in addition, important lexical significance. Since he was attempting to write regular

iambic lines, it is likely that he made a much wider use of form-shortening for meter than has previously been supposed, and that some forms
which have not yet been satisfactorily explained may really be shortened
variants of well-established words. Such form-shortening may be by apocope (I would classify *cowed and nave in M 1.2.22 here), by syncope, by
aphesis, or by a process of compression in which two words of different
meaning are combined into one.

As Dr. Johnson so well observed in his Preface to Shakespeare, "conjecture has all the joy and all the pride of invention," and perhaps I
will be pardoned if I here mention a few interpretations of words which
OED defines erroneously, in my opinion, or not at all. Thus, for example,
I suggest that Shakespeare's nonce-word *unsisting in MM 4.2.92 (F4 in-
sisting),

. . . That spirit's possest with hast,
That wounds th'unsisting Posterne with these strokes,

not defined by OED, is a derivative formed on an aphetic verb sist. It
stands, I think, for unassisting rather than for unresisting, as con-
jectured by Yale Ed.; I base this interpretation partly on considerations
of sense (the door is "resisting" entry, and not "assisting" by opening)
and partly on the evidence provided by several Shakespearean parallels in
which a prefix has been added to a word whose initial vowel sound has
been lost.

These forms include the nonce-word *unsured in J 2.1.471 'unassured,'
also not defined by OED: "For by this knot, thou shalt so surely tye /
Thy now unsur d assurance to the Crowne" (F2-4 unsur'd). Sured was an
aphetic form of assured in Shakespeare's time. Also there is *unbated

in MV 2.6.11, etc., meaning 'unabated'; <u>bated</u> is first recorded in 1596,
in Shakespeare, and the aphetic verb <u>bate</u> from ca. 1300. In addition, F
has *<u>relume</u> in O 5.2.13 (Q <u>returne</u>; Q2-3 *<u>relumine</u>), which was probably .
formed from <u>re-</u> + <u>illume</u> with loss of the <u>i</u> vowel by synaeresis, or perhaps even from <u>re-</u> + an unrecorded verb <u>lume</u>.[8]

In contrast, I have been unable to find any Shakespearean derivative
formed on a variant showing aphetic loss of <u>re-</u>, or indeed any other prefix with an initial consonant. And in fact, with the exception of
Kökeritz' conjecture *<u>cital</u> = <u>recital</u> mentioned above on p. 169, note 21,
there do not seem to be any variants at all showing aphetic loss of <u>re-</u>,
whereas there are many in which an initial <u>a-</u> vowel was dropped (e.g.
<u>greed</u>, <u>nointed</u>, <u>pothecary</u>, <u>sayed</u>, <u>stonished</u>, <u>surance</u>). Therefore I feel
that *<u>unsisting</u> was probably formed on an unrecorded aphetic verb <u>sist</u> =
<u>assist</u>;[9] a parallel would be the aphetic form <u>sistence</u> = <u>assistance</u> for
which OED gives a 1513 citation. But whether *<u>unsisting</u> stands for
<u>unassisting</u> or for <u>unresisting</u>, it is a compressed form metrically neces-
sary for an iambic pentameter line.

Meter was probably also an important factor in formations such as
<u>intrinsicate</u>, discussed above on p. 173, in which two words were conflated.
Though Shakespeare did not himself introduce <u>intrinsicate</u> into the language, he does have other portmanteau words of this type which he apparently either created or first used as compressed forms. For example,
scholars have long recognized that the nonce-word *<u>uprighteously</u>, used by
the Duke in MM 3.1.205, conflates <u>uprightly</u> and <u>righteously</u>; and that
Mrs. Quickly's <u>bastardly</u> in 2H4 2.1.55 ("thou <u>bastardly</u> rogue") is a mal-
apropism combining the senses of <u>bastard</u> and <u>dastardly</u>. Similarly,
Armado's unique <u>annothanize</u> in LLL 4.1.69 (F2-4 <u>anatomize</u>), "<u>Veni</u>, <u>vidi</u>,

vici: Which to <u>annothanize</u> in the vulgar . . . He came, See, and over-
came," is probably a pedantically erroneous form combining two verbs.
These are <u>annote</u>, a morphological variant of <u>annotate</u>, and <u>anatomize</u> 'to
analyze,' usually spelled <u>anathomize</u> in the old editions of Shakespeare.[10]

But all of these words are in prose. I suggest that, in verse also,
Shakespeare used such forms, and that there they allowed the compression
of much meaning into a form adaptable to the iambic pentameter line. For
example, <u>birth</u> and <u>kingdom</u> seem to have been conflated in the nonce-word
*<u>birthdom</u>, used in M 4.3.4 by Macduff to describe his homeland, the king-
dom in which he was born:

> . . . Let us rather
> Hold fast the mortall Sword: and like good men,
> Bestride our downfall <u>Birthdome</u>: each new Morne,
> New Widdowes howle, new Orphans cry.

(<u>Downfall</u> = <u>downfall'n</u>.) *<u>Birthdom</u> is defined by OED (and Dr. Johnson) as
meaning simply 'birthright,' but virtually all formations in -<u>dom</u> mean
either 'the condition of being [what is denoted by an adj.]' (<u>freedom</u>,
<u>wisdom</u>) or 'the domain of [a person denoted by a noun]' (<u>dukedom</u>, <u>kingdom</u>).
Thus *<u>birthdom</u> is an unusual formation on a nonpersonal noun;[11] and in my
opinion it supplies the place of an awkward and unmetrical circumlocution
such as <u>kingdom</u> <u>of</u> <u>birth</u>.

A parallel case found in Shakespeare is <u>christendom</u>, combining the
senses of the verb <u>christen</u> 'to give a name to at baptism' and the noun
<u>kingdom</u>. In AW 1.1.188, Helena refers to the nicknames affectionately be-
stowed on mistresses by their lovers as

> . . . a world
>
> Of pretty fond adoptious <u>christendomes</u>
>
> That blinking Cupid gossips.

New Arden Ed., following Schmidt, defines <u>christendoms</u> as 'Christian
names'; OED glosses as 'the giving of a name' (a nonce-use). But although
the "world of . . . " metaphor was dead long before Shakespeare's time, I
feel that it was here resuscitated for the occasion, and that the passage
is enriched by interpreting <u>christendoms</u> as including the sense 'kingdoms.'

Conclusions

All of these compressed forms, together with words arising by functional shift such as *<u>impose</u> (from the verb) = <u>imposition</u>, served as a
verbal shorthand for Shakespeare. It is my conviction that almost all of
his neologisms involving form-shortening were inspired, at least in part,
by metrical considerations. Not only did they permit compactness of expression, but also, in some cases, they replaced cumbersome polysyllables
not easily adaptable to the rhythmic requirements of the verse.

In addition, many other types of allegedly "stylistic" innovation
may in fact have originated in Shakespeare's wish to maintain the iambic
pattern. For illustration, we may look at two of the numerous lines cited
by Schmidt (pp. 1422-23) to exemplify the poet's extensive use of a rhetorical device known as <u>abstractum</u> <u>pro</u> <u>concreto</u>, the abstract for the
concrete. In C 4.6.53, <u>Information</u> is found meaning 'informant':

> But reason with the fellow
>
> Before you punish him, where he heard this,
>
> Least you shall chance to whip your <u>Information</u>,

And beate the Messenger, who bids beware

Of what is to be dreaded.

Elsewhere, Shakespeare has informer to express this sense (e.g. in VA 655), but had it been used here as a morphological as well as syntactical parallel for Messenger, an anapestic foot would have been created.

Similarly, in H 3.4.49, solidity is parallel neither to compound (being a noun) nor to masse (being an abstraction), but it is metrically exact where solid or solid thing would have been defective:

Heavens face doth glow,

Yea this solidity and compound masse,

With tristfull visage as against the doome,

Is thought-sicke at the act.

OED cites this line as the first occurrence of solidity in the concrete sense of 'a solid thing or body'; Shakespeare has the adj. solid several times in like contexts, e.g. in TC 1.3.113, "And make a soppe of all this solid Globe." It seems logical to conclude that a characteristic stylistic device may have become characteristic because of the poet's concern for metrical precision.

Anyone who has ever attempted to write in verse knows that there are at least three elements vying for dominance: the metrical framework, the ideas to be expressed, and semantic and morphological features of the language itself. Each of these carries with it certain possibilities and certain limitations, and when one element is in conflict with another, the poet takes liberties with the one which seems most flexible to him. For Shakespeare, writing at a time when linguistic categories, meanings, and forms were not fixed by lexicographers and grammarians as they are today, language seems to have been the element most frequently modified.

The briefest of glances through OED reveals how readily he assigned new

senses and functions to existing words (many of which, like solidity

'solid thing' discussed above, were adopted by other writers), thus man-

aging to preserve metrical regularity without--as far as we can perceive--

weakening the ideas expressed.

Although, as pointed out in Chapter I, all poets of the period

adapted their vocabulary to meter, only Shakespeare did it in such a

fascinating way. And he did it by his bolder, more extensive linguistic

innovations, particularly those which involve compression or ellipsis and

are therefore quite obvious to the reader. The more apparent the fact

that a poet has had to modify his language to accommodate the meter, the

more aware we become of the tension existing between meter and ideas, and

the more "poetic" (in either a good or a bad sense) his vocabulary seems.

When, as in Shakespeare's case, the innovations are unusual as well as

numerous, when they capture a complex thought in a brief, memorable word

or phrase, an extraordinary effect of intensity is produced.

Let me illustrate with several words which, according to the evidence

assembled in OED, seem to have been created by Shakespeare. All show eco-

nomical yet imaginative use of a familiar prefix or suffix. First, there

is a large group with the un- prefix expressing reversal of the action of

the root verb. Shakespeare has *unbless in the poems meaning 'to retract

a blessing,' *uncurse R2 3.2.137 'to free from curses uttered' ("Againe

uncurse their Soules"), and *unshout C 5.5.4 'to undo what has been done

by shouting.' A similar formation, but with an adjectival root, is *un-

deaf R2 2.1.16 'to free from deafness' ("My deaths sad tale, may yet un-

deafe his eare"); and Shakespeare also uses the p.p. *unwitted, based

on the noun <u>wit</u>, in O 2.3.182 to mean 'deprived of understanding' ("As
if some Planet had <u>unwitted</u> men"). A formation of an entirely different
type is <u>Moorship</u> in O 1.1.33, a title given to Othello by Iago humorous-
ly, contemptuously, or both: "And I . . . his <u>Mooreships</u> Auntient." The
meaning of <u>his</u> <u>Mooreships</u>, expressed in five syllables, is 'his lordship
the Moor's,' and yet this bulky, unmetrical circumlocution does not begin to convey the wry subtlety of Shakespeare's phrase.

It is apparent from this, and from my other definitions as well,
that in all of these cases a startling amount of meaning has been compressed into an extremely small space in the line. One pictures the poet
writing hastily, barely pausing to consider before adding a prefix or
suffix to an existing form. And yet, despite his disregard for tradi-
tional grammatical categories and delight in unorthodox verbal shortcuts,
Shakespeare does not produce an effect of bizarre eccentricity. Somehow
he manages to make the constraints and deviations from the prosaic im-
posed by meter actually enhance the power and grace of his verse. Metrical regularity, then, is only one part of the greatness of Shakespeare's
poetry, but an essential part, and perhaps even responsible for some of
the qualities most often admired in his style.

Conjectures such as these, like the lexical interpretations tentatively set forth above, cannot be confirmed by statistics. Though critical judgments are "scientific" in the sense that they are based on cal-
culated probabilities, the probabilities may not seem identical to every
reader. But even if we set all of the peripheral hypotheses aside, the
large body of evidence collected in this study remains. And it demon-
strates, beyond reasonable doubt, not only that Shakespeare chose or
created syllabic variants with meter in mind, but also that stylistic,

phonological, and sometimes even lexical characteristics of his verse

must be considered in reference to a basic iambic framework.

APPENDIX

Neologisms and their

Non-Neologistic Synonyms

in Shakespeare's Plays

195

Table I. Distribution of Neologisms and their Non-Neologistic Synonyms

(by play)

Expected Order of Incidence[a]		Actual Order of Incidence[b]			
		Neologisms		Non-Neologisms	
R3	4.7%	TC	6.3%	R3	5.9%
3H6	3.9	H	5.9	C	4.9
AC	3.7	O	5.9	H	4.6
O	3.7	H5	5.9	O	4.4
1H6	3.6	L	5.4	3H6	4.3
Cy	3.6	R3	4.5	TC	4.0
2H6	3.6	1H6	4.5	R2	3.9
R2	3.5	R2	3.6	H5	3.7
H8	3.5	M	3.6	1H6	3.7
RJ	3.5	2H6	3.6	M	3.4
H	3.4	J	3.2	J	3.4
C	3.4	TG	3.2	RJ	3.4
J	3.4	Cy	3.2	2H6	3.3
TA	3.3	MND	3.2	WT	3.1
L	3.1	T	3.2	MM	3.1
TC	3.0	1H4	3.2	TA	3.0
JC	3.0	RJ	2.7	L	2.9
TS	2.9	C	2.3	AC	2.9
MV	2.7	3H6	2.3	2H4	2.9
WT	2.4	WT	2.3	TmA	2.7
H5	2.4	TS	2.3	TG	2.4

TmA	2.3		MV	2.3		Cy	2.3
1H4	2.3		JC	2.3		H8	2.3
M	2.3		MM	1.8		LLL	2.2
P	2.2		H8	1.8		MND	1.9
MM	2.2		LLL	1.8		TS	1.7
TG	2.2		P	1.8		P	1.7
MND	2.2		TA	1.4		AW	1.7
LLL	2.2		AC	1.4		T	1.6
CE	2.0		AYLI	1.4		CE	1.6
AW	2.0		2H4	0.9		1H4	1.3
2H4	2.0		TmA	0.9		TN	1.3
T	2.0		AW	0.9		MV	1.1
AYLI	1.3		CE	0.5		AYLI	1.1
TN	1.2		TN	0.5		JC	1.0
MA	0.9		MW	–		MW	0.9
MW	0.4		MA	–		MA	0.4
	———			———			———
	100.0%			100.0%			100.0%

a. Based on each play's percentage of the total number of verse lines in Shakespeare's plays; the original figures were obtained from a table in Craig, Works, p. 38.

b. Based on each play's percentage of the total number of neologistic variants and non-neologistic synonyms.

Table II. Distribution of Neologisms and their Non-Neologistic Synonyms

(by character)[a]

	Neologisms		Non-Neologisms
HENRY V	2.3%	HENRY V	1.9%
MACBETH	2.3	HAMLET	1.7
TROILUS	2.3	MACBETH	1.3
RICHARD III	2.3	CORIOLANUS	1.3
IAGO	1.8	FRIAR LAURENCE	1.3
RICHARD II	1.8	Titus	1.3
Ulysses	1.8	TROILUS	1.1
BASTARD in J	1.4	RICHARD III	1.1
PROTEUS	1.4	IAGO	1.1
HECTOR	1.4	OTHELLO	1.1
Exeter in H5	1.4	Isabella in MM	1.1
Cassio in O	1.4	Leontes	1.0
Edmund in L	1.4	BASTARD in J	0.9
HAMLET	0.9	Claudius in H	0.9
CORIOLANUS	0.9	Duke in MM	0.9
FRIAR LAURENCE	0.9	Cominius in C	0.9
OTHELLO	0.9	Antony in AC	0.9
BUCKINGHAM in R3	0.9	RICHARD II	0.7
LEAR	0.9	BUCKINGHAM in R3	0.7
LAERTES	0.9	Caesar in AC	0.7
BIRON	0.9	Adriana in CE	0.7
Player King in H	0.9	Aufidius in C	0.7

Buckingham in H8	0.9	PROTEUS	0.6
Chatillon in J	0.9	HECTOR	0.6
Duke in TG	0.9	LEAR	0.6
Gratiano in MV	0.9	LAERTES	0.6
Henry IV in 1H4	0.9	BIRON	0.6
Kent in L	0.9	Alcibiades in TmA	0.6
Mariana in MM	0.9	Camillo in WT	0.6
Timon	0.9	Helena in AW	0.6
Ariel	0.9	Prince Hal in 2H4	0.6
Prospero	0.9	Lady Macbeth	0.6
Florizel	0.9	Petruchio	0.6
Iachimo	0.9	Polonius	0.6
Pistol	0.9	Paulina in WT	0.6
Cassius in JC	0.9	Tranio in TS	0.6
Brutus in JC	0.9	Sicinius in C	0.6
Lucy in 1H6	0.9	King Philip in J	0.6
Burgundy in 1H6	0.9	Queen Elizabeth in R3	0.6
Captain in 2H6	0.9	Talbot in 1H6	0.6
Gloucester in 2H6	0.9	York in 2H6	0.6
Clifford in 3H6	0.9	Henry VI in 3H6	0.6
Chorus in H5	0.9	Julia in TG	0.6

a. Based on each character's percentage of the total number of neologistic variants and non-neologistic synonyms; only those with more than 0.5% are included. Names found on both lists are capitalized.

Table III. Variants Included in the Tabulation

*aboded - boded

*abrook - brook

*accuse - accusation

*across - cross

*acting - act

*admirable - mirable

*aidance - aid

*alarum-bell - larum-bell

*amazement - amazedness

*ambuscado - ambush

*arouse - rouse

*attest - test, testimony

*attorneyship - attorney

*awakening - awaking, waking

*bedabbled - dabbled

*belocked - locked

*bemadding - madding

*bemet - met

*bemete - mete

*bemock - mock

*bemocked - mocked

*bescreened - screened

*besmirch - smirch

*bethumped - thumped

*betrim - trim

*blastment - blast

*brisky - brisk

*childness - childishness

*climature - climate, clime

*co-mart - mart

*co-mingled - mingled

*commixture - mixture

*composture - compost

*confixed - fixed

*conjointly - jointly

*control - controlment

*converse - conversation

*countless - uncounted

*cowed - cowarded

*crimeful - criminal

*critical - critic

*dauntless - undaunted

*deafened - deafed

*deceptious - deceitful, deceivable

*design - designment

*dispose - disposition

*dowered - endowed

*duteous - dutiful

*effuse - effusion

*embounded - bounded

*embrace - embracement

*enacture - enact

*enclog - clog

*enfettered - fettered

*enguard - guard

*enhearsed - hearsed

*enrapt - rapt

*ensnared - snared

*ensteeped - steeped

*entame - tame

*figo - fig

*fount - fountain

*futurity - future

*guardage - guard

*guardant - guard, guardian

*howl - howling

*illume - illuminate

*immure - mure

*impaint - paint

*impawn - pawn

*impawned - pawned

*import - importance, importancy

*impose - imposition

*impressed - pressed

*impressure - impression, pressure

*inclip - clip

*inexecrable - execrable

*inshipped - shipped

*interchangement - interchange

*interjoin - join

*intrince - intrinsicate

*investments - vestments

*iterance - iteration

*lament - lamentation, lamenting

*las - alas

*leagued - colleagued

*lesser - less

*lunes - lunacies

*majestic - majestical

*mechanical - mechanic

*midst - amid, amidst

*music, *musicked - musical

*neglect, *neglection - negligence

*operant - operative

*ostent - ostentation

*pageantry - pageants

*plantage - plants

*probal - probable

*profitless - unprofitable

*prophet-like - prophetically

*questioning - question

*rebel-like - rebel(ling, rebellious

*reinforced - forced

*remarked - marked

*retirement - retire

*revengive - re)vengeful, revenging

*roundure - round

*rouse - carouse

*solicit - soliciting

*superflux - superfluity

*tending - attendance, tendance

*unbefitting - unfitting

*unbegot - unbegotten, ungot(ten

*uncomfortable - comfortless

*unhelpful - helpless

*unstringed - stringless

*vasty - vast

*vaultage - vault

*villain-like - villainously

*votarist, *votress - votaress

*worthless - unworthy

LIST OF WORKS CONSULTED

In addition to the works listed below, the following standard editions of Shakespeare have been consulted:

A New Variorum Edition, Horace H. Furness and others, eds., 26 vols. Philadelphia and London, 1871- . (Var. Ed.)

The Arden Edition, W[illiam] J. Craig and R[obert]H. Case, general eds., 39 vols. London, 1899-1924. (Arden Ed.)

The [New] Arden Edition, Una Ellis-Fermor, Harold F. Brooks, and Harold Jenkins, general eds., 26 vols. London, 1951- . (New Arden Ed.)

The New Cambridge Edition, Sir Arthur T. Quiller-Couch and John Dover Wilson, eds., 37 vols. Cambridge, England, 1921-62. (Cambridge Ed.)

The [Revised] Yale Shakespeare, Charles T. Prouty and Helge Kökeritz, general eds., 11 vols. New Haven, 1954- . (Yale Ed.)

Abbreviated titles have been used in references to these editions, as indicated in parentheses above. Other books and articles have been cited, in references following the first, by giving only the author's or editor's name plus the relevant page number; if there are two or more works by the same author, the name is followed by a short title which will be found below in parentheses after the work in question.

Abbott, E[dwin] A., A Shakespearian Grammar, 2d ed. London, 1891.

Bartlett, John, A New and Complete Concordance or Verbal Index to Words, Phrases, & Passages in the Dramatic Works of Shakespeare, with a Supplementary Concordance to the Poems, London, 1927.

Bronson, Bertrand H., ed., Samuel Johnson, New York, 1960.

Browne, George H., Notes on Shakspere's Versification, Boston, 1884.

Butler, James Davie, The Once Used Words in Shakespeare, New York, 1886.

Craig, Hardin, ed., The Complete Works of Shakespeare, Chicago, 1951. (Works

———————— "Shakespeare's Bad Poetry," Shakespeare Survey, 1 (1948), 51-56.

Danielsson, Bror, Studies on the Accentuation of Polysyllabic Latin, Greek, and Romance Loan-Words in English, Stockholm, 1948.

Ekwall, Eilert, Shakspere's Vocabulary: its Etymological Elements, Uppsala, 1903.

Evans, B. Ifor, The Language of Shakespeare's Plays, London, 1952.

Franz, Wilhelm, Die Sprache Shakespeares in Vers und Prosa, 4th ed. Halle, 1939.

Gordon, George S., Shakespeare's English (S.P.E. Tract No. XXIX), Oxford, 1928.

Halliday, F[rank] E., The Poetry of Shakespeare's Plays, London, 1954.

Hulme, Hilda M., Explorations in Shakespeare's Language, Aberdeen, 1962.

Jespersen, Otto, Growth and Structure of the English Language, 9th ed.

Garden City, N.Y., n.d.

————— A Modern English Grammar on Historical Principles, VI, London, 1946. (MEG)

————— "Notes on Metre," Linguistica, Copenhagen, 1933, pp. 249-274.

Kökeritz, Helge, "Elizabethan Prosody and Historical Phonology," Annales Academiae Regiae Scientiarum Upsaliensis, 5 (1961), 79-102. ("Elizabethan Prosody")

————— "Shakespeare's Language," Shakespeare: Of an Age and for all Time (The Yale Shakespeare Festival Lectures), ed. Charles T. Prouty, Hamden, Conn., 1954, pp. 35-51. ("Shakespeare's Language")

————— Shakespeare's Names: A Pronouncing Dictionary (Yale Shakespeare Supplements), New Haven, 1959.

————— Shakespeare's Pronunciation, New Haven, 1960. (Shakespeare's Pronunciation)

König, Goswin, Der Vers in Shaksperes Dramen, Strassburg, 1889.

Koziol, Herbert, Handbuch der englischen Wortbildungslehre, Heidelberg, 1937.

McClure, Norman E., ed., Sixteenth-Century English Poetry, New York, 1954.

Marchand, Hans, The Categories and Types of Present-Day English Word-Formation, Wiesbaden, 1960.

Munro, John, ed., The London Shakespeare, 6 vols. New York, 1957.

Nearing, Homer, Jr., "Shakespeare as a Nondramatic Poet: Sonnet XXIX," Shakespeare Quarterly, 13 (1962), 15-20.

The Oxford English Dictionary, 13 vols. Oxford, 1933.

Partridge, A[stley] C., Orthography in Shakespeare and Elizabethan Drama, Lincoln, Nebr., 1964.

Pauli, Reinhold, ed., Confessio Amantis of John Gower, Vol. III, London, 1857.

Ransom, John Crowe, "On Shakespeare's Language," The Modern Critical Spectrum, ed. Gerald J. Goldberg and Nancy M. Goldberg, Englewood Cliffs, N.J., 1962, pp. 48-57.

Schelling, Felix E., ed., Ben Jonson: Timber or Discoveries Made upon Men and Matter, Boston, 1892.

Schipper, Jakob, A History of English Versification, Oxford, 1910.

Schmidt, Alexander, Shakespeare-Lexicon, 2 vols. 3d ed. Berlin and New York, 1902.

Scholl, Evelyn H., "New Light on Seventeenth Century Pronunciation from the English School of Lutenist Song Writers," P.M.L.A., 59 (1944), 398-445.

Shakespeare as Put Forth in 1623. A Reprint of Mr. William Shakespeares Comedies, Histories, & Tragedies (for Lionel Booth), London, 1864.

Simpson, Percy, Studies in Elizabethan Drama, Oxford, 1955.

Smith, G. Gregory, ed., Elizabethan Critical Essays, 2 vols. London, 1959.

Smith, James C., ed., _Spenser's Faerie Queene_, 2 vols. Oxford, 1909.

Sprott, S. Ernest, _Milton's Art of Prosody_, Oxford, 1953.

Tilley, Morris P., _A Dictionary of the Proverbs in England in the Six-teenth and Seventeenth Centuries_, Ann Arbor, 1950.

Walker, William Sidney, _A Critical Examination of the Text of Shakespeare_, 3 vols. London, 1860.

Wallrath, Hans J., ed., _William Sampson's Vow Breaker_, Louvain, 1914.

Withycombe, E[lizabeth] G., _The Oxford Dictionary of English Christian Names_, 2d ed. Oxford, 1959.

Wright, William Aldis, ed., _The Works of William Shakespeare_ (The Cambridge Shakespeare), 9 vols. London and New York, 1891-95.

NOTES

I. 1. Shakespeare quotations are from the F text unless otherwise
specified. However, the following minor alterations have been made: _u_
has been changed to _v_, _v_ to _u_, and _i_ to _j_ when necessary, in accordance
with modern typography; the final punctuation of lines has sometimes been
omitted or altered; syllabic -_ed_ has been indicated by a grave accent;
names of speaking characters have been expanded; proper names have been
given in roman type; italics have been used for emphasis. Obvious typo-
graphical errors such as _rhe_ for _the_ have been silently corrected. All
line numbers are from the Globe text. Except when two or more variants
are involved, a single line reference has been given for every passage
quoted: the number of the line in which the relevant variant appears.
When referring to variants in the body of my discussion, I adopt the
normative spelling given by OED, except that nouns which are relevant
only in the plural have been referred to in the plural form.

2. We must here, I think, disregard the fact that the play is set
in Denmark.

3. If so, this would account for the absence of other citations in
OED. A modern parallel might be the American use of _Italiano_ as a slang
term for an Italian.

4. Unless otherwise specified, all etymological information of this type has been obtained from OED. I have not thought it necessary to indicate indebtedness in each instance.

5. An opinion also held by Alexander Schmidt; see his Shakespeare-Lexicon, 3d ed. (Berlin and New York, 1902), s.v. A/an, p. 3.

6. Considerations of sense work against Dyce's interpretation of *carlot as the diminutive of carl, quoted by Var. Ed. (p. 208) along with Keightley's conjecture that the word represents the Sp proper name Carloto. The stress difference suggests that Keightley is also in error. Yale Ed. interprets the word as a proper name because it is italicized in F. But F sometimes italicizes common nouns, e.g. in MW 1.3.18 ("a Tapster is a good trade") and 4.6.31 ("a Priest attends"). Cf. MW 1.3.20 ("a fresh Tapster") and 4.6.53 ("you shall not lacke a Priest"), where the same words are not italicized.

7. We know that Macduff, Dane, hungry, and carl were familiar to Shakespeare, and therefore possible alternates, by the fact that they appear elsewhere in the plays--always, it should be noted, in regular iambic lines. It will be observed that Shakespeare could have used these forms and still achieved metrical regularity had he altered the wording slightly, e.g. "Macduff, I prythee contradict thy selfe." The implications of his decision not to do so will be discussed in Chapter VII.

8. "A Straunge Passion of a Lover," ll. 28-30, Sixteenth-Century English Poetry, ed. Norman E. McClure (New York, 1954), p. 138.

9. I use the phrase "lexical meaning" to signify the plain, unadorned dictionary definition of a word: the action, quality, or object to which a word refers. "Stylistic connotations" are the associated overtones which a word may have acquired through long use (or nonuse) in certain contexts. Thus a word may be elevated, colloquial, pedantic, affective, arcane, vulgar, etc.

10. For ease of reference, it has been necessary to use such words as "unmetrical" and "irregular" to describe lines which do not conform to a basic iambic pattern, or variants which disrupt such a pattern. I do not mean to suggest, by this terminology, that I am assuming that Shakespeare's verse was iambic. It would have been equally possible (though extremely awkward) to have regarded all variants used in accordance with an iambic pattern as "irregular," and to have compiled statistics on that basis. But even those who do not accept the idea of a strictly iambic Shakespearean prosody will agree that most of the feet in his verse are disyllabic.

11. S. Ernest Sprott, Milton's Art of Prosody (Oxford, 1953), pp. 38, 142.

12. Orthography in Shakespeare and Elizabethan Drama (Lincoln, Nebr., 1964), pp. 87, 155.

13. The Poetry of Shakespeare's Plays (London, 1954), p. 30.

14. See Helge Kökeritz, Shakespeare's Pronunciation (New Haven, 1960), pp. 274, 289-291--hereafter cited as Shakespeare's Pronunciation.

15. Partridge, pp. 83-84, 95-96. Miss Scholl discusses _patience_ in "New Light on Seventeenth Century Pronunciation from the English School of Lutenist Song Writers," _P.M.L.A._, 59 (1944), 410. Though her findings are not, in my opinion, conclusive, Kökeritz also asserts (_Shakespeare's Pronunciation_, pp. 293-294, 317-318) that _patience_ could be trisyllabic when the verse rhythm required it to be so; [s] may or may not have been assibilated. It will be understood, in connection with the lines scanned in the present study, that the system used does not permit much subtlety, and that only _relative_ stress could be indicated; here, for example, _-ence_ would receive more stress than _-ci-_, but would not be as strongly accented as _pa-_. It has not been feasible (or relevant) to analyze in each case the complex tension between speech accent and underlying metrical pattern that creates what we feel as a characteristically "poetic" effect.

16. George Gordon, _Shakespeare's English_ (Oxford, 1928), p. 275.

17. James Davie Butler, _The Once Used Words in Shakespeare_ (New York, 1886), p. 9.

18. _A Shakespearian Grammar_, 2d ed. (London, 1891), p. 333.

19. Boston, 1884, pp. 6, 16, 18.

20. _A Defence of Ryme_, in _Elizabethan Critical Essays_, ed. G. Gregory Smith (London, 1959), II, 376-377. (In quotations from the theorists, _v_ has been substituted for _u_ and vice versa in accordance with modern typography.)

21. _Certayne Notes of Instruction_ (1575), in Smith, I, 50, 55.

22. The Arte of English Poesie, in Smith, II, 70. (Greek has been transliterated.)

23. Ane schort Treatise conteining some reulis and cautelis to be observit and eschewit in Scottis Poesie (1584), in Smith, I, 213.

24. A Discourse of English Poetrie, in Smith, I, 273.

25. In Smith, II, 318.

26. "On Shakespeare's Language," in The Modern Critical Spectrum, ed. Gerald J. Goldberg and Nancy M. Goldberg (Englewood Cliffs, N.J., 1962), p. 49.

27. Kökeritz discusses this question fully in "Shakespeare's Language," Shakespeare: Of an Age and for all Time, ed. Charles T. Prouty (Hamden, Conn., 1954), pp. 48-50--hereafter cited as "Shakespeare's Language." He notes on p. 49 that although these adjs. probably were originally colloquial formations, greeny (= green) occurs twice in Queen Elizabeth's "Englishing" of Boethius' De Consolatione Philosophiae.

28. The Language of Shakespeare's Plays (London, 1952), p. 118.

29. In a comment on imperseverant in Cy 4.1.15, pp. 281-282, Var. Ed. cites Shakespeare's imbar, impaint, impasted, impawn'd, enpearced, impleached, embay'd, embounded, emmew (actually a misprint for enew, ultimately f. OF en + eau), and empoison and suggests that the prefix in these words is a late manifestation of the in- prefixed to OE and ME adjs. with intensive force (see OED, s.v. In-[4]). But this prefix died out in Middle English, and surely the prefix in the above words is derived from L in-.

30. En- as adding a (possible) locative sense will be discussed in Chapter III.

31. In an oblique way, of course, for the total effect of these words in context is not one of elevation.

32. For purposes of this study, words have been classified as neologisms if they first appear in OED in quotations from Shakespeare. (Also, words not listed by OED except in Shakespeare have been called nonce-words; meanings not listed except in Shakespeare have been called nonce-uses.) Proper names, even if they happen to be included in OED, have not been so classified. It is recognized that OED is not infallible, partly because it is necessarily based on selective reading and Shakespeare happens to be one of our most-studied authors, partly because it is based on written evidence and takes no notice of words which for various reasons may have appeared in speech but not in printed literature. Thus, words which I have marked with an asterisk may have first appeared many years before Shakespeare used them; Kökeritz comments that anyone who works with unprinted documents will almost always be able to antedate OED ("Shakespeare's Language," p. 43). However, it may be assumed that most of these words (and meanings) were at least unusual in Elizabethan English; and in some instances, most probably in the case of nonce-words, Shakespeare may indeed have introduced a new word into the language. I have included this information about a word's neologistic status because the extent of Shakespeare's concern for metrical regularity cannot be properly assessed unless we have some indication, however imperfect, of the words which he may have formed for metrical reasons.

33. I do not mean to suggest that there is never a connection between
a particular type of prefix or suffix and specific stylistic effects.   I
mean only to emphasize that there is no indication of a consistent Shakespearean preference for certain types of derivatives in certain contexts.
The fact that, relatively speaking, there are nearly twice as many neologisms involving negative particles (de-, dis-, in-, un-, -less) in the
tragedies as there are in the comedies does not negate this finding, for
the determining factor here was lexical meaning as much as style.   In any
case, the synonym of a negative word almost always has a negative prefix
or suffix also.

34. When two synonymous variants were both neologistic, or when one
variant occurred only in the poems, both were omitted.   All of the jocular
formations were excluded.

35. Evans states on p. 32 that "there is not present elsewhere the
accumulative effect of flat passages which I Henry VI presents.   So that,
all concessions having been made, one has the sense that the language of
Part I is the least exciting in the plays."   And Schmidt (p. 1472) quotes
Herford's similar reason for rejecting F nourish 'nourisher' in
1H6 1.1.50: " . . . the use of so rare a word would not be in keeping with
the straight forward, incurious style of the author of 1 Hen. VI."

II. 1. In the Hardin Craig edition, The Complete Works of Shakespeare
(Chicago, 1951)--hereafter cited as Works. Craig incorporates a few
variant readings from the quartos and folios, but these changes are always recorded in his notes. The Globe text was used at this preliminary
stage for ease of reference, as Bartlett's Concordance is based on it
and reprints of F do not have full line numbering.

2. The Lionel Booth reprint (London, 1864) was used. F is actually
much more "regular" than the Globe text, for it includes many contracted
forms which were expanded by later editors.

3. Wherever this is clearly the case (e.g. in Mercutio's "Queen
Mab" speech in RJ, printed as verse in Q), I have counted the lines as
verse, recording the change only when citing a particular line.

4. All quotations from the poems and from omitted portions of H and
L are taken from Var. Ed.; all quotations from P are from New Arden Ed.

5. Compounds have been included in my statistics whenever they appear in two forms: one containing a simplex, the other containing the
same simplex modified in syllabic value (e.g. *alarum-bell vs. larum-bell);
the other element of the compound must remain constant. Certain frequent
combinations such as upon (vs. on) have been omitted because the Concordance and Schmidt list only a small percentage of the actual Shakespearean
occurrences.

6. In a few cases, I have interpreted the word "simplex" loosely so
as to be able to include derivational, etymological, morphological, and
analogical variants whose roots actually could not have independent existence in English. For example, simplicity functions as a syllabic variant

of _simpleness_ in Shakespeare, but its root _simplic-_ could not stand alone;
the identity of the roots has been disguised by etymological change. Such
variants are included whenever, as here, the difference in syllabic value
is due to prepositive or postpositive particles (in this case, -_ity_ and
-_ness_). If one were dealing primarily with word-formation rather than
with metrics, it would be necessary to adopt a more rigorously structural
approach such as that recommended by Hans Marchand in _The Categories and
Types of Present-Day English Word-Formation_ (Wiesbaden, 1960), pp. 6-8.

7. OED sometimes states that a form could be either aphetic or a
simplex with a derivational variant, e.g. _bide_, which occurs along with
abide. In such cases I have arbitrarily chosen the aphetic classification.

8. It should be noted that unless we are dealing with a group of
synonyms in which no simplex is present as one of the variants (e.g. _heed-
less_ vs. _unheedy_ and _unheedful_), the prefixes and suffixes discussed will
necessarily be redundant or greatly weakened in meaning. Otherwise the
derivative and simplex would not be synonymous, and hence would have no
place in this study.

9. Except for a few cases in which one of the variants is statistically significant in relation to a third variant (e.g. trisyllabic
mis-shapen vs. disyllabic _shapeless_ as well as _mis-shaped_). A few variants of this type in Group 2 have also been included (e.g. _live_ vs. _living_
as well as _lively_).

10. This was due to the fact that when the OE adverbial -_e_ was lost
in Middle English, -_ly_ began to be felt as the real indicator of adverbial
function, and was increasingly used to create advs. with a more distinc-

tively adverbial appearance. See Otto Jespersen, A Modern English Grammar on Historical Principles, VI (London, 1946), 408--hereafter cited as MEG-- and Wilhelm Franz, Die Sprache Shakespeares in Vers und Prosa, 4th ed. (Halle, 1939), p. 223.

11. "Elizabethan Prosody and Historical Phonology," Annales Academiae Regiae Scientiarum Upsaliensis, 5 (1961), 92, 99-100--hereafter cited as "Elizabethan Prosody."

12. There are a few words in Shakespeare, including *fount, mead, mongst, and morn, which never occur in prose and therefore might be classified as more "poetic" in tone than their synonyms fountain, meadow, amongst/among, and morning. However, since I count only the instances of the latter which do occur in verse, I have not thought it necessary to exclude these variants on stylistic grounds.

13. This may be inferred from the evidence collected by Morris P. Tilley, who in his A Dictionary of the Proverbs in England in the Sixteenth and Seventeenth Centuries (Ann Arbor, 1950), p. 333, has only the form stone walls.

14. Schipper's theories, put forward in A History of English Versification (Oxford, 1910), pp. 210-237, are apparently based on evidence gathered from actual usage. Feminine endings, for example, occur far too frequently in Renaissance poetry for them to have been considered irregular at that time. The comments of the theorists will be summarized later in this section.

15. The doggerel lines in CE and LLL have been excluded, along with the irregularly-stressed lines in songs.

16. Those familiar with the theories advanced by Kökeritz in Shakespeare's Pronunciation will notice that this line could be reduced to ten
syllables by syncopation of the word residence to res'dence. But here
and in Chapters III-VI I have always tried to account for seeming irregularities first by means other than form-shortening or form-expansion
(permissible variation, textual corruption, etc.). This I have done in
order to avoid partial circularity of reasoning. Kökeritz bases his
theories about pronunciation on the evidence provided by puns, phonetic
and inverted spellings, and rhymes--and on the phonological possibilities
of the language--but his hypotheses about individual words are sometimes
dependent on the assumption that Shakespeare was writing iambic verse.
Therefore, if I had accepted his theories as adequately explaining the
presence of certain variants, I would often have been assuming as "given"
precisely what I was trying to prove.

17. The monosyllabic form was colloquial; the disyllabic form, conservative (see Kökeritz, Shakespeare's Pronunciation, pp. 293-294, and
cf. my discussion of Anthonio and patience above, p. 10 f.).

18. See his remarks in Smith, II, 134-135.

19. Ibid., p. 130. Puttenham marks the stresses as reproduced, but
his verbal explanation of the scansion of this line should be quoted to
show how unreliable such statements often are: "Which verse if ye peruse
throughout, ye shall finde him after the first Dactil all Trochaick &
not Iambic, nor of any other foot of two times" (pp. 130-131). It is
obviously unsafe to infer, from such analyses, that Puttenham admitted
dactylic feet everywhere in the line, yet this is what Sprott implies,
p. 47. Furthermore, Puttenham's scansions are very heavily influenced by

"quantitative" thinking; for example, on p. 131 he marks "Full manie" in
the line "Full manie that in presence of thy livelie hed" as a dactylic
foot.

20. Observations in the Art of English Poesie (1602), in Smith, II,
335. It is unfortunate that Campion does not elaborate on the word "sometime." But in all except two of the lines he cites, the extra unaccented
syllable falls in a caesura or at the end of the line. The two exceptions
are highly doubtful since Campion does not specifically say that they contain trisyllabic feet. They are "Call him with numerous accents paisd by
arte" and "Whome misery cannot alter, time devours" (pp. 336-337). In any
case, numerous and misery could easily have been printed as full forms
even though meant to be pronounced as disyllables.

21. Ibid., pp. 336-337.

22. On the other hand, variants have been included when syllabic
identity might not be admitted by every reader; for example, unmerciful
(once trisyllabic) has been discussed along with merciless.

23. It will be observed that in word-pairs such as disyllabic *enthroned and thronèd, syllabic identity coincides with a difference in
stress. All such stress variants have been excluded as, strictly speaking, irrelevant in a study attempting to disprove Shakespeare's free in-
dulgence in trisyllabic or monosyllabic feet. In addition, given the
frequent use of inversion in the line and the shifting nature of accent
in Shakespeare's time, it is often possible that an apparent stress variant may merely be occurring in a trochaic foot or showing Germanic reac-
centuation or variable stress. This possibility becomes remote in poly-

syllables such as <u>diminishing</u>, used instead of <u>diminution</u> in CE 2.2.130,

"Without addition or <u>diminishing</u>." (Notice the lack of parallelism with

<u>addition</u>.) However, for consistency all stress variants have been ex-

cluded when the variation was unaccompanied by a difference in syllabic

value.

24. A very few words which occur only at the end of a line have been

counted as statistically significant because the stress precluded the use

of a syllabic variant (no inversion being possible in the fifth foot).

Examples are the nouns *<u>impose</u> (= <u>imposition</u>) and <u>origin</u> (= <u>original</u>), and

several of the <u>en-</u> derivatives such as <u>endanger</u> (= <u>danger</u>).

III. 1. It will be understood that any etymological information of this kind applies only to the prefix or suffix in itself, and not necessarily to the words discussed. Here, for example, I do not mean to imply that prattle had an OE ancestor in -lian. All verbs included in this study are trans. unless otherwise specified.

2. OED defines recollect in the P line as meaning 'to gather' in the lit. sense; if this is correct, the word is a metrical variant of collect 1x H5 4.1.304 instead.

3. Fine is also found once (in H5 1.2.72, Q) meaning 'to refine,' but refine occurs only in the p.p. in Shakespeare.

4. Cf. also in the second sense the p.p. *congreeted (H5 5.2.31), a nonce-word.

5. I regard repast, which occurs 1x R3 4.4.396 (only in Ff) as a misprint for the Qq form orepast (= o'erpast) rather than as a syllabic variant of past 'gone, existing formerly.'

6. See Kökeritz, Shakespeare's Pronunciation, pp. 278-279 for many examples of this type of colloquial syncopation (indicated orthographically) in Shakespeare: sheel, for example, appears in RJ 1.1.215. As Kökeritz points out on p. 284, orthographic inconsistency is to be expected, for "the influence of the conventional spelling, though not so strong as today, tended to interfere with any attempt at a more phonetic rendering." Malone's emendation is certainly correct. (All lines which, like this one, show the slightest possibility of irregular use of a variant have been listed in a table to be found at the beginning of Chapter VII, p. 175 ff.)

7. It is possible, also, that medial v was sometimes lost. See
Shakespeare's Pronunciation, pp. 260, 325, note 3.

8. Letters on Reformed Versifying, &c. (1580), in Smith, I, 120.

9. Although I am convinced that internal truncation was allowable
in iambic lines in Shakespeare's time, I have not regarded it as such in
this study because almost every apparent example can be regularized by
some other means; and because I can find no evidence for its use in the
statements of the Renaissance theorists. But the argument of parallelism with initial truncation is a strong one, especially since the lines
involved always have a very heavily marked caesura. Schipper regards
internal truncation as a permissible variation (p. 210). Still another
possibility, in this particular case, is that the line could be read as
short with an extra unaccented syllable after the caesura. See below,
note 15 on p. 52.

10. Another adjectival pair is *commutual 1x H 3.2.170 and mutual,
if OED's definition of *commutual is accepted, but I feel that the word is
really being used adverbially here: "Hymen did our hands / Unite comutuall,
in most sacred Bands." Note also *corresponsive 1x TC Prol.18 'corre-
spondent,' which cannot be counted because the synonymous responsive occurs only in prose.

11. Shakespeare's Pronunciation, p. 269. On pp. 286-287, Kökeritz
also records the phonetic spellings moity (= moiety) in H 1.1.90, etc.
and ruffin (= ruffian) in 2H4 4.5.125, 2H6 1.1.188 (Q), along with the
Renaissance spellings dimond and vilet given by OED.

12. There are a few other lines which, like this one, involve the

possibly irregular use of a variant in a _being_ construction. They are
TmA 1.1.106 ("And _being_ enfranchized bid him come to me"; _enfranchised_
vs. _franchised_), RJ 1.4.87 ("And _being_ thus frighted, sweares a prayer or
two"; _frighted_ vs. _affrighted_), L 2.4.109 ("When Nature _being_ opprest,
commands the mind"; _oppressed_ vs. _pressed_), and TG 2.6.40 ("But Valentine
being gon, Ile quickely crosse"; _Valentine_ vs. _Valentinus_). Because of
the possibility of an unmarked caesura, none of these uses has been
counted as irregular. As Kökeritz points out, _being_ may have been pronounced as a monosyllable, [biːn]; he records the phonetic spelling _been_
in P 2.3.82 (_Shakespeare's Pronunciation_, p. 269), and see my discussion
of _going_ above. But it is not necessary to assume this in the lines
involved here.

13. The verb _advantage_ is also found meaning 'to benefit, profit,'
but the simplex _vantage_ occurs only in the compound *_double-vantage_ 1x
S 88.12.

14. It has been very difficult to decide how to group the _be-_ (and
_en-_) variants. I have adhered as closely as possible to the classifications suggested by OED's commentary, even when these classifications were
rather perplexing (e.g. _befriend_, _belong_, and _beseem_ placed in the "intensive" group). Thus OED's _Be-_ 4 appears here, under _Direction or Posi-_
tion; _Be-_ 1 and 2 and _En-_[1] 3 under _Intensification_; and _Be-_ 5 and 6 and
_En-_[1] 1 and 2 under _Change of State_.

15. There are several lines resembling this one which may in reality
be short instead of showing irregular use of a variant or internal truncation. They are J 1.1.161 ("Kneele thou downe Philip, but rise more
great"; _rise_ vs. _arise_), TS 3.2.168 ("What said the wench when he rose

againe"; <u>rose</u> vs. <u>arose</u>), TmA 4.3.6 ("The greater scornes the lesser.

Not Nature"; <u>lesser</u> vs. <u>less</u>), R2 1.3.84 ("Mine innocence, and S. George

to thrive"; <u>innocence</u> vs. <u>innocency</u>), TN 1.5.320 ("The Countes man: he

left this Ring behinde him"; <u>count</u> vs. <u>county</u>), AW 3.1.5 ("Upon your

Graces part: blacke and fearefull"; <u>part</u> vs. <u>party</u>), AW 5.3.60 ("Crying,

that's good that's gone: Our rash faults"; <u>fault</u> vs. <u>default</u>), AW 5.3.165

("Come hether Count, do you know these Women"; <u>count</u> vs. <u>county</u>). Uses

of a specific variant in these nine lines have not been counted as ir-

regular. Such lines can be read as tetrameter because an unstressed syl-

lable precedes and/or follows the caesura: lines in which two stressed

syllables enclose the caesura cannot be so shortened.

16. <u>Shakespeare's Pronunciation</u>, pp. 287-288. It is possible that

the <u>u</u> vowel was consonantized to a <u>w</u>-glide instead, or even that the

final vowel was suppressed.

17. Kökeritz cites <u>shee'd</u> in O 1.3.149, Q and <u>she'ld</u> in TG 4.3.3 as

instances in which such a contraction <u>was</u> indicated. See <u>Shakespeare's

Pronunciation</u>, p. 279 and my discussion of the parallel case <u>she will</u> in

P 4.1.99, p. 41.

18. In Group 2, Shakespeare also has the p.ps. <u>bedashed</u> and <u>bedaubed</u>,

but they had to be excluded because their simplexes (in the relevant

senses) do not occur in the p.p. And in Group 3, the p.p. *<u>bedazzled</u>

'overpowered with light' could not be counted because in F, <u>dazzled</u> is

trisyllabic in the relevant occurrence, TG 2.4.210.

19. Cited by Kökeritz in <u>Shakespeare's Pronunciation</u>, pp. 371-372,

along with many cases in which similar syncopations must be inferred from

the scansion.

20. Enclose and close also occur meaning 'to envelop,' but both only in the poems when statistically significant: close followed by the adv. in has been omitted from the count. (Here, and elsewhere in my discussion of en- and in- words, I exclude occurrences of the simplex with adverbial in because Shakespeare does not use en- or in- derivatives with in. This does not necessarily mean that he felt that the derivatives already contained the sense of "in" whereas their variants did not. It was probably a matter of style: enclose in is more obviously redundant than close in. This comment also applies to some of the variants previously discussed. For instance, mingle together and press down were excluded because we cannot be sure that Shakespeare would have said intermingle together or oppress down, both of which seem conspicuously tautological.)

21. New Arden and Yale Ed. retain in, but are thereby forced to change the final punctuation of the line to a dash.

22. Many parallel syncopations are orthographically indicated in the old editions, e.g. boyst'rous 2H4 4.5.192, etc., murd'rous Cy 4.3.328, etc., prosp'rous AC 4.6.6, etc., sland'rous Cy 3.3.52, etc., vap'rous M 3.5.24--all cited by Kökeritz in Shakespeare's Pronunciation, pp. 387-389.

23. Schmidt's interpretation of intend in TG 4.2.103 as = tend 'to have a tendency,' p. 593, seems to me erroneous and therefore I have excluded this pair.

24. Though Kökeritz does not specifically mention credulous, he notes (Shakespeare's Pronunciation, p. 270) that u in the suffix -ule tended to be pronounced [I] or [ə]: thus he feels that the form modell in

H5 2.Prol.16 probably stands for _module_. In addition, he lists on pp.
377-378 such words as _fortunate_, _importunate_, and _unfortunate_ as showing
loss of medial _u_ when metrically necessary. And cf. the Early ModE
phonetic spellings _fortenat_ and _fortun_ recorded by OED.

25. In this section, a few words like *_inshipped_ may show the native
prefix _in_- from the prep. and adv. _in_. But since the two prefixes are
identical in form and sense, I have not attempted to distinguish between
them here; the distinction is historical and of no great significance in
a study of this kind.

26. I have, however, excluded the use of _enclouded_ in AC 5.2.212
("In their thicke breathes, / Ranke of grosse dyet, shall we be _enclowd-
ed_") because the prefix here carries a strong locative sense not provided
by _clouded_. The meaning is 'enveloped _in_ a cloud.'

27. It should be mentioned that Q and F2-4 omit the word _then_, thus
reducing the line to pentameter with an extra unaccented syllable before
the caesura, though not affecting the irregularity in the first foot.

28. Jespersen feels that these verbs in -_en_ were originally exten-
sions of pre-existing _verbs_ derived from adjs. He believes that the -_en_
verbs were subsequently apprehended as belonging to the related adj. instead, particularly when the verbs without -_en_ went out of use. Thus in
post-Shakespearean times we find verbs such as _coarsen_ formed directly
from the adj., where there was never a verb without -_en_ at all (see _MEG_,
p. 352).

IV. 1. Walker has a full discussion of this common confusion (II, 44-50). On p. 48 he cites MND 5.1.16, "And gives to aire nothing, a locall habitation," as an instance in which the sense clearly indicates that the form airie was intended.

2. Compare also *arrivance (Qq only) - *arrivancy (Ff only), both occurring in the fifth foot, meaning 'arrivals'; competence - competency (fifth foot) 'sufficient means of subsistence'; continence - continency (prose) 'self-restraint'; and dependence (fifth foot) - dependency 'the condition of being logically dependent.'

3. OED gives the meaning of resting here as 'resting-place'; if this is correct, the word is a metrical variant of rest in P 2.Gower.26 (rhyme) instead.

4. Kökeritz, citing Luick as authority, says that at least as early as the fifteenth century, a glide had begun to develop between r and a preceding long vowel or diphthong. Therefore -dure, like sower (= sour) in CE 5.1.45, could have been disyllabic when required to be so by the meter (Shakespeare's Pronunciation, pp. 291-292).

5. Shakespeare also has feeding - feed (fifth foot) 'pasturage, pasture land'; jesting (fifth foot, pl.) - jest 'something not meant in earnest'; knowing - know (Ff only, possibly a printer's error; Qq knowing) 'knowledge'; wearing - wear (fifth foot) 'what one wears or should wear'; and weeding (fifth foot) - weeds 'weeds collectively.'

6. See my discussion of -dure above, p. 89, and note 4. No examples of elision before [dʒ] are given in Shakespeare's Pronunciation, but it is at least possible that intelligent lost its medial i instead.

7. Thus also the nonce-word *embrasure in TC 4.4.39, a synonym of *embrace and embracement, had to be excluded because it occurs in the pl.

8. The nonce-word *allayment also occurs meaning 'a mitigation,' but its variant allay is found only in prose in Shakespeare.

9. Compare also a 1387 quotation from John de Trevisa: "There is no fairenesse of body whether it be in state of body as in schap of lengthe and brede, other in meovynge as in song" (OED, s.v. State, I.9; italics mine; orthography modernized). The Latin which he is translating, however, supports OED's assigned meaning of 'bodily form.'

10. Shakespeare's Pronunciation, p. 276. Apparently either the vowel of the pronoun or the vowel of the auxiliary verb could have been elided.

11. Prediction 'prophecy, portent' is also used along with the nonce-word *predict, but only in the fifth foot.

12. Shakespeare also has discomfiture - discomfit (fifth foot) 'disconcertment'; and soilure (fifth foot; a. OF soilleure but assimilated to the -ure form) - soil 'the state of being soiled.'

13. It should be noted that the text is quite corrupt at this point and that F prints several lines following this one as prose which may have been meant to be verse. Thus, most modern editors put I wish no better of the following speech with this line. Such an emendation would not improve the meter, but it would make the superiority of nobility to nobles questionable, for if nobility were substituted, the resulting line would have seven feet.

14. In all of these instances, there is a simple noun (e.g., ease) distinct in form from the adj. (easy) to which -ness is added. But sometimes the root adj. itself is used absolutely to create a noun of identical form. This is the case with several pairs of variants in the plays, such as fairness - fair (e.g. "Where faire is not, praise cannot mend the brow," LLL 4.1.17), darkness - dark ("And that the leane abhorrèd Monster keepes / Thee here in darke to be his Paramour," RJ 5.3.105), goodness ("For Talbot meanes no goodenesse by his Lookes," 1H6 3.2.72) - good, all of which in certain contexts are synonymous. All of the variants of this type that I have found do alternate metrically. However, since synonymity is extremely difficult to demonstrate without listing each line individually, and since in a few cases there seem to have been important stylistic reasons for Shakespeare's choice of variant (for example, glad instead of gladness in P 2.Gower.38 for archaic effect as well as rhyme; white instead of whiteness in O 2.1.134 to make possible a pun on wight), I have not counted these pairs in my statistics.

15. Communicated in private conversation. Mentioning Henslowe's spelling henerie (= Henry) as evidence, Kökeritz cites several cases of the probable insertion of a parasitic [ə] between a consonant and following r (Shakespeare's Pronunciation, p. 292). In a further note (p. 520), he specifically adds secrets in the TC line under discussion to these expanded forms. It should be noted also (though it does not affect the meter) that Q has the amusing variant reading neighbor Pandar for nature, as this raises the possibility of textual corruption elsewhere in the line.

16. Cf. the parallel use of drum as = drummer in AW 5.3.253 (prose), "Hee's a good drumme my Lord, but a naughtie Orator."

17. There is actually another case: the nonce-word *sternage in
H5 3.Prol.18 'sterns collectively,' which could not be included because
stern does not occur in the pl.

18. OED classifies the one occurrence of signal in this sense, in
R3 5.3.21 (Qq only; Ff token) as meaning rather 'token, indication,' but
the two senses overlap in this case.

19. One of the OED citations is from The Troublesome Raigne of John
King of England (1591), Shakespeare's source play for J: "Lordings for-
beare, for time is comming fast, / That deeds may trie what words can not
determine" (italics mine). Shakespeare also has the sg. lording once in
the poems as a synonym of lord: "It was a Lordings daughter, the fairest
one of three," PP 211, a doggerel line.

V.   1. Trisyllabic _enforced_ in RL 668 may also mean 'powerful, charac-terized by force': "Yeeld to my love, if not _inforcèd_ hate, / In steed of loves coy tutch shall rudelie teare thee." But this word has been ex-cluded because of the possibility that it represents the p.p. ('forced, compelled') instead.

2. There is another synonym, _defendant_ in H5 2.4.8, but it is in the fifth foot. Shakespeare has several words showing the _-ible/-ive_ confusion which are not relevant in this study because they lack syllabic variants: for a full discussion, see Kökeritz, "Elizabethan Prosody," p. 94. Hilda Hulme's interesting interpretation of _relative_ in H 2.2.633 as = _relatable--Explorations in Shakespeare's Language_ (Aberdeen, 1962), pp. 30-33--is rendered unlikely by the difference between the stress patterns of the two words.

3. We also find _credible_ and *_credent_ in WT 1.2.142 used synony-mously to mean 'likely, worthy of belief,' but the latter is in the fifth foot where it is not statistically significant.

4. _Virginal_ also occurs 1x 2H6 5.2.52, but following the noun ("Teares _Virginall_"); _virgin_ would not be possible in this position.

5. Compare also the use of _admired_ 'deserving the highest praise' in AC 2.2.121, T 3.1.37 ("_Admir'd_ Miranda") along with _admirable_ in the same meaning; the latter, however, occurs only in prose. And _loathed_ is used as a synonym for _loathly_ and _loathsome_ 'disgusting' (e.g. in O 3.4.62, where Q2 and Ff have _loathed_, Q _lothely_), but this group cannot be counted because _loathed_ is frequently disyllabic. For further exam-ples of _-ed_ derivatives alternating metrically with other adjs., see p.

6. Note that in Falstaff's "If Reasons were as plentie as Black-ber-ries" (1H4 2.4.265, prose), Q has plentifull. Beautiful also occurs 10x along with beauteous 24x, but in TS 1.2.86, beauteous is trisyllabic and therefore this pair lacks statistical significance.

7. I have excluded the use of profitless in MA 5.1.4 ("Which falls into mine eares as profitlesse, / As water in a sive") because I feel that it is adverbial, though OED classifies it as an adj.

8. Though some of these -ed variants resemble forms in -ed :- OE -ede rather than past ppl. adjs., they are all satisfactorily accounted for by senses of the root verb; for example, doubt could mean 'to affect with fear.'

9. Note the juxtaposition of the two words in H5 4.1.168 (prose): ". . . there is no King, be his Cause never so spotlesse, if it come to the arbitrement of Swords, can trye it out with all unspotted Souldiers."

10. OED defines unshapen here as 'imperfectly formed; left rude or rough,' but note that the speaker (Richard III) uses mis-shaped to de-scribe himself in the 3H6 line quoted below; in any case, the two senses tend to overlap.

11. Shakespeare's Pronunciation, pp. 272, 283. (I find in addition b'example = by example in Samuel Daniel's "To the Lady Lucie, Countesse of Bedford," l. 78, quoted in McClure, p. 535.) It is possible, however, that be is merely an extra syllable in an unmarked caesura after Somerset.

12. OED defines <u>unnumbered</u> in the JC line quoted as 'not numbered or reckoned up; uncounted.' But <u>uncounted</u> and <u>unnumbered</u> may actually be formed on -<u>ed</u> :- OE -<u>ede</u> derivatives rather than on the p.p.; note the use of the nouns in such phrases as <u>beyond</u> <u>all</u> <u>count</u>, <u>without</u> <u>number</u>.

VI. 1. It is also possible to regularize the line as it stands in F by reading our as disyllabic; Abbott wishes to do so, and to read this is as a "quasi-monosyllable" (p. 372).

2. Kökeritz cites several parallel cases, in which, however, haplology is orthographically indicated: Clarence death in R3 2.1.136, Lawrence Cell in RJ 2.4.193, etc. (Shakespeare's Pronunciation, p. 265).

3. Shakespeare also has the analogical formation pyramisis as the pl. of pyramis, but only in prose.

4. New Arden Ed. of Cymbeline, p. 5. The editor is defending the use of Posthumus Leonatus in Cy 1.1.41, which is, however, not irregular (the line is an alexandrine).

5. It is possible that a few forms which I call etymological variants (such as Desdemon and Prosper) may really be apocopated variants created by Shakespeare himself. But since they coincide with what would have been the French-influenced form, I include them here.

6. I have regarded the occurrence of Desdemon (Qq Desdemona) in O 5.2.25 as in prose. And I follow Var. Ed. and Walker (I, 231) in classifying Desdemon as a syllabic variant like Helen (= Helena) rather than as an exclusively affective form: it is used by Cassio in O 3.1.56.

7. It is also possible that F Diomids was in this case disyllabic, as suggested in Shakespeare's Pronunciation, p. 286. But the presence of a F4 variant reading indicates that textual corruption may have occurred instead.

8. _Isabel_ may occasionally be disyllabic, as suggested by Kökeritz in _Shakespeare's_ _Pronunciation_, p. 286, and as strongly supported by the form _Isbell_ in AW 1.3.20, etc., but it is not necessary to assume this since all of the relevant cases are in caesuras. The same may be said of _Katharina_ and _Prospero_--they may sometimes have been syncopated, but not necessarily so.

9. And in RJ disyllabic or trisyllabic _Juliet_ occurs 46x along with the monosyllabic apocopated form _Jule_ 3x (F prints as prose; F2-4 substitute _Juliet_). But since only the Nurse uses _Jule_, it was probably a stylistic variant and has therefore been excluded.

10. _Extirpate_ 'to root out' also occurs 1x T 1.2.125, but its shorter variant _extirp_ is found only in the p.p. in verse.

11. And the spelling _deale_ 2x in H 2.2.627, Q2 may reveal an alternate pronunciation [di:l] with loss of medial _v_. See Kökeritz, _Shakespeare's_ _Pronunciation_, pp. 188-189.

12. I, 86-91. Another possibility in the Cy case would be that _to_ is used proclitically before _a_ just as before other unstressed vowels and was meant to be pronounced _t'_; cf. _t'adore_ in the preceding line, Cy 3.3.3. But the omission of _a_ seems preferable for the sense.

13. _Shakespeare's_ _Pronunciation_, p. 265 note 8; see also his "Elizabethan Prosody," p. 93. The use of _Countes_ in the TN line quoted has not been counted as "possibly irregular" because the line could be tetrameter with an extra unaccented syllable in the caesura. See above, p. 52 note 15.

14. Var. Ed. suggests the reduction of <u>hath</u> to an enclitic '<u>th</u> instead; this would also be possible, as forms of <u>have</u> in an unstressed position normally lost their initial <u>h</u> (see Kökeritz, <u>Shakespeare's Pronunciation</u>, p. 309). Note, for example, the spellings <u>h'as</u> (= he <u>has</u>) in TN 5.1.178, <u>t'as</u> (= <u>it has</u>) in P 3.2.4, and <u>s'hath</u> (which should be read <u>sh'ath</u>, = <u>she hath</u>) in H 3.2.70, Q2, all cited by Kökeritz on p. 277. ˇ

15. We also find the nonce-word *<u>cern</u> (but in prose) along with the full form <u>concern</u>. And <u>sayed</u> occurs 2x P 1.1.59, 1.1.60 as a short form of <u>assayed</u> 'tested,' but Shakespeare has only the pr.t. <u>assay</u> in this sense (I disagree with the New Arden Ed. interpretation of <u>sayed</u> in P as an active rather than a passive p.p.). Finally, <u>feated</u> in Cy 1.1.49, "A sample to the yongest: to th'more Mature, / A glasse that <u>feated</u> them," may be aphetic for <u>defeated</u> as suggested by the discussion in New Arden Ed. However, it is not necessary to assume an aphetic shortening here, since an established meaning of <u>feated</u>--'made fit'--serves quite well in the context.

16. It is possible that <u>history</u> is once disyllabic (in Cy 3.5.99, so interpreted by Kökeritz in <u>Shakespeare's Pronunciation</u>, p. 375). But since this could be a case of an extra syllable in an unmarked caesura, I have not excluded these variants on grounds of syllabic identity.

17. Cf. also the compound verb *<u>weather-fend</u> in T 5.1.10 'to defend from the weather.'

18. "Elizabethan Prosody," p. 96. It is possible, also, that <u>alarum</u> could have been syncopated to a disyllable, as is implied in <u>Shakespeare's Pronunciation</u>, p. 292.

19. Kökeritz comments that monosyllabic <u>given</u> may, however, have been pronounced [giːn] or perhaps even <u>give</u> (<u>Shakespeare's</u> <u>Pronunciation</u>, p. 327).

20. Parallels for the <u>poys'nous</u> syncopation are seen in <u>glutt'nous</u> TmA 3.4.52 and <u>rav'nous</u> H8 1.1.159, 1.2.79, cited by Kökeritz in <u>Shake-speare's</u> <u>Pronunciation</u>, pp. 387-388.

21. Shakespeare also has <u>paritor</u> 1x LLL 3.1.188 for <u>apparitor</u>, which does not occur in his works. And the form *<u>cital</u> in 1H4 5.2.62 is inter-preted by Kökeritz ("Elizabethan Prosody," p. 96) as an aphetic form of <u>recital</u>, which also does not occur. Finally, the noun <u>bate</u> (only in prose; 2H4 2.4.271) may be mentioned as probably shortened from <u>debate</u> 'strife, contention.'

22. See <u>Shakespeare's</u> <u>Pronunciation</u>, p. 278, for several parallel cases in which <u>you</u> may have been similarly apocopated before a vowel.. On pp. 276-277, Kökeritz also records forms such as <u>y'are</u> and <u>y'have</u>, in which apocopation is orthographically indicated.

23. Kökeritz also points out that disyllabic <u>easily</u> in VA 627 is ac-tually sp. <u>easly</u> only in Q5-6 (<u>Shakespeare's</u> <u>Pronunciation</u>, p. 284).

24. Cf. trisyllabic <u>reverberate</u> (F sp. <u>reverb'rate</u>) in TC 3.3.120 'to re-echo' along with the probably apocopated form *<u>reverb</u> L 1.1.156, which OED classifies rather as an irregular adaptation of L <u>reverberare</u>. The pair could not be counted because <u>reverberate</u> is in the fifth foot.

VII. 1.. Here and in the following tabulation, numbers in parentheses des-
ignate the page on which the line is discussed in full.

2. This is perhaps of no great significance, for they make up only
about 10% of the total number of variants. However, I have made an independent study of Shakespeare's approximately 500 neologistic derivatives,
most of which were excluded from the present investigation because they
had no syllabic variants occurring in the plays. None of these neologisms
are used in such a way as to create trisyllabic or monosyllabic feet.

3. A more exact (but less immediately convenient) phrase would be
"meter or another aspect of style." Metrical practice is, strictly speaking, part of a poet's style, or the way in which he chooses to express his
ideas.

4. That is, dramatically old enough; historically, he was nine years
old at the time.

5. Halliwell points out, however, that another use is to be found
in William Sampson's The Vow Breaker, or the Faire Maid of Clifton (1636):
"Didst thou not make me draw conveighances, / Did not th'assurance of thy
Lands seeme proball?" (italics mine; Halliwell's comment is quoted in Var.
Ed. of Othello, p. 150).

6. And loss of a medial unstressed vowel before -ble may have a
parallel in disyllabic terrible Cy 3.1.27, T 1.2.264 and terribly T 2.1.313,
as indicated by dialectal terble, terr'ble, tarble, turble, all cited by
Kökeritz in Shakespeare's Pronunciation, p. 267. It should be noted that
there are, in addition, two other Shakespearean occurrences of probable
(in T 5.1.249 and 2H6 3.2.178) in which the word is trisyllabic.

7. Kökeritz wishes to read _ignominy_ in 1H4 5.4.100 as so syncopated (<u>Shakespeare's</u> <u>Pronunciation</u>, p. 386). And on p. 282 he cites as a possible parallel Chaucer's colloquialism <u>astromye</u> (= <u>astronomy</u>) in "Miller's Tale" A 3451.

8. The nonce-word *<u>unplausive</u> (= <u>unapplausive</u> 'unapplauding') in TC 3.3.43 might also be mentioned here, though <u>plausive</u>, first recorded by OED in a 1600 citation, apparently was not shortened from <u>applausive</u>, whose first citation is dated five years later. <u>Unapplausive</u> is not recorded until 1837.

9. Though it is also conceivable that *<u>unsisting</u> was simply a syncopated variant of <u>unassisting</u>, as suggested by Arden and Cambridge Ed., the latter is not recorded in OED citations before 1694; <u>unassisted</u> appears in 1614.

10. It is hardly likely, however, that Thersites' <u>varlot</u> in TC 5.1.18 (describing Patroclus) is, as Schmidt suggests on p. 1310, a form compressing <u>harlot</u> and <u>varlet</u>. Shakespeare was, after all, writing primarily for stage performance rather than for the reading public, and the suffix -<u>ot</u> (even assuming that it was sp. -<u>ot</u> in his manuscript) would not have been discernibly different from -<u>et</u> in pronunciation. Note the phonetic spelling <u>Lancelet</u> in MV 2.3.5, cited by Kökeritz in <u>Shakespeare's</u> <u>Pronunciation</u>, p. 268.

11. Suggested in part by Clarendon, whose comments are quoted by Var. Ed. on pp. 226-227. The only other formations on a nonpersonal noun that I have found are a few jocular nonce-words such as <u>appledom</u>.

INDEX OF PREFIXES AND SUFFIXES

WORD INDEX

Renaissance forms not classified as distinct words in OED appear in italics. If the p.t., p.p., or pr.p. of a verb occurs along with the infinitive, only the infinitive is listed.

abate 159

abide 25n.,159,160

*aboded 58

*abodement 58

about 170

above 170

*abrook 151

accite 48

accompany 51

accomplice 155

accompt 49

account, noun 49

account, verb 48,49

accusation 95

*accuse 95

accustomed 50

acquit 26,49

acquittance, noun 50

acquittance, verb 49

*across 170

act, noun 86,95

act, verb 69

*acting 86

action 95

*acture 86

address 49

adjoined 7

*admirable 50,123n.

admired 123n.

admonishment 95

admonition 95

Adon 144

Adonis 144

adowne'a 3

advantage, noun 51

advantage, verb 51n.

advantageable 118

advantageous 118

adventure, noun 165,166

adventure, verb 165

afar 46

affect 96

affection 96

affianced 83

affied 83

affright 47n.,151,152

affront 43

afore 53

Afric 144

Africa 144

after 57

cause, noun 108

causer 108

cease, noun 7,152

cease, verb 152

*cern 162n.

*chaliced 125

chance 60

change, noun 54

change, verb 54

cheerfully 127

cheerless 135

cheerly 127

*childed 125

childishness 128

*childness 128

christendom 188,189

Christian 129

Christian-like 129

*cide 161

circle 74

*cital 169n.,187

cite 8,39,48,54

clad 149

claspings 86

clasps 86

cleped 149

climate 149

*climature 149

clime 149

clip 71

clog 69

close 69n.

Clothair 144

Clotharius 144

clouded 74n.

coequal 44

cognizance 42

cojoin 43

colleagued 20,43

collect 39

*co-mart 43,44

co-mate 44

come 1,60

comfort 28

comfortless 134

*co-mingled 42,43

command 93

<u>commandement</u> 93

commandment 93

commend, noun 96

commend, verb 40

commendation 96

commix 43

commixtion 43

*commixture 43

common 102

commonalty 102

commoners 102

commons 102

*commutual 44n.

companionship 105

company, noun 105

company, verb 51

compare 98

comparison 98

compassed 75

compensation 42

competence 85n.

competency 85n.

complain 65

complaining 65

complaint 65

complice 155

complot, noun 162

complot, verb 162

compost 99

*composture 99

compt 49

*compulsative 147

*compulsatory 147

*compulsive 147

doubtless, adv. 138

*dowered 75

drench 62

dress 49

drum 108n.

drummer 108n.

due 75

Duess' 5

Duessa 5

Duff 2,3,29,182

*duteous 127

dutiful 127

ease 103,104n.

easiness 103,104n.

east 126

eastern 126

*effuse 20,96

effusion 20,96

embalm 74

embar 74

emblaze 19,69

emboldened 79

*embounded 74

*embrace 36,93

embracement 36,93

*embrasure 93n.

empery 143,154

empire 143

enact, noun 99

enact, verb 68,69

*enacture 99

encaged 74

encamp 74

encircle 74

*enclog 69

enclose 69n.

enclouded 74n.

encompassed 75

*encrimsoned 78

end 87

endamage 75

endanger 37n.,75

*endart 68

endeared 1

ending 87

endowed 75

endue 75

enfeebled 78

*enfettered 75

enfold 75

enforce 78,119n.

enfranchised 47n.,79

enfree 74,79

engage 160

engender 31

engild 69

engirt 69

englut 69

engraft 70

engrafted 70

engrave 70

*enguard 70

*enhearsed 75

enjoy 79

enkindle 18,70

enlard 75

enlighten 79

enlinked 75

Enobarbe 182

Enobarbus 182

enraged 79

*enrapt 79

enriched 79

enring 76

enrounded 76

ensign 70

*ensnare 76

*ensteeped 69,70

*entame 79

entangle 76

entertain 93

entertainment 93

enthralled 76

*enthroned 36

entombed 76

entranced 76

entrap 76

entreat, noun 154

entreat, verb 70

entreatment 70

entreaty 154

envenom 74,76

equal 44

equality 102

equalness 102

erudition 33

escape, noun 163

escape, verb 163

especial 142

especially 142

espial 142

espy 142

esquire 142

establish 142

estate 142

estimate 96

estimation 96

eternal 120

Ethiop 116

Ethiopian 116

Europa 145

Europe 145

even 36

evening 36

example 167

excellence 84

excellency 84

except 91

excepting 91

exchange, noun 54

exchange, verb 54

excite 54

exclaim 96

exclamation 96

excuse 87,168

excusing 87

execrable 73

executioner 98

executor 98

exorcist 108

exorcizer 108

expect 84

expectance 84

expectancy 84

expectation 84

expedient 130

expeditious 130

expend 161

extern 119

external 119,120

extirp 147n.

extirpate 147n.

*extolment 19

extreme 101

extremity 101

fair, adv. 27

fair, noun 104n.

fairly 27

fairness 104n.

faith 103

faithfulness 103

fall 62,63

famed 130

familiarity 19

famoused 130

fantastic 120

fantastical 120

far 46

fault 52n.,66

fear 103,104

specially 142

speed 89,103

speediness 103

speeding 89

spend 161

spite 168

spiteful 168

spoke 26

spoken 26

sport, noun 163

sport, verb 163

spotless 135

spy, noun 142

spy, verb 142

squire 142

stablish 142

stain 62,161

stalled 161

state 97,142

station 97

stay 89

staying 89

steel 131

steeled 131

steely 131

steep 133

steeped 70

steepy 133

stern 112n.

*sternage 112n.

stir 89

stirred 64

stirring 89

stone 31,132

stonished 161,187

stony 31,132

story, noun 163

story, verb 163

stow 64

strain 44

strew 62

stride 52

stringless 135

stroyed 161

subsequent 56

success 97

succession 97

sum 115

summary 115

sunrise 91

sunrising 91

superfluity 101

*superflux 101

supply 94

supplyment 94

supposal 98

suppose 98

supposition 98

surance 169,187

surcease, noun 7,152

surcease, verb 152

surely 50

surpass 56

surrender, noun 56,57

surrender, verb 56

swart 133

swarth 133

swarthy 133

swarty 133

sweet 117

sweeting 117

Syracusa 37

Syracuse 37

taint, noun 100,164

taint, verb 163,164

tainture 100,164

take 61

talk 89

talking 89

tame 79